CRACKS
IN THE
CRESCENT

HUSSEIN HAJJI WARIO

Hussein Hajji Wario
Grandville, Michigan 49468
USA

Quotations from the Qur'an marked "Yusuf Ali" are taken from *The Meaning of the Holy Qur'an* by Abdullah Yusuf Ali (Beltsville, MD: Amana Publications, 1997).

Quotations from the Qur'an marked "Pickthall" are taken from *The Meaning of the Glorious Qur'an* by Marmaduke Pickthall (New Delhi: Taj Company, 1993).

Quotations from the Qur'an marked "Shakir" are taken from *The Qur'an,* 7th ed., by Muhammad Habib Shakir (Elmhurst, NY: Tahrike Tarsile Qur'an, Inc., 1999).

Hadith quotations marked "Sahih Bukhari" are taken from Abu Abdullah Muhammad bin Ismail bin Ibrahim bin al-Mughira al-Ja'fai, *The Translations of the Meaning of Sahih Bukhari,* Muhammad Muhsin Khan, trans., (New Delhi: Kibab Bhavan, 1984).

Hadith quotations marked "Sahih Muslim" are taken from Abul Husain Muslim bin al-Hajjaj al-Nisapuri, *Sahih Muslim,* Abdul Hamid Siddiqui, trans., (New Delhi: Kitab Bhavan, 2000).

Hadith quotations marked "Sunan Abu-Dawud" are taken from Abu-Dawud Sulaiman bin Al-Aash'ath Al-Azdi as-Sijistani, *Sunan Abu Dawud,* Ahmad Hasan, trans., (New Delhi: Kitab Bhavan, 1990).

Hadith quotation marked "Malik's Muwatta" is taken from Malik bin Anas bin Malik bin Abu Amir Al-Asbahi, *The First Formulation of Islamic Law,* A'isha Abdurrahman Bewley, trans., (Inverness, Scottland: Madina Press, 1989).

More information about this book is available at
http://www.cracksinthecrescent.com
http://www.husseinwario.com

Contents

PART II: The Confusion in Islam

Preface

No one wants to become a pariah in a culturally homogenous community, especially not in Kenya, where allegiance to a tribe is esteemed and a social misfit is shunned. The confluence of Islamic teachings and the customs of my Orma tribe makes it hard for an Orma Muslim to disagree openly with, let alone flagrantly transgress against, mores without ominous consequence. But I did. This is my story. I live to tell it courtesy of God the Father who drew me to Himself through His Son Jesus Christ.

I was raised as a Muslim who studied Islam in a *madrassa* (Islamic religious school), which equipped me with wide-ranging knowledge of the Qur'an and the Hadith. With this background, I wrote my story in this book, *Cracks in the Crescent*, to give the reader a better understanding of Islam. I use objective evidence, such as references to Islamic texts and Islamic scholars, in every analysis of a topic in Islam. In addition, I enunciate some esoteric aspects of Islam.

The first fourteen chapters of *Cracks in the Crescent* cover my upbringing as a Muslim, my conversion to Christianity, and the ensuing persecution. Various topics in Islam are discussed objectively in the context of my experience. The last two chapters are devoted exclusively to two topics in Islam that both Muslims and non-Muslims mostly misunderstand. Understanding these topics is crucial for deciphering Islam accurately. Chapter 15 is about the "Jesus of Islam," and chapter 16 examines Muslims' contention that the Promised Comforter in the Gospel of John chapters 14 and 16 is Prophet Muhammad.

My research for *Cracks in the Crescent* has taken the past six years. Much gratitude I give to God, my Savior, who predestined me to come to the knowledge of His Son, Jesus Christ, and did not forsake me when I was subjected to persecution after my conversion. I am thankful for many Christians who risked their lives by identifying with me and helping me even after my conversion became public. I also thank Amy, Annise, Cal, Cynthia, Jason, Judy,

Kirsten, Mark, Mary Anne, and Stephanie for their stupendous help in proofreading and editing this work. Their persistent encouragement stemmed some of my procrastinations.

My hope and prayer is that this book becomes an encouragement to many who deal with life's various adversities, a valuable asset to those who are striving to gain a better understanding of Islam, and a humble challenge to any Muslim willing to read it and give it an honest consideration.

Hussein Hajji Wario

Grandville, MI

November 4, 2008

PART I

MY STORY

CHAPTER ONE

My Upbringing

~~~~~~~~~~~~~~~~~~~~~~~~~~~~~~~~~~~~~

I was born in Kenya in 1975 to avowed Sunni Muslim parents. My father gave me the name Hussein, which means "good" or "handsome" in Arabic, because Islam teaches that the meaning of a name influences the character of the bearer. A name with a bad meaning not only would adversely affect the character and livelihood of the bearer, but also that of his or her descendants for as long as they bear that name.[1] When I was seven days old, my father gave me a heifer. He gave all his sons heifers as a form of investment, hoping that by the time some of his sons had grown up, the cows would have multiplied and some of them would be used to pay his sons' brides price.

1.1 My Family

My father had three wives, which was one less than what is suggested in the Qur'an—Islam's holy book—for a Muslim man to marry. Suratul Al-Nisa, 4:3, states:

> And if ye fear that ye will not deal fairly by the orphans, marry
> of the women, who seem good to you, two or three or four;
> and if ye fear that ye cannot do justice (to so many) then one
> (only) or (the captives) that your right hands possess. Thus it
> is more likely that ye will not do injustice.[2]

(This verse also advises Muslim men to marry as many slave women as they can possess.) Exceeding four wives in Islam is generally discouraged because only Prophet Muhammad was allowed to have more wives. The Qur'an states:

O Prophet! Lo! We have made lawful unto thee thy wives unto
whom thou hast paid their dowries, and those whom thy right
hand possesseth of those whom Allah hath given thee as spoils
of war, and the daughters of thine uncle on the father's side
and the daughters of thine aunts on the father's side, and the
daughters of thine uncle on the mother's side and the daughters
of thine aunts on the mother's side who emigrated with thee,
and a believing woman if she give herself unto the Prophet
and the Prophet desire to ask her in marriage—a privilege
for thee only, not for the (rest of) believers—We are Aware
of that which We enjoined upon them concerning their wives
and those whom their right hands possess—that thou mayst
be free from blame, for Allah is ever Forgiving, Merciful.[3]

Whereas the Qur'an does not aver the number of wives the
Prophet had, the Islamic traditions list their numbers as nine[4-1] and
eleven.[4-2] There is lack of consensus because Muhammad had at
least two slave concubines.

My father's wives had their own houses. Since he had many
cattle and sheep, it was not hard for him to provide for his wives
and children. He visited each home on a daily basis and spent most
nights with his youngest wife, who is my mother. The most senior
wife is considered the leader of the pack in the Orma culture. Para-
doxically, she advises her husband when to marry more wives.

My father, now deceased, had the title "Al-Hajj," which means
"the pilgrim" in Arabic, because he went on *Hajj* (pilgrimage) to
Mecca, Islam's holiest city, in Saudi Arabia. Every able-bodied
Muslim is enjoined to perform *Hajj*—one of the Five Pillars of
Islam—at least once in his or her lifetime if he or she can afford it.
The rest of the Pillars are: reciting the *shahaada* (creed), which attests
that Allah is one and Muhammad is his messenger; observing the
salat (five daily prayers); giving *zakat* (annual giving of 2.5 per cent
of one's income to the cause of the poor, converts, *jihad*, etcetera);
and *sawm* (fasting during the month of Ramadhan).

Ardent Muslims believe that *jihad* is the sixth Pillar of Islam,
which they also must perform. Even though there is a plethora of
references in the Qur'an and the Hadith to *jihad's* militaristic status,

some Muslims consider it as an individual struggle against Satan's temptation. On the other hand, there are Muslims who strive to obey Allah and Prophet Muhammad and fight.

1.2 Enrolment in *Madrassa*

Upon returning from Mecca, my father became a very devout Sunni Muslim. All of his school-aged children enrolled in *madrassa*. Everything in his family revolved around *madrassa* and the local mosque. He invested in gigantic kitchen utensils that widely accommodated the needs of the community during religious feasts. They were inscribed with his name, Hajj Wario.

When I was old enough, my father enrolled me in *madrassa* where I started learning how to read and write the Arabic language. As a result, the earliest childhood memory I have is about the Islamic school. Having mastered reading and writing the language, I embarked on reading the 30 shortest chapters (*surahs*) of the Qur'an that form *Juzzu Amma*. The 114 chapters of the Qur'an are unequally divided into 30 sections called *Juzzu*. These sections are divided such that one reads through the entire Qur'an in a month, especially during the fasting month of Ramadhan. They are also instrumental in instructing those who are young or those who are new to the Islamic faith.

Our *madrassa* teacher was extremely demanding. He flogged us whenever we got spellings or pronunciations of the Arabic verses wrong and I bear scars from his beatings. *Madrassa* students are forced to learn the Qur'an in this manner because Muslims believe that the Angel Gabriel did the same to Prophet Muhammad when he initially learned the Qur'an. The Islamic traditions say that the angel pressed him down three times causing him great distress when he failed to recite Suratul Al-Alaq as he had been instructed.[5]

Having memorized the preliminary section, *Juzzu Amma*, I moved on to the next one. I also studied Islamic history, *seerah* (the life of Prophet Muhammad) and the Islamic traditions (*Sunnah* and Hadith). The *Sunnah* is about how the Prophet lived his life, an exemplary life that every Muslim should try to emulate. The aHadith (plural for Hadith) are sayings of Prophet Muhammad. There are two types of aHadith. The general sayings and advice of

Prophet Muhammad are aHadith. The other form of aHadith is the Hadith Qudsi, which are sacred sayings of Muhammad that Allah inspired. I also studied *fiqh*, which is the Islamic jurisprudence based mainly on the four classical Sunni jurists: Ahmad bin Hanbali, Imam Shafi, Imam Malik, and Abu Hanifa.

1.3 My *Madrassa* Teacher's Question

A senior Islamic cleric from a nearby city oversaw the Islamic teacher in my hometown. Maalim Athman was an Arab who was well-versed in Islamic matters. He visited us on Thursday nights since *madrassas* have Fridays off. When he was in town, we had discussions about various topics in Islam.

One night our *madrassa* teacher asked him about Jesus. That was the first time I heard him mention *Nabi* (*Nabi* means "prophet" in Arabic) Isa ("Jesus" in Arabic) in a discussion. Our Islamic teacher wanted to know if Jesus was indeed coming back at the end of the world. When Maalim Athman answered in the affirmative, I was perplexed. Jesus had been mentioned only in passing in our class because Muslims believe his period as a prophet has passed; hence, he should play second fiddle to Prophet Muhammad. I would later learn from the Qur'an and the Hadith that his second coming is the sign not only for the end of the world, but also for the coming hour of judgment.[6]

1.4 Concurrent Enrolment in Secular School

In 1982, the Kenyan government started a new primary school in my home area. Since the law required that every school-aged child should gain a formal education, my parents reluctantly enrolled me as a first grader without my previously attending a kindergarten. I attended *madrassa* immediately after the dawn prayer, while spending time at the secular school during the day. Then at night, I went back to *madrassa* until the night prayer. I juggled the two schools, learning two foreign languages: Arabic and English.

Some Muslims in Kenya tend to be skeptical of secular education. There is a belief among them that since it does not contribute toward the hereafter, it should be shunned. Unfortunately, that was what early Islamic missionaries of Arab descent preached to the indigenous people of the area. Inconsistently, those missionaries have the most secularly educated descendants in the country, since they took their children to expensive private schools out of town, while their message to the masses was to shun what they secretly practiced. What a double standard! Sadly, Muslim parents in the Orma community still prefer taking their children only to *madrassa*.

1.5 My Graduation from *Madrassa*

When I accomplished my studies in *madrassa*, my family had a ceremony to celebrate it. My mother made coffee and delicacies for the occasion and frankincense was burned. After graduation, I helped the Islamic teacher with some of his duties in *madrassa*, filling in for him when he was sick or out of town. He gave me a special name, *Maalim Jaylo*. The title *maalim* means "teacher" in Arabic. I was also in charge of calling people for prayers.

When I was a Muslim, I used to pray at least five times a day. A Muslim must perform *wuudhu* (ablution) prior to each prayer or the prayer is considered null and void. There are two types of prayers. The first type is a set of the five daily prayers that is *faradh* (compulsory). Every Muslim must observe them to be considered a Muslim. They are *fajr, dhuhr, asr, maghrib,* and *isha* prayers. The call to prayer is called *adhan*. It is necessary for every *faradh* prayer. A *Muadhin* is the person who calls Muslims for prayers. There is a belief that when a *Muadhin* calls, Satan farts and runs away.[7] Muslims maintain silence when the call for prayer is in progress.

The second type of prayers is called *Sunnah* because Prophet Muhammad prayed them, and whoever performs them gets rewarded accordingly. They are sandwiched between the *faradh* prayers.

Muslims pray facing in the direction of *Al-Hajarul Aswad*, the black stone in Mecca. The prayer direction is called *qiblah*. Each prayer is composed of a sequence of bowings called *rakkah*. The prayer times are at dawn (*fajr*), at around noon (*dhuhr*), in mid-afternoon (*asr*), at sunset (*maghrib*), and about an hour and a half after sunset (*isha*). There are two, four, four, three, and four *rakkahs* respectively.

Every Muslim recites Suratul Al-Fatiha, which is chapter 1 of the Qur'an, for every *rakkah* (set of bowings) followed by another chapter of choice, otherwise the prayer is invalid. Even though it was revealed later than Suratul Al-Alaq—the first chapter revealed— it is the official chapter 1 of the Qur'an and has seven verses. On average, a typical devout Muslim recites Suratul Al-Fatiha at least seventeen times a day.

I fasted during the month of Ramadhan of the *Hijra* (Islamic) calendar. My family had a tradition of breaking their fast with our relatives and neighbors. After the evening prayers, we ate *iftar*, the evening meal. Later in the night, we had the *Taraweh*—prayers that are optional and are observed after *isha* (night) prayer during Rama-dhan. The whole area woke up before dawn to eat *suhr* (predawn meal) in order to observe the fast until sunset.

At the conclusion of Ramadhan, *Idd-ul-Fitri* was celebrated. On that day, my family gave to the poor in accordance with the teachings of Prophet Muhammad. The Hadith states:

> The Apostle of Allah (peace be upon him) prescribed the sadaqah (alms) relating to the breaking of the fast as a purification of the fasting from empty and obscene talk and as food for the poor. If anyone pays it before the prayer (of 'Id), it will be accepted as zaakat. If anyone pays it after the prayer, that will be a sadaqah like other sadaqahs (alms).[8]

Zaakat al-Fitr is not part of the *zakaat*—the annual obligatory giving—as the amount of money given is contingent on the number of people in a household.

We also observed *Idd-ul-Hajj*. It is also called *Idd Mubarak* or *Idd-ul-Adh'ha*. This fete comes three months after the month of Ramadhan on the tenth day of the month of *Dhul-Hijjah* (twelfth month) on the day pilgrims gather at Muzdalifah in Saudi Arabia. We went for prayer two hours after sunrise. There is no *Adhaan* (call to prayer), and *Idd* prayers have only two *rakkah*. In order to emulate the Prophet, we were encouraged to take a different route home from the one we took on the way to prayer. After that, we sacrificed sheep, goats or cows in commemoration of what Abraham did to his son Ishmael (not Isaac). The community had a big feast after the noon prayer.

The climax of all the celebrations was the one that marks the birth of Prophet Muhammad, called *Milad-u-Nabi*. Every year, we went to neighboring towns for celebrations. We had a group of people singing in praise of the Prophet during the procession. Some of us sang *casida*, religious poetry, in praise of the Prophet. The month-long celebration culminated in a grand celebration on the island of Lamu, an ancient Islamic city in Kenya, which has graveyards of many descendants of the Prophet. Muslim revelers came from as far as West Africa to mark the occasion.

1.6 Limited Exposure to Other Beliefs

When I was a fulltime student in *madrassa*, I had no exposure to people from other religions. Then at the secular school, I received a little exposure. My teachers were Christians but rarely professed their faith, primarily because the area was 100 percent Muslim, and the school's board of governors did not tolerate such talk.

1.7 The Death of My Father

My father passed away unexpectedly. He collapsed on the morning of June 15, 1987 and died before *fajr* (dawn) prayer on Wednesday, June 17. He had not been sick, and yet within days he was gone. That was a very sad day for my family. Many relatives and friends came from all over the country to console us. We were not allowed to mourn outwardly because that is contraindicated in the Islamic teachings. Muslims believe that when the bereaved wail or lament, it exacerbates the punishment of the deceased in the grave, regardless of his or her pious life on earth.[9] It was heartrending to think about my father, supposedly being punished in the grave, because his family outwardly mourned his demise.

The funeral procession took place and my father was hurriedly buried before the noon prayer. After his death, my mother observed a four-month, ten-day period called *iddah*. Every Muslim widow who is not expecting is required to stay indoors for that period of time after her spouse dies. An expectant one observes it for the entire period or until the child is born, whichever comes first. A widow can be inherited if she so desires according to the Islamic law. Islamic law, however, does not specify who may inherit her. So, in my mother's case, she did not want to be inherited.

My father had been polite and very kind to the poor. Upon returning from pilgrimage, he had spent his wealth in helping the poor and the needy. I remember how he took in a family of seven that was rejected by their own and had them live by us. He took care of them until their children grew up.

Many say that his life changed for the better after the pilgrimage to Mecca. Muslims believe that when a pilgrim, out of good intentions, kisses the *Al-Hajr-e-Aswad* (the black stone) and also spends time at the plains of Arafat while on pilgrimage, his or her sins are forgiven, and he or she becomes pure again.[10] Conversely, my father was notorious when it came to dealing with those who did things against Islam and Muslims. As a result, he had run-ins with the Kenyan government, and was thrown in jail once. He also fought against neighboring tribes who were Christians. Many non-Muslims in the area lived in trepidation of him.

His death was really hard for me because I also lost someone who regularly took me to a nearby town for the Friday prayers. There has to be a certain quorum for the Friday congregational prayer to be held. The least number of men that may attend is forty. My town had more than that but most of them were regularly out of town. In case fewer than forty men answered the call to prayer, they observed the regular *dhuhr* prayer at noon. Women, children, and the incapacitated are not required to attend.

My father wanted the best for me. He always treated me preferentially. I got the favors of accompanying him to attend the Friday prayers, where we had good talks about our religion. He was strict and did not compromise when it came to his religion. However, although I was his favorite child, he did not spare me when I was defiant.

1.8 Hardships Occasioned by His Death

No sooner did my father die than my uncles—who also had gone on *Hajj* to Mecca—proved to be difficult to deal with. We wondered what their motives were. Our Orma custom is primitive in that it allows a man to inherit a deceased brother's widow(s). Besides,

Islamic law tacitly approves this practice, which is not endemic to my Orma tribe, but is prevalent among other predominantly Muslim Kenyan tribes. Somalis, Wordei, Borana, Gabra, and Munyoyaya practice it and Islamic scholars in Kenya have not objected to it.

Since my uncles had multiple wives with some of them younger than my mother, it was illogical that any of them wanted to inherit her. It became evident within weeks of my father's demise that they were after our livestock. They made rules that were difficult for our family. We had been used to herding the cows on alternating days, but now we were forced to be the herdsmen for the entire clan. It was difficult at first, but we finally got relief when arbitrators ruled in our favor.

On a day that it was his sons' turn, one of my uncles came to my school requesting the school officials that I herd the livestock. The school headmaster summoned me to his office and instructed me to do what my uncle had requested. Knowing that it was not my family's turn, I refused to go. Consequently, I was arbitrarily punished. My uncle was angry that I defied his order, which clearly portrayed his abuse of my father's absence. But my father's death not only opened doors for our possible exploitation but also resistance on our side. My uncle persisted with his attempts to turn us into his herdsmen to no avail.

The Kenyan government posted a new headmaster, Mr. Buya, to our school. It did not take him long before he realized what was happening at the school. He resisted any attempts by parents or guardians to have school children herd the livestock. He monitored my progress and concluded that I needed to go to a better school. He approached my family with the idea, and they concurred that transferring me to a better and bigger school would help by way of competition among the students.

1.9 The Transfer to a Boarding School

A few months later, Mr. Buya informed my family about a transfer to a boarding school in Kipini, a town that was far away from my home. He thought I would fare better there, as there would also be less interference with my studies. My family was elated.

My father had a friend in Kipini who went by the title *sharif* because he was a descendant of the Prophet Muhammad. Therefore, when Mr. Buya suggested the school to my family, they thought it would be a good fit, as I would also be influenced in Islam.

He gave me the transfer letter to the boarding school in January 1988. Kipini is a town by the Indian Ocean, one of the oldest Islamic cities in East Africa. I traveled there and was received in town by the school officials. I went to my new dormitory and later met with the *sharif* family who took me on a tour around town. Kipini is a gorgeous town with lots of white sandy beaches, sand dunes, and palm trees.

School started, and one of the *sharif's* sons was my classmate. With our desks abut, Abdullah and I became close friends. We went to prayers at the mosque. We were inseparable. His family owned sprawling parcels of land with coconut and mango plantations that were a stone's throw from our school. We would bike to some of these plantations often to drop mangoes and *madafu*—unripe coconuts that are full of milk, oftentimes used as thirst quenchers in the coastal region of Kenya. We had quite an adventure.

On Fridays, Abdullah and I went to the mosque for prayers. I went to his house for meals during Ramadhan in 1988. His family was very kind and generous to me. I read the Qur'an and occasionally took instruction from the *sharif*. When I went home for a break in April that year, my family heard about my experience and was very delighted that it had worked out for me. Consequently, their relationship with the *sharif* family continued to flourish as my experience brought them closer.

Kipini was more than 95 percent Muslim. The Christians there were from other parts of the country working for the Kenyan government. They were considered outsiders by the local inhabitants' standard, hence they could not easily own land in town as most of it was passed down through inheritance. There was an old Methodist church, which was established during colonial days and was situated close to my school.

I took final exams three different times that year. Unlike in the United States, Kenyan public schools use a ranking system. All students in a class are listed in the order of their grades, and the lists are posted publicly by the staff room. It is pathetic at a term's end, as everyone knows the worst student in a class.

1.10 The Christmas Invite

My family was proud of my progress at Kipini because I was advancing not only in school, but also in my Islamic studies. Mr. Buya, who had a keen interest in my education, got frequent feedback about my progress. He was proud that one of his former students was faring well.

At the conclusion of the school year I visited him at his office. It was at that time he invited me to his home for Christmas. He lived about thirty kilometers away. He was a man of impeccable character. I felt honored, and I did not hesitate to ask my mother for permission to go, which she granted.

---

[1]   *Sahih Bukhari, Volume 8, Book 73, Number 209.*

[2]   Marmaduke Pickthall, *The Meaning of the Glorious Qur'an* (Taj Company, Delhi, 1993).

[3]   Pickthall, Suratul Al-Ahzab, 33:50.

[4]   [4-1] *Sahih Bukhari, Volume 3, Book 34, Number 283* [4-2] and *Sahih Bukhari, Volume 1, Book 5, Number 268.*

[5]   *Sahih Bukhari, Volume 6, Book 60, Number 478* and *Volume 9, Book 87, Number 111.*

[6]   Suratul Al-Zukhruf, 43:61–63.

[7]   *Sahih Muslim, Book 4, Number 753–754.*

[8]   *Sunan Abu Dawud, Volume 2, Book 3, Number 1605.*

[9]   *Sahih Bukhari, Volume 2, Book 23, Number 391* and *Sahih Muslim, Book 4, Number 2023.*

[10] *Sahih Muslim, Book 7, Number 3129.*

CHAPTER TWO

The Conversion to Christianity

Christmas means party time among many Christians in Kenya. Most of them slaughter chickens, goats, sheep, and bulls to mark the occasion. Christians flock in droves to church during the holiday for worship, which usually is relegated to a secondary role other times of the year. So long as one is named after a biblical character, a famous Western missionary, or colonialist, he or she is considered a Christian. As a result, more than half of Kenya's Christian population is nominal.

I arrived in Mr. Buya's hometown on Christmas Eve, 1988. The town was in a festive mood as its buildings were decorated with dazzling ornaments. Freshly cut plantain trees, commonly used as Christmas trees in that part of Kenya, lined the street leading to church. Residents were dressed to the nines. Families had their members joining them from as far as Nairobi. It was quite an occasion.

My host introduced me to his family, who were very cordial and accommodating. I was honored to slaughter a goat they had bought for the occasion. They were aware of my religious beliefs that I could not have eaten the meat of an animal a non-Muslim had slaughtered.

After a sumptuous meal with his extended family, Mr. Buya told me about their plan for the evening, a Christmastime family tradition. It was at that time he invited me to the Christmas Eve program at his church and I downright declined to attend.

My mind started racing after I declined his invitation. At that time, the Somali government was having problems with inter-clan

27

skirmishes that oftentimes spilled into Kenya. Occasionally, heavily armed Somali bandits crossed the border into Kenya to cause mayhem by abducting, maiming, robbing, or raping Kenyans who lived close to the border. Thoughts of an August massacre were fresh in people's minds as they talked about that bizarre incident. Bandits struck in broad daylight and shot at pointblank range two hapless elderly people. Fear got the worst of the town dwellers; so much so, that whenever a tire burst in the debilitating heat, residents scampered for safety fearing an attack. The town partly bore the brunt of the Somali turmoil due to its proximity to the border. Consequently, I was terrified to stay at my host's home alone while they attended the Christmas program that night. Had the bandits hit, I thought I would be a victim.

2.1 "The Stamp"

One probably wonders why I was so hesitant to go to a church program with the family. It is fine to be respectful and do what your host asks, but when the request has some religious ramification that deeply violates convictions, the thought of any concession is unlikely. In this case, the cliché, "When in Rome do what the Romans do," did not apply.

Muslims in Kenya widely believe that if people go into a church and sit in the pews, they get a stamp on their buttocks, which earmarks them for hell. Muslims believe Christians will go to hell because Christians ascribe partners to Allah by believing in the Trinity, the most grievous sin by the Qur'an's standard. They heed this teaching in Suratul Al-Nisa verse 171:

> O followers of the Book! Do not exceed the limits in your religion, and do not speak (lies) against Allah, but (speak) the truth; the Messiah, Isa son of Marium is only a messenger of Allah and His Word which He communicated to Marium and a spirit from Him; believe therefore in Allah and His messengers, and say not, Three. Desist, it is better for you; Allah is only one Allah; far be It from His glory that He should have a son, whatever is in the heavens and whatever is in the earth is His, and Allah is sufficient for a Protector.[1]

The above standard explicitly forbids belief in a triune God. Therefore, many Kenyan Muslims believe anyone who attends church has a stamp on his or her buttocks and hence goes to hell on the Last Day. Conversely, the Qur'an sends a damning gesture to Muslims because it declares that they would likewise go to Hell.[2] This subject is addressed later in the book.

The unrest in Somalia dominated my mind that evening. I knew well from history that Somali militiamen might raid the town as they had conducted hit-and-run raids in the past. The potential of being kidnapped was part of the reason I chose to go to a Christian church that evening. The consequence of getting my buttocks stamped and eventually going to hell did not deter me. I thought that since Allah was fully aware of my predicament—countless times the Qur'an talks of his omnipresence—he would understand on the Judgment Day.

2.2 The Christmas Program

Having exhausted pondering about the stamp and its consequence, I decided at the last minute to attend the Christmas Eve service. Mr. Buya and his family were already there. With jitters I walked into the church. That was my first time to set foot in a Christian church. My deep thoughts about the stamp were suddenly interrupted by the commencement of the program with the choir singing Christmas carols. The songs were in Swahili and Pokomo, my host's tribal language. Young people from the church recited Bible verses from memory. These verses included the creation story in the book of Genesis, prophecies about the coming of Jesus in the prophets, and his virgin birth in the gospel according to Saint Luke. A song of similar theme followed each recital. The last song of the program was about how Jesus Christ came to earth to save his people from their sins.[3] The young people tied the story about the prodigal son from the fifteenth chapter of Luke's gospel to Jesus' saving work. The program, which I thought took hours, actually lasted about an hour and a half. No sooner did the program end than I hurried out of the church with my mind preoccupied with thoughts about the stamp.

2.3 Sleepless Nights

Mr. Buya heard that I had been in attendance. He asked me about the program, but I did not divulge much as I was quite remorseful about going into a Christian church. Thus I went to bed right away. I lay in bed that night but could not sleep. Whenever I attempted to sleep I heard church songs. It was like I was having nightmares. I was disconcerted the whole night. When I got up the following day, I asked him whether the church choir had sung that entire night. Apparently it had disbanded right away for security reasons.

From that day on, my typical night was filled with lack of sleep. Almost every time I closed my eyes to sleep, I revisited the church scene. The songs continued to haunt me, and my nights were never the same. When Christmas was over, I dejectedly went home, where I experienced similar episodes.

My younger brother and I once discussed my plight. We concluded that I worked within my Islamic teachings' paradigm by going to a church service to save myself from possibly being kidnapped. There are passages in the Qur'an that encourage Muslims to lie or outwardly compromise their beliefs in order to protect themselves from possible danger.[4] This practice is called *Al-Taqiyya*. It means that a Muslim is at liberty to lie when faced with danger. After all, what I did was not as bad as lying about my religious affiliation or compromising it; all I did was take refuge in a church.

2.4 The Onset of My Interest in Christianity

The strange dreams continued for some time despite my coming home. Before long, the holiday break was over, and I left for school. By the time I reported to school, I had an interest in Christianity. I yearned to learn about *Isa* ("Jesus" in Arabic). I thought it was unfair to not read his *Injil* (gospel) that Islam teaches was given to him. Muslims believe that Abraham, Moses, David, Jesus, and Muhammad were prophets who were each given a holy book.

The Methodist church adjacent to my school had choir practice on Saturdays in preparation for Easter. The church was located between my school and the Indian Ocean. Since I was afraid to go in, I listened to the choir from my dormitory. The breeze from the ocean made it easier for me. The songs were about the passion of Jesus Christ.

Cecilia, a Christian girl in my class, had a Gideon International New Testament Bible. I thought it was fair enough to find out what the Bible taught about Jesus Christ but was hesitant to do so partly because Abdullah was always with me. Having pondered the consequences, I plucked up some courage to borrow it. It was in English. I thought it was written from right to left like the Qur'an. For that reason, I opened the back of the Bible expecting it to be the front. At that time I came across John 3:16, which was inside the back cover. That was the first Bible verse I had ever seen in print, and it caught my eyes right away. I perused through the pages trying to locate in what context it was written.

On Easter 1989, I went to a solitary place to hang out. Bahongo was on the Indian Ocean, and its serenity and tranquility was conducive for ruminating. Intermittent sounds of soaring waves occasionally interrupted the calmness of the evenings. Its sunsets were breathtaking. I frequented Bahongo after school to behold its charming panorama.

Nonetheless on that particular day, I went there solely to contemplate about Jesus and how he gave up his life for me. I was still a Muslim who was praying five times a day and observing the Ramadhan, but my mind was constantly on him. It seemed quite outlandish that I had thoughts about his passion. Muslims do not believe in the original sin; they "believe that human beings are born without sin..."[5] rejecting "the notion that one human being can take on the burden of the sins of another."[6] They believe that Jesus is a mere human being. I continued contemplating about him that evening. Within minutes I was crying. I spent the whole evening alone, meditating. Afterward, I went back to my dormitory. For fear of reprehension, I did not share my experience with anyone.

I continued reading Cecilia's Bible. It dawned on me after some time that my sins were gargantuan and only Jesus could forgive me. At that time it did not matter if Islam made any sense. One thing

I needed that my religion did not offer was the eternal sacrifice for my many sins. Muslims believe that as long as they obey what the Qur'an teaches and stay away from sin, they are right with God. But at that juncture my mind was on Jesus Christ.

And what came of the stamp on churchgoers' buttocks? The whole thing is a shenanigan Islamic Arab missionaries cleverly used to scare people away from exploring the Christian church as an alternative to the Islamic teaching. Indeed that myth still keeps the curious faithful at bay. What a deceptive way to hinder multitudes from their quest for the truth! In reality, going to church did not give me a mark of any kind. On the contrary, it shed light on a mark I had since my conception. That mark is sin that only the blood of Jesus Christ can wash away.

I also learned that the Islamic teachings about Jesus and the Trinity are skewed. The context in which Jesus is mentioned sometimes is in a form of accusation, as in Suratul Al-Maidah verse 116, "And behold! Allah will say: 'O Jesus the son of Mary! Didst thou say unto men, worship me and my mother as gods in derogation of Allah'?"[7] This is one of the instances that depict less respect for Jesus as Allah, supposedly the All-Knowing, accuses him of lying to people. How could he accuse Jesus of something he did not say? One wonders if Allah indeed knew what Jesus told his followers six hundred years earlier.

2.5 The Desire to Get Saved

Days turned into weeks, weeks into months, and I still kept what I had experienced at Bahongo to myself. Then one morning toward the end of July 1989, I approached my math teacher, who was a born-again Christian. (In Kenya, it is very easy to tell practicing Christians from nominal ones. Practicing Christians tend to salute one another with slogans like "Praise the Lord!" and "Hallelujah!") My math teacher, Mr. Asahel, and I were close partly because I spent time with him solving complex equations. One morning, I approached him after class and told him about my desire to have Jesus forgive my sins and to convert to Christianity. Since I knew that for a person to convert to Islam he or she has to follow a certain protocol, I thought the same applied to someone who wished to convert to Christianity. He responded rather mesmerized. He asked me to give him time so that he could consult with his pastor. He belonged to a Pentecostal church that was located some miles away from town.

A fortnight elapsed without a word about my request. Many Christians in predominantly Muslim areas are wary of Muslims who approach them about converting to Christianity. Most "seekers" tend to be spies for Muslim leaders. I was not surprised that Mr. Asahel took a while to get back to me.

In the weeks that followed, he responded. The plan was to meet at his friend's house, a teacher in another town. He was worried that should the locals find out that I was meeting with them about converting to Christianity, they would be in danger. Besides, his friend was a tenant of a *sharif* (descendants of Prophet Muhammad) family. He was fully aware of the consequences of proselytizing a Muslim, especially in that predominantly Muslim community. To his credit, much caution was exercised.

2.6 The Meeting with Church Leaders

I went to the meeting, which was close to my school, that Saturday afternoon in August 1989. Although students were typically observing the August holiday, the school administration extended the term for eighth graders that year to prepare us for the impending national examinations that November. When I walked into the house, there were a handful of people—the host, Mr. Asahel, the pastor, and two other elders. I learned later that Mr. Asahel was also an elder at that church. They asked me questions about the decision I was about to make.

After I answered all their questions, the pastor asked me to kneel down. They all laid their hands on me and prayed. At the conclusion of the prayer, the pastor led me through a prayer for repentance. After that, he gave me a Gideon International Bible that contained both the Old and New Testaments. I was elated to have my own copy of the Bible. But they forgot to advise me where to start reading. They urged me not to tell anyone I was a Christian, because they understood how dangerous the area was for ex-Muslims.

2.7 My Exploration of Christianity

I carefully tucked my new Bible under my shirt and took it to my dormitory where I read it when no one was around. It was hard to read, as I did not know where to start. I launched into the Old Testament, reading through the book of Genesis. I learned many stories about the Old Testament patriarchs. One other thing I learned was that, unlike the Qur'an, its stories were mostly in chronological order.

My adventure in exploring the Bible continued. When school reopened, I continued going to the mosque while secretly attending church on Sundays. I sneaked out to go to a church that was five miles away in some coconut plantations. It was easier for me to go there for church since the area was considered predominantly Christian. However, with a scarcity of Muslims converting to Christianity in the area, I was concerned that news of my conversion might be announced, thus jeopardizing my safety should the news spread, but I trusted in the Lord to carry me through.

I continued spending so much time with Mr. Asahel that some teachers became suspicious. The deputy headmaster made a comment one time that if I were not cautious, I would convert to Christianity. I shrugged off his comments and I ignored him whenever he advised me against joining Christianity. I continued going to church secretly. It became a trend that I was always missing from school on Sundays. There was a roll call at lunchtime, but I was always gone. I had the excuse of being with Mr. Asahel, which was within the rules governing the school.

2.8 The Answered Prayer

The Kenya Certificate of Primary Education (KCPE) exam was around the corner. Students tirelessly prepared for the examination week. Our teachers had review sessions round-the-clock. In Kenya, all eighth graders who wish to proceed to secondary school (high school) take the KCPE exam. It is a standardized exam administered nationwide for a week in November. The KCPE is graded in Nairobi. Examinees wait six weeks for their examination results.

Since there are many cases of cheating, the government posts police officers armed with rifles to man the classes. When students sit for exams, they see a mean-looking officer either sitting at the entrance to a classroom or strolling back and forth in the corridor peering into the classrooms.

We had the examination rehearsal on Monday, November 13, 1989, and everyone was assigned a seat. I sat for my first paper, the math exam, that was two and a half hours long, on Tuesday morning. No sooner did the proctor put the exam paper on my desk, than I started sweating, panting, and shivering. I was scared that I would fail the exam. What a shame that would have been! Years of painstaking preparation would have gone down the drain! At that point I prayed in the name of Jesus Christ about my sudden plight. Surprisingly to me then, the Lord alleviated my anxiety and with a deep sigh of relief, I started working on the exam. I was grateful to Jesus and my faith in him got a boost. I took the remaining exams without any hitch.

2.9 Life as a Secret Christian

While awaiting my exam results, I went home for the holidays. My family was excited to have me home. I kept a low profile by being always gone, running errands. I mentioned to Mr. Buya—the one who had invited me over for Christmas—that I had converted to Christianity. He was flabbergasted. He was so euphoric that he invited me to a meeting at his home with his pastor friend. I asked my mother for permission to visit him, and she granted it not knowing what had transpired. I went to the meeting. While there, I attended a church service and met with other Christians. They were thrilled to see someone from a Muslim tribe that is considered hard to evangelize, going to church with them. After my visit, I went back home and continued keeping a low profile.

2.10 The Question of My Religious Affiliation

My exam results came out, and I was selected to attend a secondary school about a hundred kilometers away from my home. My family was excited about the good news. My elder brother sold some cattle, gave me the money to buy school supplies and pay the school fees.

Since I had never done that kind of shopping in the past—my family always shopped for going to religious schools—I asked Mr. Buya to help me. He bought all the things I needed and advised me not to pay the whole year's fees, as it was a risk. I did not know what he had in mind then but heeded his advice by paying only the term's fees and put the rest away.

He put me on the bus and I was off to school by myself. My family trusted that I would be okay.

The Kenyan school system was really hard on its students. An Associated Press writer once likened Kenyan high school students' living quarters to "a military barracks."[8] Once students were admitted, they were not allowed to leave the fenced compound without the school administration's permission. The only exceptions were during midterms or holidays or to allow those who owed money to collect the fee arrears. There was a gate to my school that was guarded 24/7 by watchmen on the government's payroll. In spite of many attempts by students to abuse the system using fabricated stories, some teachers were kind enough to let students go home for genuine family emergencies.

The Kenyan high school system was quite laborious. Students would take ten subjects of study and sit for two papers for each subject at the end of four years of study. The standardized high school final exam—Kenya Certificate of Secondary Education (KCSE) exam—had a few multiple-choice questions and several essays. A typical Kenyan student studied many hours out of the classroom per day. Quizzes and midterms never counted toward the final grade. Some students were forced to repeat some grades to fare better. Due to the demand for round-the-clock studying, most high schools were boarding schools.

Heavy course loads coupled with the lack of breaks often led students to riot. Many students were also unhappy with the meals at school, and illicit drugs on campus were another cause of restlessness. Students frequently went on rampages in various parts of the country. Some cases received international attention on account of their atrocities. Students burned their teachers' houses, administration buildings, libraries and their own dormitories with their fellow students trapped inside. On three occasions many students died. The most recent one was in Kyanguli Secondary School where a few hooligans using petrol bombs burned sixty-eight students to death.[9] The dormitory was locked from the outside. The *Daily Nation* further reports that after that gruesome incident, parents were barred from getting into the school compound, because the gates were locked and armed guards were posted as a formality. What a ghastly way to deal with grieving parents! Rioting in Kenyan schools baffled experts; and it was a norm.

The Kenyan government frantically tried some measures to curb high school violence. One of the ways in which it had somewhat succeeded was to have new students declare on their admission forms what religion they belonged to. This declaration was in force when I was in high school. That move would concern civil liberties organizations in some countries because it is considered an invasion of privacy, but in Kenya it worked to impede high school violence. The government mostly used that information for roll calls at night, since students were expected to be at certain places for studies and prayers.

I declared on the admission form that I was a Christian. Had I known what declaring my new religion entailed, I would have had some second thoughts. Little did I know that the government used roll call to account for students. Absence without leave was a serious offence that was punishable by caning and menial labor. Repeat offenders were suspended from school.

That evening after the mandatory studying, I was invited to a Christian Union (CU) prayer meeting. CU is an organization very popular on high school and college campuses in Africa that tends to the spiritual needs of Christian students. It is student-led with one staff member overseeing the student leaders. All boarding students went to some form of a prayer meeting at night. Muslim students went to the mosque, while Adventists, Catholics, and Protestants each gathered in their own place. These prayer meetings were a new thing for me. Roll calls were taken. After that, we dispersed to our respective abodes where dormitory prefects took another round of roll calls.

2.11 Secret no More—My Conversion Becomes Public

In the days that followed, some students from my home area noticed that I was missing from the mosque. They confronted me about it and I told them of my conversion to Christianity. Within minutes, word spread throughout the school that a Muslim had converted to Christianity. The prefect from my dormitory let Muslim students jeer me that night. Senior students beat me up. In Kenyan high schools, it was common that upperclassmen mistreated the freshmen. However, I experienced more than the mere hazing or bullying that typically befell freshmen.

News of a Muslim converting to Christianity spreads fast in my district. Sure enough, my family learned of my conversion to Christianity through my friends. Within days, threatening letters that urged me not to go home as a Christian streamed in. Some begged me to denounce my new faith. At midterm, I gave a letter to a friend to deliver it to my family. It confirmed the rumor they had heard about my conversion to Christianity. Since I had converted to Christianity out of conviction, I felt that I should live up to that conviction. Paying lip service to my new faith was not on my agenda because I had wholeheartedly decided to follow Christ at whatever cost.

1   Muhammad Habib Shakir, *The Qur'an*, 7th ed. (Elmhurst, NY: Tahrike Tarsile Qur'an, Inc., 1999).

2   Al-Maryam, 19:69–73.

3   Matthew 1:21.

4   Suratul An-Nahl, 16:106, and Al-Ghafir, 40:28.

5   Sheikh Muhammad Sarwar and Brandon Toropov, *The Complete Idiot's Guide to the Koran* (Indianapolis: Alpha Books, 2003), 41.

6   Sarwar and Toropov, *The Complete Idiot's Guide to the Koran,* 41.

7   Abdullah Yusuf Ali, *The Meaning of the Holy Qur'an* (Beltsville, MD: Amana Publications, 1997).

8   Chris Tomlinson. "Locks, window bars hindered escape in suspected arson," *Seattle Post-Intelligencer*, March 27, 2001. Retrieved

on August 6th, 2004 from http://seattlepi.nwsource.com/national/kenya27.shtml.

[9] The Nation Team, "68 Die in Night Dormitory Fire," *Daily Nation Newspaper*, March 27, 2001. Retrieved on December 10, 2004 from http://www.nationmedia.com/dailynation/oldarchives.asp?archive=True.

CHAPTER THREE

God's Faithfulness through Persecution

~~~~~~~~~~~~~~~~~~

L etters continued streaming in from my family, friends, and members of the Muslim community persistently urging me to forsake my new religion while I was at school. Some of them dared me to go home as a Christian. At the same time, Muslim students upped their persecution of me. Some of them demanded proof of the Christian assertion that Jesus Christ is the Son of God. They also inquired of his hierarchy in the Trinity in relation to God the Father and God the Holy Spirit. As I mentioned earlier, these are classic examples of the questions Muslims have about Christianity. Seemingly, what Prophet Muhammad grappled with in ages past still lingers in their minds.

When angry students confronted me with those questions, I recited *Suratul Al-Ikhlas*, which vehemently denies Allah's physical birth or his fathering of an offspring. It also commands Muslims to speak of his oneness, an attribute commonly known as *Tawheed*. Contrastingly, I accentuated before them my belief in a God who has a Son of supernatural birth. In addition, I drew their attention to the biblical view of the Trinity, which in every facet is diametrically opposite to Muslims' idea derived from the Qur'an.[1] Finally, I implored them to learn from the Bible themselves.

My answers, and the appeal that ensued, enraged them. Some of them threatened me. The Kenyan school system, which threatened trespassers with prosecution, saved me from outside threats. The armed guards and the late night roll calls that many students abhorred thankfully kept my would-be assailants at bay. Accordingly, no threats could be carried out when I was least expecting them. Nonetheless, even that late in the term, I was still subjected to the beatings and menial job assignments that typically befell freshmen earlier in the term. Abbas, an alumnus who had attained the excellent grades necessary to proceed to the university, came all the way from his home 150 kilometers away to beat me up. He evaded the security system by pretending to visit his former teachers and friends at school.

Then one night after the Christian Union prayers, I was taken aback to discover my belongings were missing from my dormitory. I reported the matter to the school administration, and an investigation was launched. I went to bed that night fearing that the perpetrator would come after me next. It was extremely difficult, but the following morning I was grateful for an uneventful night.

The search for my belongings continued over the next two weeks. My friends and I combed through shrubs and bushes on the periphery of the school compound in vain. Finally, we found them two kilometers away in shambles. I was disconcerted. I was worried partly because I lacked the wherewithal to replace them. I seethed with anger for a while, but was thankful nothing had been physically done to me.

One night while I was asleep, an intruder came into my dormitory and struck me in the lower abdomen with a blunt object. I groaned in debilitating pain. By the time the guard and prefects came, the attacker had escaped.

In spite of all the persecutions, I continued attending the Christian Union nightly prayer meetings and the Sunday services. These gave me the needed impetus to endure the adversities that arose from my conversion to Christianity. At the same time, however, I was anxious about the looming holiday break, but I resolved to face the persecution for Christ's sake.

3.1 Persecution Abates

The Muslim students began observing the fast in the Islamic holy month of Ramadhan toward the end of the first term, the last week of March in 1990. The month-long fast, also known as *sawm*, is one of the five Fundamental Deeds compulsory for every able-bodied Muslim who attains the age of puberty. Expectant women, the sick, and travelers are exempt from fasting but are obliged to make up for missed days once their "status" changes.

Muslim students' observance of *sawm*, to an extent, decreased my persecutions because the Qur'an calls for a lull in violence during the sacred month.[2] They also were too tired and hungry from fasting to persecute me during the day. Their shunning of violence was probably reminiscent of what Prophet Muhammad said, "When the month of Ramadan starts, the gates of the heaven are opened and the gates of hell are closed and the devils are chained."[3] Since they believed that the devils were chained and the gates of heaven were opened, they were busy trying to get in by observing Ramadhan and the activities that accompanied it.

The end-of-term exams started a few days into the month of Ramadhan and at their conclusion we were dismissed to go home for the April holiday. While I prepared to leave for home, thoughts flooded my mind about letters I had received daring me to go home as a Christian. I was scared to go also because of events that had transpired while I was growing up.

3.2 Flashbacks

When I had started primary school, I had often listened to the radio in hopes of learning Swahili. I had tuned in occasionally to the only Swahili radio station that at that time had the lessons. Whenever I sang songs that I had learned in the presence of my family, they made ghastly comments. That happened often while they milked cows and I helped. Each time a cow refused to be milked or failed to yield enough milk, it was attributed to my singing of the "bad songs," and I was admonished. Because I was quite young, I did not even know some of them were Christian songs.

The Orma culture calls for older siblings to discipline the younger ones. My older brothers beat me up many times before my conversion to Christianity over philosophical disagreements. My brother Saidi was unfortunate in the same way. My elder brother, who is very impulsive, beat him up so badly that he suffered broken ribs and ruptured internal organs. Consequently, he suffered and died of his injuries. My mother still blames my elder brother for his role in Saidi's death. The matter was dealt with from within the Muslim community and forgotten. The Kenyan government is still unaware.

One day, my sister Fatuma and I set out for my mother's garden. She was twice my age. As the day wore on I became tired and laid underneath a tree. Fatuma crept up to me as I napped and slashed my neck with a machete. I bled profusely. The four-inch-long laceration on the left side of my neck scarred and healed. When the few who notice it ask me how it happened, I fail to ease their curiosity because it hurts too much to recount it.

3.3 An Encounter with My Sister

Remembering the violent "discipline" of my brother and sister, and thinking of the letters I had received, I was scared to go home for the first time as a Christian. Then I mustered up some courage, gathered myself, grabbed my meager belongings, and left for home. The journey started at the crack of dawn when I boarded the bus at school. My sister Halima received me when I arrived in Garsen. As a businesswoman, she knew school was closing that day. She had taken a day off from work to find out whether I was coming home for the April holiday.

She was a devout Muslim and was observing Ramadhan that day. After a little conversation I asked her to buy me a soft drink. Muslims in Kenya do not let people drink or eat in front of them during Ramadhan. If one is a visitor and does not share in their beliefs, one has to literally fast along with them till they break their fast at dusk.

Halima was outraged that I asked her for a drink. She all along had thought I was fasting as well. Then she reluctantly gave me some money to buy it but urged me not to drink it in public. I did not make any promise. I bought a soft drink and quenched my thirst while standing next to her. I was being insensitive but thought my sister should not have imposed on me her beliefs. We squabbled on the way home.

3.4 The First Arrival at Home

We arrived in time for *iftar*, the main meal after the *Maghrib* (evening) prayer during Ramadhan. I was invited to join the males in my family among relatives and neighbors who traditionally ate together, but I declined. Instead I went to my mother's house. She was incensed when I confirmed to her that I was a Christian. My mother talked to me at length till late into the night without reaching a compromise.

I went to bed that night and was awakened before dawn to eat in order to observe the fast. Due to my family's insistence, I got up, ate, and later that morning devoured the leftovers. That ignited my mother. She summoned me to her house and admonished me for my actions. She had every reason to chide me per her religious convictions since she thought she was acting in my best interest. The words of Prophet Muhammad, "When Ramadhan begins, the gates of Paradise are opened"[4] reverberate in every Muslim's mind during Ramadhan. That perhaps led her not to compromise, but to try winning me back to Islam.

To her disappointment, I remained adamant and defiant. At that time she told me that I had ceased to be her son and asked me to leave her home before the worst thing happened to me. I was petrified. I gathered myself, took my belongings and left not knowing where to go. Once a beloved son, I was now a pariah without a place to call home. I was hurt deeply but the words of Jesus Christ in the Gospel according to Saint Matthew 10:35–37 comforted me:

> For I have come to 'set a man against his father, a daughter against her mother, and a daughter-in-law against her mother-in-law'; and 'a man's enemies will be those of his own household.' He who loves father or mother more than Me is not worthy of Me. And he who loves son or daughter more than Me is not worthy of Me.[5]

I set out for Garsen. I prayed about the situation while on the road and decided to go to Mr. Buya's home.

When I arrived at his house that evening, I shared with him what had happened earlier in the day. He was very sympathetic with me and asked me to stay at his home until my mother asked me to return. Those words were just what I needed to hear. Words could not express how grateful I felt. I stayed with his family for about a week without hearing from my family.

3.5 The Government Letdown

Then one Saturday evening a hand-delivered missive from a Kenyan government official flabbergasted us. It was from the Chief of my location falsely accusing me of leaving my home without my mother's permission. Mr. Buya was also charged with hosting me, an underage child, without my mother's consent. The Chief summoned us to appear before him the following Monday.

The Kenyan government has three branches, namely, the executive, the legislative, and the judicial. The executive branch, headed by the president, exudes the most power, arbitrarily applying the law. The Office of the President—through its vital organ notoriously known as the Provincial Administration—oversees the eight provinces that comprise Kenya.[6] A provincial commissioner heads a province. A province is made up of districts, which are governed by district commissioners. A district is made up of divisions with district officers as their leaders. Locations make up divisions. The head of a location is a chief. Political appointees without merit mostly filled these positions.

The colonial government subdivided Kenya into small administrative units to squelch local uprisings. When the country received its independence from Great Britain in 1963, the indigenous leaders embraced the colonialists' ideology; hence nothing was done to ameliorate the deplorable condition of the vast majority of the ordinary citizens. On the contrary, the same apparatus that the imperialists had used to keep the indigenous people in check, the postcolonial government adopted to further impoverish its subjects.

Chiefs have had immense powers at the grassroots level since the advent of colonialism. If one defies a chief's order, the Administration Police (AP)—police officers under his or her jurisdiction—make the arrest. Amnesty International reported, "The Administration Police Act allows the Provincial Administration direct control over a section of the police, reinforcing the powers of local chiefs... [And] The Chiefs' Authority Act gives local Administrative Chiefs wide powers including those of arrest and detention and restriction of movement."[7] Chiefs also preside over domestic problems, and at times cases go to judicial courts at their discretion.

The fact that our Chief was a Muslim made it harder for me to get justice because his beliefs prejudiced his judgment. I am not implying that Kenyan Muslims necessarily disregard the rule of law, but as it turned out, the Chief of our location clearly flouted it in my case for the cause of Islam.

Mr. Buya defied the order to appear before the Chief. Since he hailed from a different location, the Chief's wrath could not have easily befallen him. However, even though the allegation against me was fictitious, I had to obey the order to avoid being jailed.

A Christian evangelistic team from Nairobi was in my host's town that weekend and was scheduled to have an open-air meeting in Garsen, the town where the Chief's office was located. I hitch-hiked with the group. The team members introduced me to a Kenyan missionary pastor, an indigene of western Kenya, who had some connections with the top government officials in the area. He kindly asked me to see him whenever I encountered problems on account of my conversion to Christianity. I narrated to him the story of my impending hearing and hurried to court.

When I arrived at the hearing, I saw my siblings, relatives, and Muslim leaders waiting for the Chief's arrival. I waited along with them while a gun-toting police officer stood guard. We waited for a while for the Chief to arrive.

Then an Administration Police officer sent us into the chambers for the hearing. I was falsely accused of leaving my home without my mother's consent while underage. I testified in court about what had happened at home and my mother's ensuing threat. My sister Halima, who was on the forefront of the effort to have me convert back to Islam, refuted my claim.

3.6 The Banishment to My Hometown

Shockingly, the Assistant Chief who was present at the hearing threatened to testify against me should the Chief allow the case to proceed to a judicial court. But at that time, the Chief ruled that I go home per my family's request. I was gut-wrenched by the verdict.

The Kenyan Constitution in Chapter V §78(1) guaranteed my right to exercise my belief by stating:

> Except with his own consent, no person shall be hindered in the enjoyment of his freedom of conscience, and for the purposes of this section that freedom includes freedom of thought and of religion, freedom to change his religion or belief, and freedom, either alone or in community with others, and both in public and in private, to manifest and propagate his religion or belief in worship, teaching, practice and observance.[8]

However, the constitution had not come to my aid that day because one of its custodians was a renegade. Since I knew my safety was at stake, I challenged the court to guarantee in writing that my family and the Muslim community would not do anything to harm me. To that effect, a statement that the Kenyan government would be liable for my safety was written, and the Chief, the inspector of the Administration Police (AP), my siblings, and I duly signed it. I thought that it was a genuine gesture.

3.7 The Verdict's Aftermath

The Muslim leaders and my family rejoiced at the verdict. They, along with an Administration Police (AP) officer, escorted me home. I walked quietly through the town center in their company. There were onlookers as we headed toward the River Tana. The town of Garsen had not previously experienced a grotesquely odd story of a Muslim converting to Christianity. Some of them called me names while others jeered at me as we embarked on the awaiting canoe. I soon overheard Halima bragging about a bribe that had tilted the verdict in their favor. I was devastated. I plucked up some courage and asked the Administration Police officer whether that had actually happened. He gave me the cold shoulder. Having been convinced that I was headed home, the police escort retreated.

Then we crossed the river. My siblings, relatives, and Muslim community leaders walked me home. No sooner did we approach the first bridge—one of the two before my home—then I was told by one of the Muslim leaders that it was time for me to renounce my faith in Jesus Christ. He added that the promises made in court were not binding. I was stopped in my tracks and told to carry out their demand. Failing to comply, I was threatened with death. I was petrified. I knew too well that that could be the end of me, considering my tribe had had a checkered past.

My tribe, the Orma—also derogatorily called the Galla—was one of the fiercest tribes in Kenya. History books allude to their invasion of ancient towns as what is behind the presence of many ruins in the Coast Province. The world-famous Gede Ruins partly came into being as a result of their invasions.[9]

In spite of their militaristic culture, the Kenyan government still licensed them to carry knives and spears so as to protect their herds from lions, hyenas and other predators. The knife—considered an article of clothing by many—is always carried in a sheath on the right side for easy access in case a wild beast attacks. Many legendary figures in my tribe fearlessly fought lions with their knives while braving the cruel hands of death.

Knives also were convenient when slaughtering the animals that are lawful by Islamic standards. Muslims are prohibited from eating any kind of meat of a lawful animal that is not properly slaughtered. For that reason, they only eat what a fellow Muslim slaughters. He must utter, "Bismillah," which means "In the name of Allah" in Arabic, before he slaughters the animal. That kind of meat is called *halaal*, which means "permissible" in Arabic.

My tribesmen occasionally settled scores by taking the law into their own hands. Stabbings were common during fights. Since the local Chiefs settled most of their disputes, many cases went without proper legal redress. The tribal clashes of the years 2000 and 2001 pitting farmers (Christians) against pastoralists (Muslims) are recent examples of how easily knives and spears were used to attack enemies in my home area. The Ormas killed scores of Pokomos, a neighboring tribe. The British Broadcasting Corporation (BBC) reported, "The ongoing dispute is between the Orma pastoralists and Pokomo farmers in the Tana River District. The death toll is being put at 38 for the week with more than 100 people estimated to have died this year."[10] Sadly, one of the victims of the clashes was my third grade teacher, Mr. Hiribae, who was stabbed to death at his farm. Thus I was worried about the consequence with which I was being threatened. If I failed to comply with their demand to renounce Jesus, I would surely not live to see another day.

I asked my detractors for a moment to mull over their demand. It was granted. I pondered while inwardly praying. I thought about the words of Jesus to his disciples in the Gospel according to St. Matthew 10:19–23, 28–33:

> But when they deliver you up, do not worry about how or what you should speak. For it will be given to you in that hour what you should speak; for it is not you who speak, but the Spirit of your Father who speaks in you. "Now brother will deliver up brother to death, and a father *his* child; and children will rise up against parents and cause them to be put to death. And you will be hated by all for My name's sake. But he who endures to the end will be saved. When they persecute you in this city, flee to another. For assuredly, I say to you, you will not have gone through the cities of Israel before the Son of Man comes... And do not fear those who kill the body but cannot kill the soul. But rather fear Him who is able to destroy both soul and body in hell. Are not two sparrows sold for a copper coin? And not one of them falls to the ground apart from your Father's will. But the very hairs of your head are all numbered. Do not fear therefore; you are of more value than many sparrows. "Therefore whoever confesses Me before men, him I will also confess before My Father who is in heaven. But whoever denies Me before men, him I will also deny before My Father who is in heaven."[11]

The words of Christ are explicit. Thus I was convinced to uphold them. I thought if I rejected Jesus Christ as my Savior, he would deny me before his Father in heaven as he had told his disciples. So I prayed.

3.8 The Lord's Intervention

I felt that I should tell them what I thought about their demand. I knew on that day that denouncing Christ was not an option. I was determined to pay the ultimate price if it came to that. There is no *Al-Taqiyya* (dissimulation) in Christianity. Jesus commanded his disciples to adhere to what they believed by telling them, "For whoever desires to save his life will lose it, but whoever loses his life for My sake will find it."[12]

After the prayer, I started out by telling them how they successfully won the case to take me home. I told them it was pointless for them to force me to renounce my faith on the way home, while they could do it in the privacy of their own home. I even reasoned with them that had I failed to comply and they in turn killed me, the Kenyan government could possibly hold them liable.

Startlingly, they welcomed my idea, and we proceeded with the journey home. I was relieved. As we approached my home, I became more nervous, not knowing what awaited me. We arrived in time for *iftar*. My relatives invited me to join them for the meal, but I was too nervous to eat. Instead, I went straight to my mother's house. She acted quite differently and was not as belligerent as when I had initially arrived as a Christian. She talked to me less about my conversion. I went to bed that night quite nervous because I did not know whether I would be coerced to embrace Islam.

My family woke me up before dawn for a meal so as to fast the following day. I ate this meal at my mother's insistence and then the following morning ate the leftovers. She was enraged by my actions, but did not threaten me or ask me to leave her home. Days went by without anyone raising the issue about the postponed attempt to coerce me to deny Christ. I was grateful to God for keeping them from bringing it up. Even my impulsive brother was restrained. God is good! But my anxiety made the nights go by very slowly.

In the days that followed, my family continued to wake me up for the meal at dawn, but I refused to comply, as I was content to eat leftovers in the morning. My actions were an embarrassment to my family. Our entire clan was also not spared from the aftermath of my conversion because rival clans had new lines of insult. My brothers fruitlessly tried to change my mind about Christianity. They took me away at night pleading in vain.

They did not give up with their tireless efforts. They were convinced that I was treading on the wrong path. Muslims believe that Islam is the straight path. That is why they pray at least five times a day and recite *Suratul Al-Fatiha* (Chapter 1) at least seventeen times a day in order to ask Allah to show them that straight path.

The sixth verse of the abovementioned chapter pleads, "Show us the straight path."[13] They believe anyone who does not subscribe to Islam is doomed. I asked my brothers why Muslims ask Allah that many times a day to show them the straight path if Islam is indeed that path. "Isn't it about time that you offered a prayer of gratitude for being on the path?" I quipped. They ignored my question.

3.9 The Punishment of an Apostate in Islam

My family and the entire Muslim *ummah* (community) were convinced that I was going to hell. In keeping up with their duty, they tried everything to save me from what they believed was my ultimate punishment for leaving Islam. Prophet Muhammad had also prescribed physical death as the punishment for an apostate. The Hadith states:

> Allah's Apostle said, "The blood of a Muslim who confesses that none has the right to be worshipped but Allah and that I am His Apostle, cannot be shed except in three cases: In Qisas for murder, a married person who commits illegal sexual intercourse and the one who reverts from Islam (apostate) and leaves the Muslims." [14]

The Qur'an also has a chilling message for an apostate stating:

> Why should ye be divided into two parties about the Hypocrites? Allah hath upset them for their (evil) deeds. Would ye guide those whom Allah hath thrown out of the Way? For those whom Allah hath thrown out of the Way, never shalt thou find the Way. They but wish that ye should reject Faith, as they do, and thus be on the same footing (as they): But take not friends from their ranks until they flee in the way of Allah (From what is forbidden). But if they turn renegades, seize them and slay them wherever ye find them; and (in any case) take no friends or helpers from their ranks.[15]

It is clear from these verses that Muslims should be hostile toward people who reject Faith—Islam. Nevertheless if they "flee in the way of Allah," that is, embrace Islam, and later become apostates, they should be killed.

Prophet Muhammad not only called for the killing of Muslims who apostatize, but also set a precedent by killing some of them.[16] I am an apostate, and any Muslim who carries out the commands of Allah and his Prophet to kill me, is fighting for "Allah's Cause," which is a form of *jihad*. The Prophet said the following about Muslims who participate in *jihad*:

> Whoever believes in Allah and His Apostle, offer prayer perfectly and fasts the month of Ramadan, will rightfully be granted Paradise by Allah, no matter whether he fights in Allah's Cause or remains in the land where he is born. Paradise has one hundred grades which Allah has reserved for the Mujahidin who fight in His Cause, and the distance between each of two grades is like the distance between the Heaven and the Earth. So, when you ask Allah (for something), ask for Al-firdaus which is the best and highest part of Paradise.[17]

This Hadith is clear that a Muslim doesn't necessarily have to fight for "Allah's Cause" to be granted paradise. On the other hand, there is a greater reward in paradise for a Muslim who fights against Allah's enemies, who include apostates.

It is sad that an honest decision by a Muslim to follow his or her conviction to leave Islam has to result into death if some ardent Muslims have their way. That universal sentiment in Islam on a Muslim's inability to choose another religion is summed up in the Qur'an, which states, "It is not fitting for a Believer, man or woman, when a matter has been decided by Allah and His Messenger to have any option about their decision: if any one disobeys Allah and His Messenger, he is indeed on a clearly wrong Path."[18]

Once my family realized that their efforts to convert me back to the "right Path," Islam, were proving futile, they resorted to a plan that baffled me. I never had thought they could do such a thing. One of my brothers went missing for a few days. I wondered where he had gone, and when I asked my mother, she told me that he had gone to a nearby village to bring home some cows our family had bought. I wondered how he could leave the family at such a time, when they had called meetings to discuss my conversion to Christianity. When some of their stories failed to add up, I suspected he had gone to consult with some Muslim leaders about my fate.

I am grateful to God for carrying me through the aftermath of the court verdict. He indeed gave me words to say to my adversaries at the opportune time. The Lord God surely neither leaves us nor forsakes us.

---

[1]   Suratul Al-Maeda , 5:116.

[2]   Suratul Al-Baqara, 2:194.

[3]   *Sahih Bukhari, Volume 3, Book 31, Number 123.*

[4]   *Sahih Bukhari, Volume 3, Book 31, Number 122.*

[5]   NKJV.

[6]   In early 2008, an interim coalition government was formed to avert further bloodshed occasioned by the disputed 2007 presidential election results. Despite the introduction of the position of the Prime Minister, the power of the Provincial Administration virtually remains intact.

[7]   P. Brown, "Kenya Violations of Human Rights: Communications Between Amnesty International and the Government of Kenya," *Amnesty International* (September 1997): 3. Bracket mine.

[8]   *The Kenya Constitution*, Revised Edition (1998), 1992 Printed and Published by the Government Printer, Nairobi.

[9]   Kwame Appiah and Henry Gates, *Africana: The Encyclopedia of the African and African American Experience* (Philadelphia: Running Press, 2003), 332.

[10] "Fresh land clashes in Kenya," *British Broadcasting Corporation (BBC),* December 7, 2001. Retrieved October 6, 2004 from http://news.bbc.co.uk/2/hi/africa/1697529.stm.

[11] NKJV.

[12] NKJV, Matthew 16:25.

[13] Pickthall.

[14] *Sahih Bukhari, Volume 9, Book 83, Number 17.*

[15] Yusuf Ali, Suratul Al-Nisa, 4:89.

[16] *Sahih Bukhari, Volume 9, Book 83, Number 37.*

[17] *Sahih Bukhari, Volume 4, Book 52, Number 48.*

[18] Yusuf Ali, Suratul Al-Ahzab, 33:36.

CHAPTER FOUR

An Assortment of Challenges

~~~~~~~~~~~~~~~~~~~~~~~~~~~~~~~~~~~

My brother who had gone on a family errand was still at large. He had been gone for a while now, and I was worried because I did not know what was in store for me. Since the Chief's verdict restricted my movements, there was not much I could do but entertain the inquiring minds. Muslims who had questions about Christianity kept me busy. As we saw earlier, many Muslims' knowledge of Christianity is skewed because it is based entirely on what they learn from the Qur'an and the Hadith.

One of my inquirers happened to be a prominent man who went on pilgrimage to Mecca in the 1970s. Hajj Guyole came to me with a copy of the Qur'an in hand. He started by attacking who Jesus is. He went on to various places in the Qur'an and quoted from the Hadith, trying to show me how Jesus Christ could not be anyone's savior. He tried to prove that Jesus was a mere human.

The Hadith states that Prophet Muhammad told his followers about Jesus as "a man of medium height and moderate complexion inclined to the red and white colors and of lank hair."[1] In another instance he described Jesus as a "man of brown color the best one can see amongst brown color and his hair was long that it fell between his shoulders. His hair was lank."[2]

Although Prophet Muhammad and Jesus lived centuries apart, Prophet Muhammad actually claimed to have seen Jesus in order to convince his audience that he was a genuine Prophet and should be heeded. In contrast, the writers of the four Gospels were actually with Jesus but did not divulge any information about his height, skin color, hair texture or appearance in general. These physical traits were irrelevant to what Jesus came to accomplish.

Hajj Guyole continued with reading from the Qur'an and quoting the Hadith while disregarding my objections. When he finished his discourse, I shared with him the Biblical account of Jesus Christ and raised some questions about Islam.

4.1 Islam's Mixed Messages about the People of the Book

Many Muslims, including Hajj Guyole, are confused about Christianity partly because they do not like to learn from Christians and the Bible. Most of them unreservedly believe in their leaders, who relentlessly quote the Qur'an's and the Hadith's ad hominem accusations against Christianity. They claim that the People of the Book (Jews and Christians) changed the Bible's content and context, making it fallacious.

Their accusations are in line with Prophet Muhammad's rhetoric. He capitalized on Jews' and Arabs' hatred for one another to charge the former with corrupting the Torah. And he succeeded by further exacerbating the historically delicate situation that dates back to the time of Abraham that still looms large. The message in Suratul Al-Maida verse 13 lucidly states:

> And because of their [the Jews] breaking their covenant, We have cursed them and made hard their hearts. They change words from their context and forget a part of that whereof they were admonished. Thou wilt not cease to discover treachery from all save a few of them. But bear with them and pardon them. Lo! Allah loveth the kindly.[3]

This verse accuses the Jews of breaking their covenant with God, because Muhammad was unhappy with them that they did not recognize him as a Prophet. He went to the extent of charging them with committing one of the most heinous sins in the Old Testament—the sin of altering God's Word—just to try to have the Jews listen to him. When they rebuffed his preaching, he, through the revelations he had received, called them accursed and started getting hostile toward them. The tone of sayings recorded in the

Hadith and many verses in the Qur'an tend to depict Jews and Christians as untrustworthy and evil.

The above quoted verse also accuses the Jews of changing the context of the Torah and forgetting a part of it. The part that was allegedly forgotten or changed supposedly contained the foretelling of Muhammad's coming as a prophet. He claimed that he was the one who had been prophesied to come because his name was also written in the Gospel.[4] Muhammad made that claim in Medina, where he had encountered large numbers of Jews and Christians who opposed his prophethood. It was while in Medina that he "continued to receive revelations but their tone and content changed [negatively] in this new context."[5] Anyone who intently reads and studies the Qur'an and the Hadith will hear the consistent denigration of the Jews and Christians.

How could Prophet Muhammad declare that his name was in the Torah and Gospel when he could not corroborate by reading the scriptures? The Qur'an and the Hadith both testify that he was illiterate. The Hadith quotes him at least three times telling the angel who appeared to him, "I do not know how to read."[6] Muhammad's own word reveals his illiteracy and lack of education. If he could not read Arabic, his native language, how could he read the Torah and Gospel that were originally written in Hebrew and Greek respectively?

Ironically, the Qur'an charges the Torah with lack of context. However, when one peruses the Qur'an, most of its chapters are lacking in context. The chapters are simply random compilations of sayings. Its accusation against the plausibility of the Torah and Gospel is unconvincing because it is inconsistent. Some of its verses advise the people of the Book (Christians and Jews) to practice their religions as revealed in their sacred books. A good example is in Suratul Al-Maida, 5:68a, which reads, "O People of the Book! Ye have no ground to stand upon unless ye stand fast by the Law, the Gospel, and all the revelation that has come to you from your Lord."[7] Some revelations Prophet Muhammad received admonished the Jews and Christians to read their own scriptures. What a contrast with the accusation of treachery in the above quote from Suratul Al-Maida!

Reading these mixed views confuses Muslims who rely on the Qur'an and the Hadith to understand Christianity. Even when their account drawn from Islamic sources is debunked, they still typically conclude that the Torah and Gospel are flawed. Hajj Guyole, who supposedly knows Islam, is not an exception. However, when one asks Muslims to produce a copy of the original scriptures that they have as a reference to ascertain their claim, they refuse to produce one. One wonders how Islam—a religion that came almost six hundred years after Christianity and several thousand years after Judaism—repudiates the religious events that preexisted it. Reading conflicting views in the Qur'an and the Hadith does not help Muslims in the quest for an unequivocal answer. It seems they are happy pointing fingers at the Bible.

The Qur'an is full of contradictions. One of them is when it endorses the Torah and Gospel in Suratul Al-Yunus, 10:94:

> And if thou [Muhammad] art in doubt concerning that
> which We reveal unto thee, then question those who read the
> Scripture (that was) before thee. Verily the Truth from thy
> Lord hath come unto thee. So be not thou of the waverers.[8]

It is perplexing that the Qur'an endorses what it also challenges. What an oxymoron! One thing worthy to note in this verse is that Muhammad was not asked to read the scriptures that were revealed before him but advised to ask the Jews and Christians about them. Could it be that the authors of the Qur'an were fully aware that even at that point and time in Islamic history—at least nineteen years had elapsed since the first revelation—that Muhammad was still illiterate? No wonder the Qur'an contains some half-finished Bible narratives with bizarre twists because Muhammad could not verify the hearsay. For instance, Moses, the Virgin Mary, and Aaron are siblings. The story of Mary and her newborn son, Jesus, is similar to the story of Hagar and Ishmael in the desert in Genesis 21:8–21.

Had the writers of the Qur'an and the Hadith devoted their time to articulating what Islam really stands for, perhaps there would have been less confusion among Muslims. Their account of Islam is as incoherent as their account of Christianity.

4.2 The Qur'an and its Authorship

The Hadith incriminates the Qur'an by exposing its dubious authorship. It states that Arab Muslims in Iraq and Sham (present day Syria) were at war over differences in the recitation of the Qur'an. Uthman, the Third Caliphate, was asked to take charge in ensuring that the Qur'an was compiled into one language, the language of the Quraish—Prophet Muhammad's tribe. He in turn asked Hafsa (one of Prophet Muhammad's wives) to send him the manuscripts of the Qur'an so that they could compile it. Hafsa responded to Uthman's request. He ordered three Muslim men, among them Zaid bin Thabit, to rewrite the manuscripts in perfect copies. When the writing of the Qur'an was complete, Uthman sent a copy to every Muslim province and ordered all the other Qur'anic materials in fragment manuscripts or whole copies to be burned.[9]

Uthman was not appreciated for what he did. He paid dearly for his actions to compile the original Qur'an because angry Muslims later killed him for putting together the current Qur'an. The Hadith states that they besieged his house and killed him.[10] Perhaps some of the obscure topics in the Qur'an and the Hadith would have been illumined had he not burned the other manuscripts. Or did he burn them to cover up some of their major inconsistencies? We are left to speculate.

The compiling of the Qur'an as stated in the Hadith is unknown to most Muslims. The Muslims I know, including Hajj Guyole, tend to believe that the chapters in the Qur'an were revealed intact directly from Allah to Muhammad, with no errors and human involvement in compiling and propagating them. The Hadith confirms their belief in stating, "When Allah completed the creation, He wrote in His Book which is with Him on His Throne."[11] In addition, the Qur'an alludes that humans should not write Allah's book.[12] On that account, most Muslims are willing to sacrifice their lives for the Qur'an, especially when one criticizes its content or goes to the extent of desecrating it by either handling it improperly or destroying it.

4.3 Who May Touch the Qur'an?

Ardent Muslims are offended if non-Muslims touch the Qur'an. Apparently this notion is lax among some Muslims nowadays, because a Christian friend of mine received a copy of the Qur'an from the Saudi Arabian Embassy in Washington, DC. This is contrary to the belief that "unless one has performed the rite of ablution, one may not touch the Qur'an."[13] Prophet Muhammad told his followers, "Most surely it is an honored Qur'an, a book that is protected none shall touch it save the purified ones."[14] The message is clear that without a ceremonial cleansing that includes the ablution no one should touch the Qur'an. If this guideline is followed, non-Muslims, however clean they are, should not touch it because only a Muslim who has recited *niyat*—purpose in his or her heart—and performed the ablution can touch it.

This condition of purity could be a deterrent to Muslims who try to decipher the Qur'an because it is very hard for them to be in this state of purity at all times. A mere fart would nullify this state of purity because Prophet Muhammad said, "The prayer of a person who does Hadath (passes urine, stool or wind) [sic] is not accepted till he performs (repeats) the ablution."[15] An ablution is necessary for not only performing prayers, but also handling the Qur'an. If a Muslim who has performed *wuudu* (ablution) and is in a state of *tahara* (purity) farts, he or she has to repeat the ritual of ablution in order to handle the Qur'an. Thus Muslims have a difficult time reading the Qur'an without natural interruptions and washings.

4.4 A Red Herring

The honored Qur'an contains many apparent inconsistencies. Since its contradictions are obvious, Muslims who proselytize Christians tend to compare it with the Bible. They go to the extent of searching the Bible for evidence that it is also flawed. While intentionally avoiding the New Testament, which disproves some of Prophet Muhammad's claims, they rummage through the Old Testament looking for some discrepancy. The Book of Jeremiah 8:8 is the focal point of their assault. Muslims who bring up this issue are normally interested only in verse 8, but for the sake of clarity, let us look at both verses 8 and 9. Prophet Jeremiah said:

> How can you say, 'We *are* wise, And the law of the LORD *is* with us'? Look, the false pen of the scribe certainly works falsehood. The wise men are ashamed, They are dismayed and taken. Behold, they have rejected the word of the LORD; So what wisdom do they have?[16]

Muslims claim that verse 8 proves that the scribes had lied when writing the law, hence the Bible is fallible. That allegation is easily refuted when one consults the entire chapter. Verse 9 clearly shows that the scribes did not change the law, but rejected it. Jeremiah the prophet was "contrasting his proclaimed word of the Lord with the written tradition (law) misinterpreted by those administering it (scribes)."[17] Bible commentaries on the chapter show that the scribes were not writing the Law at that time as alleged by Islamic scholars because the Law was already written. Jeremiah "refers to the false interpretation"[18] of the Law.

4.5 The Offer to "Buy Me" Back

Hajj Guyole did not like some of my explanations and quickly changed the topic, contending that Jesus, before his Ascension, predicted Prophet Muhammad's coming. Muslims I know seem to be quite confused about the promised "Comforter" whom Jesus said in the Gospel of John would come. If they read chapters 14 and 16 of this Gospel, they would learn that Jesus promised the coming of the Holy Spirit.[19] According to John, God sent the Holy Spirit because Jesus asked for him to be sent. If that spirit were Muhammad, then Muslims would never accept it because it would seem like Jesus requested for Muhammad to be sent. The prophecy being about Muhammad is even beside the point because the Holy Spirit came a few days after Jesus' ascension—more than five hundred years before the birth of Muhammad.[20]

Hajj Guyole gave up on trying to convince me because I had an answer or rebuttal for every question or claim he had raised. I even showed him passages in the Qur'an which spoke well of Jesus. The attributes and accolades ascribed to Jesus far exceed those accorded to Prophet Muhammad.[21] Suddenly Hajj Guyole asked me how much I was paid to join Christianity.

Many Muslims believe that Christianity buys converts. It could be that they are confused about the central theme of Christianity that centers on Christ's redeeming power. I told Hajj Guyole that no one paid me to convert. I reiterated that the only price that was paid was the death of Jesus Christ on the cross for my sins. When Jesus died on the cross he said, "It is finished!"[22] The Greek word used by Jesus was also used in the first century Greco-Roman world to mean, "Paid in Full."[23]   Hajj Guyole shook his head in disgust and talked to me about a family in Bahrain whom he claimed was willing to pay me to convert back to Islam.

Muslims in Kenya falsely accuse Christians of buying converts, but apparently they are the ones who practice it. It is not new that Muslims provide enticement to people so that they become interested in Islam or even convert. The African Muslim Agency (AMA)—a Kuwaiti-funded Islamic charity organization—is busy influencing people in Kenya with handouts to join Islam. In some countries, the almsgiving, *zakat*, is also distributed to non-Muslims "whom Muslims hope to win over and convert to Islam."[24] For instance, the Malaysian government gives "2 percent [of 2.5 percent collected from every Muslim earning an income] to converts."[25] With that knowledge, I knew that Hajj Guyole was serious about his offer. At that point, I felt I had heard enough of his desperate appeals. I dismissed his frantic efforts, closed my religious books, and went on with my schoolwork for the rest of the day.

My brother who went on the family errand returned home a few days later. I asked him where he went. His account was similar to my mother's: he was gone to bring home some cows that our family had bought. Evidently he did not bring any cows home because I didn't see any new ones. I wondered what had happened.

4.6 Continued Debate

The evening came, and my brothers and I went to the cow corral to see how our herd was doing. It is part of our tradition for males to visit the cow herd every evening. After the sun had set, the call to Maghrib prayer sounded. The faithful hurriedly broke their fast.

The Hadith recommends that Muslims break their fast with fresh dates during Ramadhan. Muslims believe that they will be rewarded for emulating the Prophet this way. If fresh dates are unavailable then dry dates are recommended. As a result of this practice, the date market soars during Ramadhan. Muslims believe they also get rewards for hastening to break the fast. They hurry to break their fast because they believe that the devils would otherwise do it before them. But this practice seems a bit incongruous because the devils are supposed to be chained during Ramadhan.[26]

My brothers and male members of the Islamic community went to the mosque for the prayer. I was alone in the cattle corral that evening, gazing into the distant horizon, marveling at the magnificent sunset. We had a fire burning to keep the cows warm and ward off mosquitoes. I kept busy feeding it.

Women went to milk the cows after *iftar* before the *isha* (night prayer) and *taraaweh* prayers. The *taraaweh* is observed only during Ramadhan after the *isha* prayer. It is not compulsory but those who observe it believe they are rewarded. Men joined me for a time to chat about the daily happenings before *taraaweh*. Some of them were hostile toward me because of my conversion to Christianity. Fights often broke out because most of those who had the audacity to ask questions about Christianity had no basis for most of their arguments. They occasionally charged at me when I asked questions about Islam that they could not answer.

My tribe is considered 100 percent Muslim. Some of their neighboring tribes are Christian. I heard many bizarre stories about Christians when I was growing up. Many Muslims in my home area and throughout Kenya hate them because they believe that Christians will fuel the fire of hell.

I was not surprised that Muslims had a strong aversion for Christians because some Christians I met staggered home drunk. Some of those who lived near my hometown were not good witnesses. There was a story going around that a drunken Christian man staggered home one evening and fell into a ditch that was infested with mosquitoes. He passed out for the night. The following day his tribesmen found him quite anemic and in need of a blood transfusion. They say that mosquitoes sucked most of his blood. Although the story could not possibly be true, it pictures how Muslims in my home area view Christians, which sadly does not reflect the teachings of Jesus Christ.

Muslims in my home area still bring up that story. However, there is one thing that most of them do not know: although Islamic teachings prohibit alcohol consumption here on earth, they also teach that it will be in ample supply in paradise. Alcohol will be flowing like a river, and Muslims will be enjoying it. The Qur'an promises wine that tastes delightful.[27]

Why would Islam ban the use of alcohol here on earth but sanction its use in paradise? There are a few reasons. The Hadith states, "Some people drank alcoholic beverages in the morning [of the day] of the Uhud battle and on the same day they were killed as martyrs, and that was before wine was prohibited."[28] Wine was popular among Muslims even in 625 AD—fifteen years after the advent of Islam. Even on an important day of a battle it was consumed in large quantities. Many Arab Muslim warriors drank in the morning before fighting and as a result were killed. The companions of Muhammad enjoyed it until the fateful day of Uhud. But another reason that the Hadith gives for banning alcohol was the scarcity of dates in Arabia during that time. Instead of importing some dates from neighboring territories to continue the production, alcohol was banned outright by Muhammad.[29] What an indirect economic sanction against those who were not receptive toward Islam!

Muslims in my home area were hypocritical for continuing to bring up the story of a drunken Christian man. Aside from the fictitious additions to the story, his sin should not have become the laughing-stock of the village, especially not for what they believe they will practice in paradise. But reasoning with them did not alleviate their entrenched hatred for Christians. Even though I was one of their own, and they knew my way of life, I was not spared from their hatred on account of my conversion.

4.7 The Attempt to Poison Me

I continued debating Muslim men at the cow corral in spite of their reactions. To my surprise, later that evening my younger brother joined us. He was not expected to be there because the young ones were excused from that cultural practice. Since children of his age were not obliged to observe the fast, they ate later. I was surprised that he cleared his share of food rather quickly to join us. He walked toward me and informed me that my sister Halima had invited me over for a post-fast meal.

It is normal in my culture for one to be invited over for a meal or a beverage within a short notice. The fact that I was home for the school holiday gave credence to many invitations. I thought Halima had invited me in order to save me from debating unruly Muslims. Many a time one who declines an invitation or fails to consume what is served is considered egregious. Having that in mind I unsuspectingly left for her house.

When I got there, Halima, her husband, and some of my relatives were waiting for me. The group did not raise my suspicions because the gathering was normal since most of them stayed up for the *taraaweh* prayers. Some of them would stay up until a few hours before dawn for *suhur*, the predawn meal eaten during Ramadhan.

Halima offered me a drink that she set up on a mat with some delicacies to follow. I sat down and was ready to consume it. Then I felt uncomfortable. My conscience was telling me not to consume it. I asked if it was all right if I offered it to somebody else. Halima told me that they would keep it for me. I did not suspect what that implied but kept it in mind. I inquired once again if it was okay to feed it to some poor neighbors. There was a poor family a stone's throw away whom I thought would have enjoyed it. She insisted that they would save it for me.

I walked out of her house into the expansive darkness of the night heading toward the cow corral, not knowing that I had just dodged a bullet. When I was halfway, my conscience told me to go back to the house. And hesitatingly, I walked back. As I was approaching the house, I heard a large group of people arguing. They were accusing each other of something. When I moved closer, I could hear that they were accusing each other of telling me about the poison in my drink. My heart sank. I could not believe what I was hearing. My mind began to race. I was running out of ideas of how to act. It was a nightmare. I stood outside the house motionless listening to them.

My tribe's houses are built such that there is natural air ventilation. I listened to all their arguments and discussions about their next move. I stood outside in shock, not knowing how to act. My heart was thrusting against the walls of my chest cavity, and chills ran down my spine. I was shocked but at the same time felt that they should be confronted.

The Qur'an advises against violence during the holy month of Ramadhan. I had known right from the outset that they would do something to me because I converted to Christianity. But I was obviously mistaken to think that they would wait until the end of Ramadhan.

Their discussion and brainstorming ended. No sooner did they agree on the next step than I plucked up some courage to storm the meeting. To their dismay I walked into a house full of them and went straight to the point. Their mouths dropped open. I said, "You planned to poison me, but the God I believe in is powerful. If you do not give up your aspiration, my God will destroy you." I unabashedly talked to them, showing no sympathy. They were speechless and looked at each other wondering what had befallen them.

The group was bigger than when I had gone into the house initially. Some of them probably had hidden in the darkness waiting for me to consume the drink and food I was offered. Had I ingested the poison, perhaps they would have mocked me to death.

I walked out of the house that night with some leverage. One thing stood out inescapably clear: they poisoned my food, but providentially I did not eat it. Instead I caught them fighting over their failed attempt and devising another strategy. Galano, one of my loquacious relatives, was in their midst that night. He has another wife who resided in a different town. He told Muslims there not to persecute me because it seemed like God spoke to me. One of his sisters-in-law was my classmate in high school. She told me what he had said when I returned to school after the April holiday.

I praised God for saving me from consuming the poisoned drink. The abortive attempt to poison me stymied my detractors. I take no credit for the good amidst the gloom that I lived through since my conversion to Christianity became public. Were it not for the hand of the Almighty, I would not even be alive. I live to offer praise and gratitude to God. I live to give glory and honor to His name.

[1] *Sahih Bukhari, Volume 4, Book 54, Number 462.*

[2] *Sahih Bukhari, Volume 4, Book 55, Number 649.*

[3] Pickthall.

[4] Suratul As-Assaf, 61:6.

[5] John Kaltner, *Ishmael Instructs Isaac: An Introduction of the Qur'an for Bible Readers* (Collegeville, MN: Michael Glazer Books, 1999), 14. Bracket mine.

[6] *Sahih Bukhari, Volume 1, Book 1, Number 3; Volume 6, Book 60, Number 478;* and *Volume 9, Book 87, Number 111.*

[7] Yusuf Ali.

[8] Pickthall.

[9] *Sahih Bukhari, Volume 6, Book 61, Number 510.*

[10] *Sunan Abu-Dawud, Volume 2, Book 8, Number 2680* and *Volume 3, Book 34, Number 4487.*

[11] *Sahih Bukhari, Volume 4, Book 54, Number 416.*

[12] Suratul Al-Baqara, 2:79.

[13] Don C. Locke, *Increasing Multicultural Understanding: A Comprehensive Model* (Thousand Oaks, CA: Sage Publications, 1998), 218.

[14] Shakir, 56:77–79.

[15] *Sahih Bukhari, Volume 1, Book 4, Number 137.*

[16] NKJV.

[17] Footnote. *The New Oxford Annotated Bible, New Revised Standard Version* (New York: Oxford University Press, 1989), 975.

[18] John Calvin, *Jeremiah* (Christian Classics Ethereal Library).

[19] This subject is addressed in chapter sixteen.

[20] The Acts of the Apostles chapters 1–2.

[21] This topic is addressed in chapter fifteen.

[22] NKJV, John 19:30.

23   Retrieved from http://www.bible.org/qa.asp?topic_id=5&qa_id=28
     on July 13, 2007.
24   Creighton Ainsworth, *The Truths: The Shameful, Deceit, Arrogance,
     and Corruption of Religion* (Philadelphia: Xlibris, 2002), 173.
25   Timur Kuran, *Islam and Mammon: The Economic Predicament
     of Islamism* (Princeton, NJ: Princeton University Press, 2004), 25.
     Bracket mine.
26   *Sahih Bukhari, Volume 3, Book 31, Number 123.*
27   Suratul Al-Muhammad, 47:15.
28   *Sahih Bukhari, Volume 6, Book 60, Number 142.* Bracket mine.
29   *Sahih Bukhari, Volume 7, Book 69, Number 486.*

CHAPTER FIVE

Iddul Fitr and the Planned Forced Conversion

After the botched poisoning incident, people of the Orma community—my tribe—spoke in low voices whenever I crossed their path. Some of them glanced at me but maintained only minimal eye contact, which was strange behavior for a typically gregarious people. They knew what had transpired that night because the news had spread like wildfire in the community. My relative Galano also told people everywhere he traveled. Consequently, my enemies were confounded by the turn of events. My family loathed the attention the aftermath of my conversion had brought onto the parochial community.

Galano continued spreading the news. He was honest about what he had witnessed that night. Muslims I have known tend to see ex-Muslims as conspirators, hence would not have believed had I been the one telling the story. Whatever the case, I believe God spared me that night because He was proving to my family and relatives that it was not yet His time for me to die. Perhaps He was making it clear to them that I should be left alone.

Although I experienced God's protection that night, I was worried about the possibility of subsequent attempts to poison me. Thus, whenever I was invited to a meal or a drink, I refused to eat or drink unless my host shared his or her dish or drank from the same container with me. Some of my Muslim friends and relatives thought that was awkward and poked fun at me, but I took no chances in light of what had happened. That precautionary approach became a routine for me also during feasts.

My family was quite upset at how things had unfolded. Some of my relatives tried to deflect the attention from what my sister and others had unsuccessfully attempted to do to me. The month-long fast during Ramadhan that year was coming to an end. A huge celebration, *Iddul Fitr*, follows the conclusion of the fast, which takes place after the sighting of the new moon.

Muslims look forward to the end of Ramadhan because they are not restricted in how they conduct themselves in matters pertaining to sex with their spouses, eating, drinking, and prayer. Ramadhan is a time to forgo some luxuries and observe extra prayers; thus, *Iddul Fitr* is welcomed with ecstasy.

The day starts with festivities beginning as early as dawn. Women bake specialty bread and make all sorts of delicacies. Men and women observe the mandatory daily prayer at dawn. They perform the *Iddul Fitr* prayer about two hours after sunrise. Most people adorn themselves in the newest clothes. Adults give candy to children.

I was worried that the huge *Idd* celebration would be used as an avenue for more persecution. I thought many Muslims had so far patiently put up with me since my conversion became public only because they were heeding the Qur'an, which urges restraint during the sacred months. I was hoping that nothing out of the ordinary would happen to me.

Little did I know, there was already a plan in place to persecute me. On the eve of *Iddul Fitr*, my brother-in-law Dokota and my half-brother Godana informed me that I would be converted back to Islam the following day. (Dokota had also been present when my food was poisoned.) They informed me that it made no difference whether I complied or not. I was taken aback by their bold warning. I prayed about the situation and consulted with a Christian friend, Raphael, who frequented my village. He was an adult education teacher in the area with whom I had secretly met after my conversion; his father is a pastor. They lived about seven kilometers away from my village.

5.1 Taking Refuge at a Friend's House

It was evening and my mind was fixated on the threat ushered in by the duo. I knew that if I stayed around I would be tortured. Then I recalled what Jesus Christ told the devil when he was being tempted in the desert. When the devil appeared to him in the form of a serpent quoting from the Book of Psalms and taunted him, if he was the Son of God, to jump from the top of the tower because God would send His angels to protect him, Jesus said to the serpent, "You shall not tempt the LORD your God."[1] Since I knew what was coming, I thought it would be imprudent of me to stay because that would have amounted to putting God to the test.

One thing Dokota and Godana did not know was that I had a plan that would keep me some miles away from them during the *Idd* prayer. They had given me an advance warning and I took advantage of it. I knew that the duo would have carried out their threat because they had such an influence on the masses.

I found out that my mother was not apprised of the plan, so I asked her for permission to leave my home for the night. The Chief's order required me to ask her for consent whenever I left home, and she gave me permission to spend the night at Raphael's house. He belonged to the Pokomo tribe.

I trudged toward his home early that evening. It was a long walk, but that did not deter me considering what I was fleeing. I arrived after sunset. His family was glad to host me that night. His father read some scripture passages, talked to me about my persecution from that perspective, and prayed with me after dinner. The family devotion inspired me. Then we went to bed.

I thought I had kept the duo's plan to convert me by force at bay. I lay in bed that night with my mind wandering through all sorts of scenarios they would use since I had beaten them to the punch by eluding them. I thought about how horrifically they would treat me for running away. All along I was persuaded that I had foiled their plans by being away at a location known only to my mother. I thought it would take them time to figure out my whereabouts and they would be discouraged from making the trip, considering that they had so much at stake on that special day. I also thought the requirement for Muslims to pray at stated times would discourage them from pursuing the idea. Islamic prayers are normally offered within certain time frames, otherwise they become time barred. The Qur'an in Suratul Al-Nisa, 4:103, states, "When ye have performed the act of worship, remember Allah, standing, sitting and reclining.

And when ye are in safety, observe proper worship. Worship at fixed times hath been enjoined on the believers."[2]

5.2 A Knock on the Door

Then at around 6 a.m. a knock on the door broke the tranquility of the night. Raphael's mother answered the door. She was shocked to see my tribesmen. We were caught completely off-guard. My brother-in-law and half-brother, accompanied by a whip-brandishing policeman, were at the door. Dokota and Godana had hired a police officer and were ready to take me home for the planned conversion. No sooner did Raphael's mother see the odd visitors than she announced in her tribal language who they were. She was so terrified that she asked her son to talk to them.

Men from my people group are usually armed at all times. Given that there was a prevailing enmity between Ormas and Pokomos, it did not surprise me that Raphael's mother was that scared. It was petrifying enough for the Pokomos to have my tribesmen at their doorsteps in broad daylight, let alone at the crack of dawn.

I lay in bed terrified, trying to come to terms with how my run had ended. The thought of having a police officer present somewhat comforted me. But as is the case nowadays, corruption was rampant in my country, and police officers were known as the most corrupt public servants. People were scared of them and hardly talked with them. Many a time policemen had planted evidence on people against whom they had a vendetta in order to charge them with crimes. Had the police officer taken a bribe? What if he did not give me a chance to tell my side of the story and forced me to go home and face the forced conversion? Those were the kind of questions that engulfed my mind.

I imagined how I would be beaten with all sorts of canes, shaved by force—shaving of pubic, armpit, head, and facial hair is part of the Islamic conversion ritual—and possibly be beaten to death. I had heard horror stories of what Muslims who converted to Christianity faced in some parts of Kenya and other countries. I was afraid.

Raphael went to the door to talk to the visitors. I was more scared when the police officer did the talking. He told Raphael that he was looking for a young man who was insane, and had left his home without his mother's knowledge. (That was a gambit that my relatives and the Muslim community widely employed to cover up or lessen the impact of my conversion to Christianity, with which they could not come to terms. That propaganda tactic could make anyone who had never met me think that I was indeed insane.) My half-brother Godana added that my mother had gone berserk over my alleged disappearance and was crying uncontrollably. I lay in bed nervously listening to all their stories.

Godana and Dokota had hired the police officer from a nearby police station in order to flush me out of Raphael's parents' house. The fact that I was in a different Location—a government administrative unit—did not deter them from pushing their case against me. I was appalled that they had gone to the extent of breaching the Kenyan law governing case jurisdictions in order to have me home to convert back to Islam. I had done nothing wrong because, per the court order, I had asked my mother for permission to go away for the night.

Emotions were running high. My heart was beating fast as I did not know what the day held for me. I said a silent prayer leaving all in God's care. I was confident that if it were His will, I would be liberated unscathed from my tribulations.

Raphael listened to all the men's allegations against me, then he asked me to come and talk to them. I reluctantly got up, walked over to the door, and greeted Dokota and Godana by name. The police officer was perplexed. He asked in disbelief if I were indeed insane. That was just the opportune moment I needed, so at that point I commenced talking. I told the officer that my brother-in-law and half-brother were there that morning to take me home for a forced conversion back to Islam. It did not seem to make sense to him. I explained to him how my family and the Muslim community were having difficulties coping with my conversion to Christianity. I went on to tell him that the duo had vowed to follow through with their threat and had come to take me home to face the conversion during the *Iddul Fitr* prayer that morning.

The cop was bewildered by my version of the story. I further elucidated how the situation he was dealing with had already been in Chief's court and a ruling had been made. I added that since the court had the jurisdiction, he should not tamper with it because I had obeyed the court order by asking my mother for permission. I warned him that should he comply with their request and send me home with them, I would file a grievance with the relevant party, and that could lead to him losing his job. Desperate times call for desperate measures.

5.3 Police Ineptitude in Kenya

Most police officers in Kenya turn a deaf ear to complaints by citizens. There have been cases in which they were called to intervene when crimes were in progress and they failed to come because they had excuses. The common one was that they lacked fuel to make the trip. But when the money to refuel was provided, the cruisers made the trip without going to a filling station. Some officers also abetted in crimes. That fact underscored how rife corruption was in Kenya.

As is the case today, the police officers in my home area were worse than most because they derided the local residents whom the government had marginalized since the country attained its independence. The proximity of my district to war-ravaged Somalia did not help the cause for justice either. Many a time police cornered pedestrians and asked them for their national identity cards. Those who lacked the documents or merely forgot to carry them were charged with being illegal aliens. They were bundled into a police Land Rover and taken to jail, where they secured their release only after money had changed hands. The *East African Standard* reported, "A survey by the corruption watchdog, Transparency International, lists the Kenya Police as the most corrupt public institution, followed by political parties and Parliament."[3] The U.S State Department in its annual country reports on human rights said, "[Kenya] Police often arrested citizens arbitrarily, sometimes with the sole purpose of extorting bribes."[4] Corruption in the police force was rampant and entrenched in Kenya. It was quite sad.

The Kenya police force's recourse to sleaze stemmed from their dissatisfaction with their meager salaries, which were not commensurate with the high standard of living. Most of them were forced into the profession out of desperation because there was no other employment opportunity. A Kenyan weekly newsmagazine, the *East African*, states:

> It must be borne in mind that most police officers joined the force as the only option available, at times buying recruitment. Therefore, to them, being a police officer is more a way of earning a living than a vocation. They owe their allegiance to their benefactors rather than to the laws and principles that should govern their conduct.[5]

I was quite nervous that morning because I had been a victim of bribery when my family took me to court, an experience that was still vivid in my mind. Since I did not want to live through that again, I was on the lookout to ensure that that did not happen.

I talked with the police officer because I did not want to face the forced conversion. I thought if he became cantankerous and failed to fulfill his duty, then I was better off languishing in jail than to be at the mercy of my persecutors. I let the police officer know that I would not let my right to freedom in religion granted by the Kenyan Constitution be infringed.

Surprisingly, he was judicious. He told me that he would not mess with the case that the court had already dealt with. He left it to me to decide when to go home that morning. That was just what I needed to hear. I did not dare to go home right away because I would have arrived around the time for *Iddul Fitr* prayer and would have played right into the forced conversion.

5.4 Islamic Teachings on Religious Freedom

Avowed Muslims go to great lengths to forcefully convert one of their own who reverts to *kufr* (unbelief) or to kill him or her as commanded by Prophet Muhammad. His message in the Hadith on how to treat ex-Muslims is explicit. On the other hand, many Muslims who do not know the Hadith have no idea how to act toward apostates because the Qur'an gives contradictory messages on the subject.

Prophet Muhammad was for religious freedom according to what he recited as revelations from Allah in the Qur'an when

Islam was in its preliminary stages. An earlier chapter of the Qur'an revealed in Mecca shows that trend. Suratul Al-Kafiruun, 109:1–6, on religious freedom states:

> Say: O disbelievers!
>
> I worship not that which ye worship;
>
> Nor worship ye that which I worship.
>
> And I shall not worship that which ye worship.
>
> Nor will ye worship that which I worship.
>
> Unto you your religion, and unto me my religion. [6]

Allah's revelation to Muhammad in the above chapter of the Qur'an let the people of Mecca continue with their idol worship— 360 gods in the Kaaba alone—while Muhammad worshipped Allah during the advent of Islam. Neither Muhammad nor Allah initially condemned the widespread idolatry in Arabia. Nevertheless, their position changed when Islam gained some followers. When Muhammad became an opponent of idolatry, he was severely persecuted by idolaters in Mecca and as a result fled to Medina in 622 AD, which marked the beginning of the Islamic calendar, Hijrah.

The inhabitants of Medina accepted Muhammad because they sympathized with him. He built his political base and later attacked the people of Mecca who had earlier rejected his message. He waged war against them to convert them to Islam. Suratul Al-Baqara, 2:193, states, "And fight with them until there is no persecution, and religion should be only for Allah, but if they desist, then there should be no hostility except against the oppressors."[7] This blunt and to-the-point command to fight is a stark contrast to the earlier abstruse message given in Mecca.

In this verse Muslims are called to fight till religion is only for Allah. There are many peace-loving Muslims who argue that Islam only calls on Muslims to fight to defend their religion. This rules out the preemptive-strike approach widely employed during Muhammad's time. This more peaceful approach is obviously not founded on the Qur'an's teachings, because this verse clearly gives the definition of peace as a time in which all religions competing against

Islam are obliterated. The Arabic word for religion, also mentioned in this verse, is الدِّينُ [Al-Diinu], which "is the sum total of Muslim's faith and the code of conduct necessary to obey sharia."[8] An ardent Muslim believes, just as the above Qur'anic verse implies, that there is only one *Diinu*, Islam, and anything short of living the *Al-Diinu* is gross error.

The Hadith drives this point home in the passage where Muhammad addresses his followers:

> The Prophet (peace be upon him) said: I am commanded to fight with men till they testify that there is no god but Allah, and that Muhammad is His servant and His Apostle, face our qiblah (direction of prayer), eat what we slaughter, and pray like us. When they do that, their life and property are unlawful for us except what is due to them. They will have the same rights as the Muslims have, and have the same responsibilities as the Muslims have.[9]

This Hadith is very lucid. Muhammad was commanded by Allah to fight until the Jews, Christians, and pagans of Arabia converted to Islam, or at the very least acted like Muslims: by praying like them, eating what they slaughtered, and facing the direction of Mecca to pray. This Hadith confirms what the Qur'an in 2:193 called for—the eradication of other religions. If Islam were for religious freedom, Allah should not have advocated for the use of force to gain converts to his religion.

It is quite offensive to a Muslim to be offered meat of an animal that has not been properly slaughtered by a Muslim. When Muhammad and his contemporaries went to fight at his command, they enforced a rule that everyone should only eat what a Muslim had slaughtered. Muslims are already achieving this goal in some countries. For instance, in some parts of Kenya Muslims slaughter all animals that are sold to the public. They are indirectly forcing people to espouse their way of life by having them eat what they slaughter, thus attempting to achieve the gradual conversion to Islam. They are a minority group in the country, but once their population soars they hope to eventually demand the Shariah law. They are already lobbying for a broader Khadis Court—a court system in Kenya that attends to Muslim matters—that would be independent to adjudicate Muslim affairs based on the Shariah law.

Non-Muslims who resisted embracing Islam suffered immensely in Arabia during Muhammad's time. Their properties were commandeered. Those who refused to accept Islam were either killed or taken as captives. They were also subjected to paying taxes to Prophet Muhammad. The Qur'an states the case:

> Fight those who believe not in Allah nor the Last Day, nor hold that forbidden which hath been forbidden by Allah and His Messenger, nor acknowledge the religion of Truth, (even if they are) of the People of the Book, until they pay the Jizya with willing submission, and feel themselves subdued.[10]

The Hadith clarifies it by stating that:

> It has been reported from Sulaiman b. Buraid through his father that, when the Messenger of Allah (may peace be upon him) appointed anyone as leader of an army or detachment, he would especially exhort him to fear Allah and to be good to the Muslims who were with him. He would say: Fight in the name of Allah and in the way of Allah. Fight against those who disbelieve in Allah. Make a holy war, do not embezzle the spoils; do not break your pledge; and do not mutilate (the dead) bodies; do not kill the children. When you meet your enemies who are polytheists, invite them to three courses of action. If they respond to any one of these, you also accept it and withhold yourself from doing them any harm. Invite them to (accept) Islam; if they respond to you, accept it from them and desist from fighting against them. Then invite them to migrate from their lands to the land of Muhairs and inform them that, if they do so, they shall have all the privileges and obligations of the Muhajirs. If they refuse to migrate, tell them that they will have the status of Bedouin Muslims and will be subjected to the Commands of Allah like other Muslims, but they will not get any share from the spoils of war or Fai' except when they actually fight with the Muslims (against the disbelievers). If they refuse to accept Islam, demand from them the Jizya. If they agree to pay, accept it from them and

hold off your hands. If they refuse to pay the tax, seek Allah's help and fight them.[11]

Non-Muslims who flirted with the idea of joining Islam because of the mounting pressure were treated favorably. They attained the same status as Muslims, and they were exempt from paying Jizya (taxes).

When all the surrounding areas in Arabia were conquered and Islam had no rival religion to challenge it, Muhammad received yet another revelation from Allah. Suratul Al-Baqara verse 256 reads, "Let there be no compulsion in religion: Truth stands out clear from Error: whoever rejects evil and believes in Allah hath grasped the most trustworthy hand-hold, which never breaks. And Allah heareth and knoweth all things."[12] That was quite a change in stance. The Jews, Christians, and pagans whom Prophet Muhammad and his associates had steamrolled for resisting conversion to Islam were probably astounded to hear the new revelation.

This verse alleges that the truth stands out clear from "error." It depicts the Christian and Judaist doctrines as the error distinct from the Islamic message. How Islam downright claims the Christian message is an error, a message it misrepresents throughout the Qur'an and the Hadith, is confusing. We saw earlier that the Qur'an's idea of the Trinity—the core doctrine of Christianity—is flawed because it is utterly in contradiction with the Bible. Many Muslims discuss Christianity from that angle. Once they are disproved, they resort to using the same rhetoric Prophet Muhammad used, that the Christian Scripture is corrupted.

The above translation of the Qur'an is the Meaning of the Holy Qur'an translated by Yusuf Ali. This verse begins, "Let there be no compulsion in religion," whereas two other prominent translations, Shakir and Pickthall, begin with, "There is no compulsion in religion." This trend is confusing because Yusuf Ali portrays that compulsion in religion was practiced in Islam for some time during Muhammad's lifetime—a contradiction to his own commentary quoted below—but was later outlawed. In the latter case, however, the same verse in the two translations outright denies the practice in Islam. The Yusuf Ali commentary on this verse states that:

Compulsion is incompatible with religion: because (1) religion depends upon faith and will, and these would be meaningless if induced by force; (2) Truth and Error have been so clearly shown up by the mercy of Allah that there should be no doubt in the minds of any persons of good will as to the fundamentals of faith; (3) Allah's protection is continuous, and His Plan is always to lead us from the depths of darkness into the clearest light.[13]

This commentary is far-fetched and clearly misrepresents the mission of Muhammad when he was spreading Islam, because coercion was widely used. When he died, the men who succeeded him (caliphs) carried on his mission of converting people to Islam by force. Those who accepted Islam but later changed their mind were killed. Umar was one of the four caliphs. The following is what the Hadith states about a conversation between Umar's son and fellow Muslims regarding religious freedom in Islam:

Narrated Nafi (through another group of sub-narrators): A man came to Ibn Umar and said, "O Abu Abdur Rahman! What made you perform Hajj in one year and Umra in another year and leave the Jihad for Allah's Cause though you know how much Allah recommends it?" Ibn Umar replied, "O son of my brother! Islam is founded on five principles, i.e. believe in Allah and His Apostle, the five compulsory prayers, the fasting of the month of Ramadan, the payment of Zakat, and the Hajj to the House (of Allah)." The man said, "O Abu Abdur Rahman! Won't you listen to why Allah has mentioned in His Book:'If two groups of believers fight each other, then make peace between them, but if one of then transgresses beyond bounds against the other, then you all fight against the one that transgresses. (49.9) and:"And fight them till there is no more affliction (i.e. no more worshiping of others along with Allah)." Ibn Umar said, "We did it, during the lifetime of Allah's Apostle when Islam had only a few followers. A man would be put to trial because of his religion; he would either be killed or tortured. But when the Muslims increased, there were no more afflictions or oppressions."[14]

This Hadith shows when Muslims have to fight in order to convert people by force. It also gives provision on how to deal with a renegade. The reason that is given by the Sahaba (companions of the Prophet) for *jihad* to cease is when Islam has more followers. Once that goal is achieved, Muslims do not need to fight to spread Islam because the Shariah law that governs an Islamic state would force non-Muslims into embracing it. And those Muslims who live in countries where they are a minority would remain compromised, similarly to how Prophet Muhammad acted when Islam had only a few followers.

Had Islam advocated against forced conversion, non-Muslims would not have been subjected to the Shariah law in some Islamic countries to discourage them from exercising their religious freedom. Saudi Arabia would have given carte blanche to Christians, Jews, Hindus, and Buddhists to practice their religions. Disgruntled Muslims would have been allowed to change religions. Unfortunately that is not the case in Saudi Arabia. Religious police round up people for the five daily prayers. Non-Muslims are harassed, and "non-Islamic practices still lead to jail and deportation."[15]

The Taliban rule in Afghanistan, however gruesome it was, was the prime paradigm of authentic Islam. It was established under the auspices of the Saudi Arabian and Pakistani governments. The Saudis later were opposed to it only because Osama bin Laden had the ambition to overthrow their kingdom. Had the Taliban rule been against Islam, it would not have gained any support among Muslims. In fact, Saudi Arabia, Pakistan, and the United Arab Emirates recognized it as Afghanistan's government.[16]

Suratul Al-Baqara verse 256 leaves a huge area uncovered and hence open to interpretation. It is possible that my relatives and Muslim leaders interpreted it differently since many Qur'an translations abound, as it does not address how a Muslim who embraces another religion should be treated. Perhaps this is what led Dokota and Godana to pursue taking me home for the forced conversion that morning.

5.5 Spared from Forced Conversion

To their utter dismay, the police officer gave me my freedom, and I decided to stay with Raphael's family for part of the day, a decision that infuriated them. They had hired a cop early that morning and had been determined to bring me home in time for the planned forced conversion during the *Idd* prayer, but the outcome was not what they had desired. They dejectedly walked home. On the other hand, Raphael was enraged. He was upset because the duo had embarrassed his family by bringing a cop to his home.

Idd prayers are normally held around 8 a.m.—two hours after the sunrise—in Kenya. The Muslim community waited for me in vain because I was not "delivered" for the forced conversion as they had expected. That altered some of their plans. As mentioned earlier, Muslims pray at specific times. Once that time frame passes, it is worthless to observe the prayer. Only travelers and those at war are excused from observing prayer at the appointed time. I wondered what excuse the community had for delaying to pray. They definitely missed an appointment with Allah that morning.

That failed forced conversion just exacerbated the Muslim community's hatred toward me. I was afraid to face them again that day but found solace in the Word of God. I was also concerned for Raphael's life. I wondered for some time what would have happened had the duo not brought a cop along. I would have probably been taken by force, and Raphael and his family would have been beaten up. What a dreadful day that would have been!

5.6 The Journey Home

No sooner did Godana and Dokota take off than Raphael and I planned for our trip to my home. We left later in the day as we agreed to avoid the angry mob after the *Iddul Fitr* prayer. We nervously discussed how we would deal with different potential situations. Raphael assured me that he would eat with me what I would be offered. He added that if the food were poisoned, then we would face it together. I do not know if that was a wise idea, but I was grateful to have him by my side because he was a great encouragement to me.

When we arrived at my home, my mother was gone fetching some water. She seemed unaware of how Dokota and Godana unsuccessfully came to Raphael's home to take me to face the forced conversion. Raphael and I could not believe our eyes. The woman who was supposedly berserk was going about her business getting ready for the festivities.

We went on an eating spree, carefully consuming what was set before us. The way we played it safe did not go very well with some Muslims. They joked about how we were cautious. Some of them still bring it up even though it had happened almost two decades ago.

Raphael and I devoured what was set before us in every home in which he was invited to eat. Muslims are very hospitable to others but hostile toward one of their own who reverts to *kufr* (unbelief). Thankfully, the afternoon went by without an incident, but I dreaded facing the night alone.

Raphael went home when the night fell. I was alone once again to deal with my persecutors. I slipped into the darkness of the night to the cattle corral. I mused over the fire that was made for our cows. An evening at home used to be my favorite pastime until my persecution started and all my friends spurned me.

The event of that day of how God intervened to save me from the forced conversion gave me the courage to endure. The odds were against me because I was going against the wishes of the entire Muslim community (*ummah*), but with Jehovah on my side I was confident of everything panning out in accordance with His will, even if that meant dying for His sake.

---

[1] NKJV, Luke 4:12.

[2] Yusuf Ali.

[3] John Oyuke, "Most Corrupt of Them All," *The East African Standard*, December 10, 2004. Retrieved from http://www.eastandard.net/archives/cl/hm_news/news.php?articleid=7898 on December 3, 2005.

[4] U.S. Department of State's Country Reports on Human Rights Practices-2004 Released by the Bureau of Democracy, Human

Rights, and Labor, February 28, 2005. Retrieved from http://www.state.gov/g/drl/rls/hrrpt/2004/41609.htm on December 5, 2005.

5   Catherine Riungu, "Culture Change Must Follow Better Police Pay," *The East African*, August 11, 2003. http://www.nationaudio.com/News/EastAfrican/11082003/Opinion/Opinion2233454.html Retrieved December 23, 2005.

6   Pickthall.

7   Shakir.

8   Wikipedia. http://en.wikipedia.org/wiki/Din_(Arabic_term) (Accessed May 21, 2006).

9   *Sunan Abu Dawud, Volume 2, Book 8, Number 2635.*

10 Yusuf Ali, 9:29.

11 *Sahih Muslim, Book 19, Number 4294a.*

12 Yusuf Ali.

13 Yusuf Ali, Commentary Number 300.

14 *Sahih Bukhari, Volume 6, Book 60, Number 40b.*

15 *Agence Française de Presse (AFP)* "Most Christians Expats in Gulf Can Celebrate Christmas." December 23rd, 2005. Retrieved from http://news.yahoo.com/s/afp/20051223/lf_afp/gulfreligionchristmas_0 51223151714&printer=1;_ylt=AsxE1p5HUjjJwfHL2h.5wUP2_sEF;_ylu=X3oDMTA3MXN1bHE0BHNlYwN0bWE- on December 24, 2005.

16 Tony Karon , "Understanding Bin Laden's hosts, the dilemma he poses for them, and the politics of the neighborhood," *Time Magazine,* September 18, 2001.

Chapter Six

The Escape

M y brothers continued meeting with me at night, hoping to convince me to quit Christianity. They always knew where to find me because I spent the evenings by the cow corral. Again, however, the meetings did not materialize into what they desired.

The Orma tribe enjoys a great loyalty. People mean what they say and are always there for each other. They listen to one another and rarely make an individual decision that goes against their family or community consensus. And they were quite upset with me for my unrelenting stubbornness.

An essential aspect of the Orma loyalty is that people go to great lengths to save one of their own whom they think is in harm's way. There is a well-known Orma saying, "A straying man the community redirects to the right path, but a straying community only God redirects." My family and the Orma Muslim community tried their best to redirect me to the path of Allah. They were also trying to avert a fracture in our bond of unity—a bond that had remained unaffected since time immemorial due to the continuous homogeneity of the Orma tribe.

Aside from the skewed idea of Christianity that they gathered from the Qur'an, they also had a wrong perception that it was a religion that belonged to "other tribes" they occasionally fought against. To them, converting to Christianity amounted to joining ranks with an enemy, which would be a recipe for disaster in a time of intertribal conflict. They were afraid for my safety since they did not trust the "Christian" tribes.

They looked out for clues as to who had influenced me to become a Christian. It did not take long until they identified a culprit in the form of my former headmaster Mr. Buya. They were bitter at him for having instigated my transfer to a secular boarding school when I was in seventh grade. Thankfully, by this time the Kenyan government had promoted him to a supervisory position, and he had been transferred to a station hundreds of miles away. He was informed of the new pejorative perceptions of him among my people. Accordingly, he avoided my home area during his vacations.

My brothers continued arguing their case with me that I should not have converted to Christianity without consulting our family. They said after I realized that Jesus Christ is a Savior, I should have discussed with them and urged them to come along. They insisted that it should have been a communal decision. I listened to their desperate pleas and told them that my decision to follow Christ was personal and nonnegotiable. That provoked their indignation and did not help even though I simply was expressing my beliefs and convictions. I was now in more trouble for being honest with them.

A family feud in the Orma community often results in a fight. Males in a clan beat up a person who fails to conform to the norm, a norm that mainly reflects the teachings of Prophet Muhammad. Cases of beatings-by-committee are common and comport with the Qur'an, which states:

> If two parties among the Believers fall into a quarrel, make ye
> peace between them: but if one of them transgresses beyond
> bounds against the other, then fight ye (all) against the one that
> transgresses until it complies with the command of Allah; but
> if it complies, then make peace between them with justice, and
> be fair: for Allah loves those who are fair (and just).[1]

If you have ever wondered why Muslims fight one another, this verse is just one of the many instances that command them to fight over philosophical differences. Those who lived during Muhammad's time heeded it to the point that they killed the four caliphs, men whom he had appointed to succeed him in leading Islam. Even the command that forbids the shedding of a Muslim's blood—a punishment exclusively reserved for one culpable of adultery, murdering a Muslim or apostasy—did not deter them.[2]

For me to entertain their idea of a communal decision without individual repentance would have been to flout the scriptural guidelines for conversion to Christianity. This was not an option for me to consider, because the Word of God never calls for a whole family or community to become Disciples of Christ just as a result of one member pressing the Gospel message on them.

Community consensus was their attempt to slow my conversion, hoping that I would change my mind. However, I knew that they would not have listened to me had I gone to consult with them before embracing Christianity. The Bible clearly states that it solely is the prerogative of God the Father to draw people to becoming disciples of His Son, Jesus Christ.[3] That criterion will never change. Therefore, despite their anger toward me, I pressed on, brushing aside all their pleas to reconsider my decision.

Thus a rift grew wider between us that I could do nothing to mend without compromising my beliefs. My brothers appeared helpless as I defied their advice. However, there was a looming danger of my being disciplined by committee. Nevertheless I did not flinch.

6.1 A Pretext for Spiritual Nourishment

The Chief's verdict required me to ask my mother for consent whenever I left home. There was an exception to that ruling, however, because the Orma's cultural expectation of duly attending to their livestock—our livelihood—took precedence. My family owns a herd of cattle that goes grazing on a communal land every day around 10 a.m. The herdsmen need help with driving the herd to the pasture. It is a formality that the males in the community escort their herds. As a youth I helped drive the herd to the pasture and afterward I would swim with others in the River Tana. We were always home in time for the *dhuhr* (noon) prayer.

The horror stories I had heard of some Muslims drowning ex-Muslims in some parts of the country made me reconsider the morning swim. Swimming was a perfect opportunity for me to display my stampless buttocks to those Muslims who believed in the "stamp." But since I was outnumbered, I was concerned that they might drown me as likely as they would appreciate my display. I had to think of something else to do with my free time.

Then an idea came to my mind that I should use that opportunity to go to a church service in a nearby village on Sunday and visit fellow Christians other days of the week. That Sunday I hid my Bible underneath my shirt when I left home with the cattle. I felt there was nothing wrong with attending a church service or visiting with my Christian brethren because my mother expected me to escort the cattle and do something afterward without her approval. Since others went swimming, I felt justified in getting some spiritual nourishment in the meantime, and besides, I was home with the others when they were done with their swim.

6.2 The Palpable Tension in My Family

My family was displeased with me when they found out that I had attended church after escorting the cows that Sunday. My family was embarrassed also because Christian tribes were joyous that an Orma had joined them at their worship service. This worsened the problem.

My other relatives were also infuriated. One of my uncles who had gone on his pilgrimage with my father was incensed. He harangued me for not heeding the call to convert back to Islam. I had immense respect for my uncle Hajj Boneya, but when it came to religious matters I kindly asked him to mind his own affairs. I recited the sixth verse of chapter 109 of the Qur'an, where Prophet Muhammad recited, "You shall have your religion and I shall have my religion."[4] That resulted in him calling me a terrible name that drew the ire of his third wife. In spite of all the persecutions, I held on to what I believed.

Pressure was mounting on my family. By that time, news had spread all over the Ormaland and parts of the Coast Province that an Orma young man had converted to Christianity. The area Islamic preachers and teachers were so concerned that they invited a delegation of Muslim scholars to visit. The pressure on my family resulted into my younger brother Ali being pulled out of a secular school. Since my conversion to Christianity was blamed on my enrolment in a secular school, Ali had to pay the price. He was compelled to drop out in sixth grade.

My mother gave in to the scholars' demands partly because they falsely promised her that Ali would get a formal education alongside his Islamic studies. He was taken to the Safa Academy in Lamu to study Islam under a tough regimen. He was closely monitored and did not get a chance to further his formal education. That upset me immensely. He was denied access to outsiders. I thought I would never see him again. I threatened to bring the matter to the attention of the government officials because the action was against the Kenyan Education Act, which guaranteed a child's right to a formal education at least through the eighth grade. However, I was advised by my fellow Christians to jettison the idea because it would make matters worse for me. I took their advice but continued to be upset.

My mother, who had had no involvement in the botched poisoning incident or the plan to convert me to Islam by force, was concerned. The palpable tension that my conversion had brought onto my family and this parochial Muslim community was obvious. She approached me. I was afraid that she was becoming involved. She had always thought I was bewitched and should look for some help. Many tribes in the area believe someone can be bewitched. Most sudden deaths and terminal illnesses are attributed to witchcraft and magic.

6.3 A Plan to Visit an Exorcist

My mother asked me if I was interested in visiting one of my brothers-in-law about fifty kilometers away. Molu is learned in Islam and has a reputation for healing people who are affected by magic and witchcraft. He is credited with healing many people.

I initially turned down her request, but later I changed my mind. At the outset, I was reluctant to visit Molu because I was afraid. However, a Scripture passage I recalled, "He who is in you is greater than he who is in the world,"[5] challenged me to go. I also felt that this visit might be the long-awaited opportunity to escape my miserable situation. At that point I did not have even the slightest expectation that my family would send me on the trip alone. Thinking that the plan to escape might not work, I resolved that I would then take comfort in the Word of God and face Molu. I was confident that I would overcome his antics. I knew that his treatment would not affect me because with the Spirit of Christ in my heart no evil spirit would enter. I looked forward to witnessing to Molu.

Muslims believe witchcraft and magic are effective, but Islam bans their actual use. It was not out of the blue that witchcraft and magic were suspected for my errant behavior that did not comport with Islam. First of all, I had been a quiet child while growing up. I was soft-spoken and rarely raised my voice. But once I converted to Christianity, my quiet side faded away under my constant questioning of Islam. My mother knew that the sudden difference in me was strange and alleged that some unseen evil force was behind it. Like her fellow Muslims, she believed that every child is born a Muslim and either changes to another religion or remains a Muslim depending on the influence of the parents.[6] Since I had once zealously followed the religion of my birth, she thought it inconceivable that I had abandoned it on my own. She was convinced that magic or witchcraft was involved.

Second, the Hadith teaches that magic actually affected Prophet Muhammad, and he acted awkwardly. He went to a point where he thought he had performed actions that were only imaginary. In Sahih Bukhari, Aisha, Muhammad's wife, narrated "magic was worked on Allah's Apostle so that he used to think that he had sexual relations with his wives while he actually had not."[7] In response to Muhammad's suffering at the hands of magic, Allah revealed some chapters in the Qur'an to help him cope. Suratul Al-Falaq (113) states:

> Say: I seek refuge in the Lord of the Daybreak
> From the evil of that which He created;
> From the evil of the darkness when it is intense,
> And from the evil of malignant witchcraft,
> And from the evil of the envier when he envieth.[8]

Suratul An-Nas (114) likewise states:

> Say: I seek refuge in the Lord of men,
> The King of men,

The god of men,
From the evil of the whisperings of the slinking (Shaitan),
Who whispers into the hearts of men,
From among the jinn and the men.[9]

Muhammad got better after reciting these chapters. Muslims today emulate him by reciting the same verses to either ward off the evil eye, magic, and witchcraft or try to obtain a cure if they have already been affected. Unlike Muhammad, I knew what I was doing, but my mother still insisted that I was "bewitched" and should see Molu, an expert in Islamic religious healing.

Many Muslims in the area believe that Molu uses verses from the Qur'an to effect his treatment. They also believe that he is married to a *jinni*, who gives him the unique ability to "cure" people. (A *jinni* is "a spirit capable of assuming human form and exercising supernatural influence over human beings."[10]) They think that the *jinni* affects his personality by making him really quiet and telling him to avoid public functions. Since he does not go to funerals, many think his *jinni* "wife" contraindicates that as well. Their belief is serious. Molu did not attend my father's funeral in 1987.

Muslims believe in the existence of *jinnis*. They believe *jinnis* were created from "intensely hot fire"[11] that was "smokeless"[12] for the sole purpose that they worship Allah.[13] Islamic teachings indicate that they are of two kinds. The good *jinnis* are Muslims[14] whereas the bad *jinnis* are devils who mislead Muslims from the path of Allah. Chapter 72 of the Qur'an is named after the *jinnis*. Prophet Muhammad was heard saying, "There is none amongst you with whom is not an attaché from amongst the jinni (devils)." When his Companions asked, "Allah's Messenger, with you too?" He responded, "Yes, but Allah helps me against him and so I am safe from his hand and he does not command me but for good."[15]

Prophet Muhammad appeased the *jinnis* by granting their request on what Muslims should use to answer the call of nature. The rule used to specify bones, dung or charcoal, but he ruled in *jinnis'* favor when they petitioned him that those substances were their food.[16] Thus Muslims were commanded to clean themselves with three stones.[17] I was taught when growing up that Prophet Muhammad forbade urinating in holes because they were the residence of the *jinnis*.[18] As a youngster I believed that urinating in a hole would flush the *jinni* out.

Molu had such an influence on the Muslim masses that many sick ones thronged to his home for treatment. On previous visits to his home, I had seen many clients who came from all walks of life and from various parts of the country. He always read the Qur'an and many Islamic books while working on the medications. I had seen him write verses of the Qur'an on pieces of paper and put them in a glass of water for the sick to drink.

I thought about my mother's idea to visit Molu, which was quite promising as my ticket to freedom. Almost two weeks had passed since the court ruled against me and placed me with my family, infringing on my right to freely practice my new religion. I yearned for freedom, and it seemed now to be within reach. My freedom depended on my accepting the offer to visit Molu. I told my mother that evening that I would do it. She was ecstatic. Everyone was excited. They claimed that my decision to visit Molu must have been the answer to his *dua* (a short prayer). I went to bed that night with a lot on my mind. At that time I still did not know whether I would be sent on the trip alone.

6.4 The Day of the Escape

I woke up very early the following day and asked my mother for permission to visit my friend Raphael before I embarked on the trip to visit Molu. She conferred with others and granted my request. I borrowed a bike from my cousin Omar and left to see Raphael and his family. They were glad to see me. I shared with them what my mother had suggested. They advised me to go on the trip even if it meant traveling as far as the intended bus stop. They thought that this could be the long-awaited opportunity for me to escape my persecution. Molu's home was a trek from the bus stop. Since there was no known arrangement for someone to meet my escort and I at the bus, Raphael thought I should try to locate some Christians he knew in the area. We also discussed contacting the authorities. Raphael and his family were fairly concerned for my safety. They prayed with me. I returned home that morning ready to catch the lunch-hour bus for the trip to visit Molu.

My family was happy to see me going on the trip. They packed my bags and deliberately left out my Bible. I asked them to pack it for me because I needed it to deal with Molu's *jinni* wife. They retorted that I would return home a changed person—a Muslim— and would not need a Bible. They were confident that Molu would convert me back to Islam. Their certainty was not a surprise to me because he impressed many with his ability to "cure" people.

My mother gave me some money for the round trip bus fare. My family members escorted me to the bus stop. At that point, however, contrary to my cousin Omar's concern, they allowed me to continue on the journey without the escort that would have ensured that I arrived at Molu's. That was a mistake they still regret making. I wondered if it was God who made them act that stupidly, or if they just trusted that strongly in my Molu's powers. Since they believed that he could convert me back to Islam, they also thought he would make me go on that trip unaccompanied. Who would deliberately face an adversary if he or she knows a way to avoid the clash? I praise God for helping me get out of my persecution.

The bus took off, and I started rejoicing. The bus conductor came toward me, and I paid the bus fare to the nearest town. At that time the bus was approaching the town where the Chief had ruled against me a fortnight earlier and put me with my family. I had all along yearned for a day when I could go back to that court and challenge its statement. Now that day was fast approaching.

6.5 The District Officer Takes My Case

I alighted from the bus and headed straight to see the Kenyan missionary pastor who, about two weeks earlier when I was taken to court, had told me to see him in case of any problem. We met then only briefly due to a time constraint because I was on my way to court. We had not had time to talk after the verdict, however, because I had been under a police escort to go home with my family. When I arrived at his house, he was eating lunch. I reminded him of his promise to help me with my suffering. He recalled our initial conversation and agreed to help me. No sooner did he finish eating than we embarked on our journey to go see the highest government official in the area, the District Officer. These officials sometimes handled disputes of cases that Chiefs had ruled on. Although it was a Saturday afternoon, we knew that many government officials spent many hours at the office, not necessarily working, but taking advantage of the amenities that came with their positions. For example, it was very common in Kenya for most of them to rack up enormous long distance telephone bills, which the government footed without questions.

The missionary pastor and I raced down to the government office on his motorcycle. The District Officer (D.O.) was occupied with a visitor in his office, so I waited, grateful that I would soon be talking to an official who would put an end to my persecutions. The missionary pastor approached the D.O. about my case and he promised to deal with it the first thing on Monday morning. Although disappointed at having to wait, I was thrilled to get an appointment with the anticipation that this opportunity would immediately put an end to my suffering. This turned out to be wishful thinking, however.

The missionary pastor was now faced with the daunting task of hiding me for two days until my hearing. It would be difficult for me to walk around for very long unnoticed. For one thing, my sister Halima frequented that town. She was a businesswoman and bought her merchandise from a wholesale shop downtown. Most people in town also knew who I was because it was so rare to see a Christian who converted from Islam. Just a fortnight earlier, after the court ruling, I had walked through the town with Muslims calling out names at me. I was certain that the incident was still fresh in their minds.

Circumstances could become very frightening if the case dragged on. I was worried for the missionary pastor who dared to associate with me, knowing how the community was hostile toward Christians who proselytize Muslims, even though the Kenyan constitution guarantees that freedom. It was impossible for Christians to get permits to hold public gatherings in some areas. My hometown is even worse in this aspect because it is off-limits to Christian activities because of implied threats. The missionary pastor had been posted in this volatile area by his church with the intent of reaching out to Muslims. Up until he met me he had never met another convert even though he had been in the area for at least four years.

The missionary pastor and I brainstormed for some time about where I should hide until the hearing on Monday. We decided that it was safe to go to Mr. Buya's town, which was about thirty kilometers away. We left on his motorcycle that afternoon. I stayed with Mr. Buya's family until Monday. I was at a loss for words, as words could not express how much being with these friends meant to me. I went to church with them that Sunday, where all the church members prayed with me, many sobbing. The experience was quite moving. They exhibited deep love to me. Their actions contradicted all the negative stereotypes my tribe held against them.

I got a ride with the missionary pastor back to see the D.O. the following day. To my utter dismay, the secretary informed me that he was out of town. I was dumbfounded because he had promised to be there that day to address my case.

The waiting and guessing game began. One never knows when government officials in Kenya will actually do what they have committed to. Many a time it is necessary for money to change hands in order for things to be done promptly. Should the official ask for a bribe I knew there was no way I could outbid my family for my life because they had the money. Besides, they were committed to either minimize or eliminate the impact of the humiliation that my conversion had caused. I left all in God's hands for His will to be done.

I went to the office again that Tuesday and was frustrated to learn that the D.O. was not around for the second consecutive day. The secretary, who supposedly knew his itinerary, had a day earlier told me that he would be in the office. It seemed like he was not sure when his boss would come to work.

In the meantime, I came across two church leaders in the area who had heard of my conversion to Christianity. One of them was the overseer of a large charismatic denomination in the area. They sent me to a convenience store to buy soft drinks for them. I expressed my concerns to them about how risky it was for me to get out of the safe government compound and go downtown during the day to run a meaningless errand for them. I asked if they would wait to quench their thirst because it was dangerous for me to be downtown in broad daylight. I told them the reason I was at the D.O.'s office. They objected and insisted that I go.

It is expected for the young to serve the old in my country, and I did not want to be disrespectful. I thought they were testing me to see if I was genuinely a Christian. They were probably checking to see if I would run away with their money. What a pathetic way of testing someone's genuine conversion! Even as a Muslim I would not have run away with their money. It was ridiculous that I was sent in the line of danger just to prove to them whether I was converted. Thankfully, the trip to the store and back went without any incident, and none of my family members or the Muslim leaders learned that I had discarded the plan to visit Molu.

I continued to wait for my hearing. By that time my family was growing anxious to find out how my visit with Molu had turned out. There was no access to telephones then to confirm whether I had made the trip. It was usually travelers who disseminated news. We were now in the fourth day since I left home, and time was becoming my enemy. I frequented the D.O.'s office for most of the day on Tuesday, hoping that he would come to work. I was disappointed to retreat to the missionary pastor's house by the end of the day without result.

I am thankful to the Lord that the missionary pastor's house was a little far from the downtown. It was also on the same side of town as the D.O.'s office and probably was the last place any Muslim who was looking for me would think I was hiding. The mission station—which was comprised of three houses—was ramshackle and devoid of glamour that characterizes many Christian mission stations in Kenya.

The missionary pastor taught me how to be a disciple of Jesus Christ during the day. I also spent most of the day reading the Bible and also discipleship materials. Other than frequent visits I made to the D.O.'s office, I did nothing else during the day, fearing that I would run into my family or Muslims who knew me. Due to the immense danger I faced, I only ventured outside the compound at night.

The wait for a hearing continued. I looked forward to that Wednesday hoping that the D.O. would finally come to work. It was really hard knowing that all I could do was wait.

On the other hand, I was grateful to God that He had delivered me from my assailants' hands unscathed. I was away from my home, and the family I was staying with was very welcoming. It had taken three weeks of sufferings, but I was thankful that He did not let me be tested beyond what I could bear. He indeed saw me through when I needed Him. He neither left me nor forsook me. It all worked out in accordance with His divine will.

So I hoped for that day that the D.O. would rule in my favor, thus alleviating my persecution that contravened my rights granted by the Kenyan constitution. I longed for that Wednesday.

[1] Yusuf Ali, 49:9.

[2] *Sahih Bukhari, Volume 9, Book 83, Number 17.*

[3] The Gospel of John 6:44.

[4] Shakir.

[5] NKJV, 1st John 4:4b.

[6] *Sahih Muslim, Book 33, Number 6426.*

[7] *Sahih Bukhari, Volume 7, Book 71, Number 660.*

[8] Pickthall.

[9] Shakir.

[10] Gerina Dunwich, *Candlelight Spells: The Modern Witch's Book of Spellcasting, Feasting, and Healing* (Secaucus, NJ: Citadel Press, 1988), 161.

[11] Shakir, 15:27.

[12] Pickthall, 55:15.

[13] Pickthall, 51:56.

[14] Al-Jinn, 72:1,2.

[15] *Sahih Muslim, Book 39, Number 6757.*

[16] *Sunan Abu Dawud, Volume 1, Book 1, Number 39.*

[17] *Sunan Abu Dawud, Volume 1, Book 1, Number 40–41.*

[18] *Sunan Abu Dawud, Volume 1, Book 1, Number 29.*

CHAPTER SEVEN

My Family Ties Officially Severed

It was Wednesday, May 2, 1990. I was scheduled to appear for a hearing at the District Officer's office in Garsen. I got up early that morning to pray with the Kenyan missionary pastor whom I had known only for six days, including a brief encounter a fortnight earlier. I left for the hearing with him by my side. We rode his motorcycle to the government office hoping that the D.O. would be there.

I was quite scared and nervous that day because I did not know if the D.O. would send me back to my family. My previous experiences with government officials made me very pessimistic that morning. I thought about how my family would treat me because I had been defiant and did not go to Molu's place. I thought they would probably kill me should the D.O. go against my objection and send me home. I walked into the office hoping that he would rule in my favor. At the same time, however, I prayed for God's will to be done. I believed that if it were His will that I was sent home, He would give me the endurance to handle persecution.

The D.O. showed up at his office that day. I was grateful to have a hearing finally. The pastor went with me into the hearing when my name was called. The D.O. asked me questions about my persecutions at the hands of my family and members of the Muslim community. Unlike the previous government officials I had dealt with, he was very easy to talk to. No sooner did the D.O., Mr. Muhoro, finish hearing my side of the story than he summoned the Chief's office to bring forth the statement that was recorded earlier regarding my case.

7.1 Altered Statement from the Chief's Verdict

At that time we discovered that the statement had been altered. The statement that the members of my family and I had signed was missing that day. The new one I saw was written such that the Chief was not held liable for his decision to send me home against my raised concerns. He would have gone unpunished for his decision had my family or other Muslims hurt me.

I told the D.O. what I had gone through since I left the Chief's office that Monday afternoon. I explained to him that within hours my detractors tried to force me to denounce my faith. They had also poisoned my food, planned a ceremony to convert me to Islam by force on the day of *Iddul Fitr*, and sent me to face exorcism. I went on to tell him that the Chief had promised me the freedom to worship at home, but my family allowed nothing of that sort.

Mr. Muhoro was a Christian. He reviewed my case and eventually made a decision that was tough for me. He officially severed the ties between my family and me. He told me in the presence of the Kenyan missionary pastor that it was easier for him to make that decision because all the talk that week in marketplaces in the Division—a government administrative unit he oversaw—had been about my conversion to Christianity. A government representative of his caliber had the privilege of being regularly briefed by undercover agents called the Special Branch. (These officers usually gathered intelligence to foil cattle rustling and banditry, two major menaces which were prevalent in the Tana River District.)

He told me that he would not let me live with my family. It was hard for me to stomach the separation from my family because I loved them. The pastor offered to take me in. The prospect of living with strangers was hard for me. However I really appreciated the pastor's help. Since I was in a boarding school, it was a little easier to put up with the family because I was only "home" a total of three months a year, spread over three holiday breaks. Nevertheless it was still hard dealing with the thought that I probably would not see my family again.

I thought Mr. Muhoro had made a wise decision. I really loved my family, but my security was too compromised for me to try to work things out with them. It was difficult, but I tried to cope with the separation. The pastor I had known only for a week took the responsibility to support me.

We went back to the mission station and shared the information with other believers. There I met Christians who were members of the pastor's church. Some of them had a hard time grasping my suffering because even though Scripture is full of examples of persecutions, they could not imagine that I would become an "orphan" overnight. Although the pastor had only been in the area for about four years, he was considered successful in his work because he had planted about twelve churches in three Divisions. However, none of his church members were from the Islamic background at that time.

The pastor's family was nice to me as well. His brother-in-law Francis and I did a lot together in the mission compound. I made some adjustment to the food but it was still hard not to have my family around me. The pastor taught me discipleship classes during the day. I was mostly holed up indoors all day and took walks near the mission compound at night.

7.2 Accidental Encounter with My Sister

My family did not know where I was at that time. Considering the way my tribe passed information by word of mouth, no doubt they knew that I had not gone to Molu's place for "treatment." Since it was paramount that I got the treatment, they probably asked travelers from that area if they had seen me.

When I thought things had cooled down a little bit, I began walking as far as the downtown, a distance of about a mile, at night. One morning I went that far to visit a shopkeeper on the outskirts of town who was keeping some of my belongings. Joseph is a brother-in-law to Mr. Buya. When I arrived in town from school at the beginning of the April holiday, I had left some of my belongings and money with him. My brother had given me enough money to pay the whole year's tuition when I first reported to high school as a freshman. Per Mr. Buya's advice I did not pay for the whole year. I was grateful that I heeded his advice because I used that money to go through some perilous times.

I stopped by that day to check how things were going and also to give Joseph an advance notice that I was going back to school the following Monday. Since money was not kept at the shop due to security reasons, I wanted him to have it ready when I came back to pick it up.

Visiting that shop did not go well that day because I accidentally ran into my sister Halima. She was shocked to see me, and I confirmed to her that I had never made the trip to visit my brother-in-law. Trying to get the attention of other Muslims, she screamed and wailed. I slipped into the crooked streets and ran for my dear life. I ran all the way to the pastor's house because I was very scared.

I let the pastor's family know that my sister had seen me downtown. They prayed for my safety, and we left it all in God's hands. Then a Christian lady Habona told my family and Muslim leaders that I was hiding in a pastor's house near downtown. Her information was inaccurate, however, because she pointed to the wrong house, which was about a kilometer from the parsonage. Instead, the house of an elder from the pastor's church was searched. That family bore the brunt of frustrated Muslims. I avoided that house from that time on.

Word spread that I was hiding in other Christians' homes. My family, with some help from the Administration Police, used a "search warrant" issued by the Chief to ransack the homes for me. Even though the government officially severed my ties to my family, the Chief, a Muslim, indirectly helped my family to try to find me, disguising the operation as one to salvage some of my belongings. Thankfully, all their frantic efforts to find my belongings and me were fruitless. Nevertheless, their searches of Christians' homes caused tension between Muslims and Christians. I am thankful to God that my family did not know with whom I associated because they were grossly enraged and probably would have killed them.

While I was hiding at the parsonage, I received information on how things were going in town. The week was winding down to an end. It had been a long one due to the uncertainties I faced. However, I looked forward to going back to school. I longed for the Christian Union fellowship at school where I would not be under constant attack. I yearned for a time at school where I would be distracted not only by homework but also by some spiritual nourishment at the nightly prayer meetings and Sunday services. Although the thought of not having my family helping me with the tuition was constantly on my mind, I had no regrets about being a Christian. I had learned that I was called to suffer for the sake of Christ.

7.3 An Undue Criticism

Sadly, however, I did not suffer only at the hands of Muslims. Some Christians I met made life worse for me by criticizing me for disobeying my mother. They contended that I had broken the fifth commandment, "Honor your father and your mother, that your days may be long upon the land which the LORD your God is giving you."[1] It was difficult to hear that from a Christian. They wanted me to heed my Muslim parent's advice on how to lead a godly life in Christ. What a quandary that was.

But the Word of God calls on children to obey their parents only if the parents' call is within the paradigm of the Scripture. The apostle Paul said, "Children, obey your parents in the Lord, for this is right. Honor your father and mother, which is the first commandment with promise: that it may be well with you and you may live long on the earth."[2] Both Muslims and Christians accused me of disobeying my mother, but I chose to honor God's Word, which is greater.

I was saddened that my Christians critics insisted that I heed my mother, who was outright opposed to my conversion. Jesus Himself had said He came to bring divisions in a household. Since this obviously states that there is a risk to being a Christian, I wondered what that meant to my Christian critics. Every believer faces rejection by the world because the unbelieving world will never endorse Christian living.

My Christian critics did not need to go very far in Scripture to find a rebuttal of their criticism. Jesus was twelve when he obeyed God and stayed at the synagogue without his earthly parents' permission. There is no comparison between Jesus and me but He set a precedent for me to follow. I was almost fifteen when I converted to Christianity.

I maintained my allegiance to Jesus Christ even when I was bombarded with criticism from Muslims and Christians alike. Muslims urged me to reconsider my decision because I was born a Muslim. Those from my tribe argued that I should have made a communal decision with my family.

I suffered immensely at the hands of Muslims and, to a certain extent, Christians. Jesus was calling me to take up my cross and follow Him. He called me to count everything worthless for His sake. He promised, "Assuredly, I say to you, there is no one who has left house or brothers or sisters or father or mother or wife or children or lands, for My sake and the gospel's, who shall not receive a hundredfold now in this time—houses and brothers and sisters and mothers and children and lands, with persecutions—and in the age to come, eternal life."[3]

When I had put everything in the aforementioned verse into perspective, I thought more on the persecution. I realized that as a Christian I am called to receive a hundredfold of persecution since it is one of the rewards apportioned for me. I expected to run away from persecution if I could, partly because as Jesus Christ advised, "When they persecute you in this city, flee to another. For assuredly, I say to you, you will not have gone through the cities of Israel before the Son of Man comes."[4]

7.4 My High School Headmaster's Visit

It was Saturday. The pastor's church had Christ's Ambassadors—a weekly youth meeting for praise, worship and Bible study. The church was far from the parsonage. I decided to stay home that afternoon because I did not know how extensive the search for me was.

The youth came to the parsonage afterward to visit the pastor and also spend some time getting to know me. Some other church members also came. It was a night on which the compound was bustling with activities. We ate dinner and afterward were sitting around the fire discussing various issues when we saw a vehicle coming in the direction of the parsonage. It was late at night, and we wondered if it was one of the elders from church who had stopped by earlier. A white Toyota Hilux pulled up. We wondered who the odd visitors were because the vehicle was not familiar to us. My heart was pounding. I wondered if my family was using a government vehicle to come after me.

The door opened and out stepped Mr. Muchilwa, my high school headmaster. I was overjoyed. I was so thrilled to see him. We were surprised because not many people knew my whereabouts. Then we spotted an elder from church and we knew that that was how he had learned where I was.

It is amazing how God works in ways that we cannot fathom. This elder owned a mechanic shop. My high school, Mau Mau Memorial Secondary School, had bought a four-wheel drive vehicle in Mombasa during the holiday break. The roads in my home area were treacherous and did not spare even a vehicle in good condition. My high school headmaster told us that he had experienced a car problem and had stopped in Garsen to get help. He said that if he had not encountered that problem he probably would have proceeded with his journey to school. The elder from my church turned out to be the one who repaired the vehicle. I believe God brought Mr. Muchilwa to town that night so that he could help me. He was a Christian and was familiar with my predicament quite well. He knew about the threatening letters I had received while at school.

Mr. Muchilwa told me that he had been constantly worried about my safety during the April holiday but had not known where to look for me. He went on to say that he was burdened on his holiday break and really wanted to see how I was doing. I was thankful to be reunited with him because he was a great encouragement to me. It was wonderful that we were able to be together within only a short time of his arrival in town.

Although he was a native of the Western Province, a province the width of the country away, he had been transferred to our high school. The Kenyan government transfers around the country teachers in the public school system and some civil servants at will.

The elder from church who brought Mr. Muchilwa over that night always played Christian music at his mechanic shop because he tried to be a Christian witness in an area where the Muslim community restricted proselytizing Muslims. When my head-master arrived at the shop that evening, the elder was playing the Faustine Munishi tapes, a musical recording well-liked by many Christians in Kenya. Hearing the music, Mr. Muchilwa assumed the mechanics were Christian. Since he knew the general area from which I hailed, he asked the mechanics whether they had heard of a Muslim boy who had converted to Christianity. Amazingly, that was how he learned where I was staying that night. No one else could have located me, save the pastor's family and a few members of his church.

Mr. Muchilwa asked me about my holiday break, and I told him all the ordeals I had faced. Even though it was a few days before the school's opening day, he asked me to ride with him to school that night because he was concerned for my safety. I declined his request and decided to stay with the pastor's family for the remainder of the holiday. I knew that going to school a few days early would not have been beneficial to me because Muslim students in form-four—an equivalent of twelfth grade in some countries—would also be there. The school required them to report early to prepare for the final exams, the Kenya Certificate of Secondary Education, which was administered by the Kenya National Examination Council. They surely would have persecuted me. Another factor was that I enjoyed the discipleship that the pastor was teaching me. Thus it was worth staying in Garsen for a few more days. Mr. Muchilwa ended up taking my big luggage and setting off for Hola, the Tana River District headquarters, where my school was situated.

7.5 An Appointment with a Muslim Landlord

The Kenyan tradition enjoins that visitors be escorted. I set out with Francis to escort some church members home. It was in the dead of the night and the thought of encountering a Muslim who recognized me never crossed my mind, let alone meeting one who would notify my family.

The church members we were escorting arrived safely at their homes. Then on the way home, we stopped by to visit a gentleman from church who was renting a place in town. We talked to him for a little bit, giving each other the long greetings that are the custom of Kenyan Christians. Such greetings include testimonies that are as long as fifteen minutes. Speculations that a believer is backslidden normally creep in if one fails to give a testimony.

Francis gave his testimony and then it was my turn. I was just getting used to the mores. As I was speaking, the landlord heard my story and came out of his quarters. (Most landlords in Kenya live on the premises they rent out.) This man was from my tribe and knew who I was. Francis began witnessing to him and he seemed interested in Christianity. He asked me for an appointment so that I would talk to him more about Christianity, so we agreed to meet the following night at the same venue.

We rejoiced at the event that a Muslim was interested in Christianity. My Christian brethren told me that should the landlord convert, Muslims' attention would be divided, thus resulting in less persecution for me. I thought about their inferences and went back to the parsonage. I was grateful to be surrounded by people who were looking out for my good and who wanted an end to my sufferings. However, their interpretation of the landlord's interest in Christianity turned out to be premature.

Unaware of the landlord's motives, we broke the news to the missionary pastor. He was thrilled to hear that the night was bringing forth more good news. First, it was Mr. Muchilwa visiting us after dinner, who ended up taking my belongings to school. Then, at the pinnacle of the night, a respected Muslim man was interested in Christianity. I had thought that if the landlord would convert, Muslims who persecuted me would respect him. I was a mere high school student at that time at whom many elders from my tribe only sneered.

7.6 Uneasiness about the Appointment

It was late at night but we prepared for the appointment with the landlord and went to bed. When I woke up the following day, I felt quite uneasy. Thoughts of going to school that day flooded my mind. I was uncomfortable for some reason about the upcoming appointment. My heart was telling me that I had to go to school that Sunday morning. The experience was similar to that of when my food was poisoned and also when my family and members of the Muslim community had tried to force me to renounce my faith in Christ after the first court hearing. I was troubled that morning. I felt I had no choice but to approach the pastor regarding my concern.

I explained what I had experienced to him, and he was quite unhappy with me. Since I was being severely persecuted, he thought one other Muslim converting would result into less persecution for me. We discussed for a while, and in the end I stubbornly decided to leave for school that day.

Instead of preparing for the appointment that morning, I was putting the rest of my belongings together. The pastor was quite upset with my decision. I asked him for a ride to Mr. Buya's town. We set off for the short trip. I bade Mr. Buya's family farewell. We returned to the parsonage in Garsen, met up with an elder from church and prayed for my trip to school.

7.7 The Trip to School

Then we brainstormed about how I would leave for school unnoticed. Muslims owned all the buses plying that route, and we expected my family and Muslim community to be watching for me to board any of them for school. My sister Halima had already told them that I was in town. At that time I did not know that the landlord who had an appointment with me had also told them about me. Either way, they knew that I was still in town. The fact that I had an appointment probably eased how vigilantly they looked for me. It is possible that they were banking on the landlord's plan to turn me in.

Our first plan was that I should ride the motorbike to Mnazini, a town about forty kilometers toward Hola, and board the bus from there. The second idea was for me to ride the bike incognito wearing riding gear and using the back roads, and to hide in a shop owned by a Christian next to the bus terminal. We unanimously agreed on the latter plan, which was quite precarious but we hoped that it would go well. I was nervous that day. I rode the motorcycle into town as planned and waited for the 11 a.m. bus that came from Mombasa.

It was not hard to hear the bus coming even when I was hiding. Kenyan drivers always blared the horn, making all sorts of obnoxious noise, which would warrant a citation for noise pollution in some countries, but Kenyan travelers reveled in it. I especially appreciated it that day, because when the bus came, I did not even need to come out of the shop to make sure it had arrived. No sooner did the blaring horn stop than I ran out of my hiding place toward the bus and boarded it even before other passengers had a chance to alight. I found an aisle seat and waited apprehensively for departure.

While seated I noticed one of my half-brothers circling the bus as if he were looking for me. My heart began racing. It was the climax of the traveling season that time of the year, and the bus was crowded with many passengers standing in the aisle. To date I do not know whether God hid me from being seen by him or whether he did not even look inside the bus for me. Had my half-brother spotted me, I would have been removed from the bus.

The bus departed a short time later, but I waited for a while before I celebrated my departure from Garsen. It had been a long holiday break for me, and I was ready for a change. In spite of the persecution, I cherished my time at school because it was the only place I felt safe to freely practice my religion.

I arrived at school safely. It was hard to reflect on what had transpired the previous few days and to accept the outcome. I loved my family, but it soon became a reality to me that it was not possible for us to reconcile unless either they changed their minds or I reconsidered my position. But reverting to Islam was not an option for me. Maintaining my stance now meant my safety was an issue wherever Muslims were present.

My finite mind wandered for answers to the questions that engulfed me. I recalled that Jesus Christ said He had come to bring a sword and not peace, divisions and not harmony within a family.

I was reminded again of Jesus teaching, "He who loves father or mother more than Me is not worthy of Me. And he who loves son or daughter more than Me is not worthy of Me."[5] It was tough but I had to accept the reality that my love for God ought to supersede my love for my family.

It was initially difficult for me to acknowledge our strained relationship. But as time went on, I learned that it is written, "all who desire to live godly in Christ Jesus will suffer persecution."[6] That passage comforted me as I learned that I was called to suffer for Christ's sake.

7.8 The Landlord's Motive

I am grateful to God that I did not honor the appointment with the landlord and that the pastor and his church members did not go there on my behalf. God was good in letting me feel uncomfortable about that situation. Thankfully, we did not ask the landlord to come to the pastor's compound for the meeting, a situation which would have been more of a disaster.

I learned from the pastor, who was informed by the tenant after I reported to school, that the landlord had notified my family of the impending appointment. My family in turn mobilized men from our clan. The pastor told me these men were lying in wait. Providentially, their wait was in vain.

What an awesome God! He brought me to the knowledge of His Son Jesus and did not leave me like an orphan, but guided me with His Holy Spirit when I needed counsel. He never let me suffer when it was not in accordance with His purpose. For this reason, I live to praise Him. In retrospect, it is quite phenomenal that this was the third time in as many weeks that God worked in my conscience to save my life. I am forever grateful to Him!

I braced myself to face more persecution because I was bound to face it, hoping for the Lord's second coming while I was still living. Otherwise, if I died before He came, I was confident that I would meet Him. I prepared my mind for the difficulties ahead, trusting that He would carry me through unscathed if that were His will.

1   NKJV, Exodus 20:12.
2   NKJV, Ephesians 6:1–3.
3   NKJV, Mark 10:29–30.
4   NKJV, Matthew 10:23.
5   NKJV, Matthew 10:37.
6   NKJV, 2nd Timothy 3:12.

CHAPTER EIGHT

More Hardships with Some Respite

My elder brother was not amused by the outcome of the vigil on the landlord's premises. The fact that he was at my high school early the following day suggested that he had left as soon as it became evident that I had abandoned the appointment.

It started out a normal day for me at school, and I went to my classroom not knowing what had transpired in Garsen. (I reported to school on Sunday, May 6, 1990, one day before school officially reopened for the second term. Even though classes had not started—they officially start on Tuesdays—I was required to be in my classroom, studying.) I did not know that my elder brother had made the trip to my school.

The deputy headmaster, who under normal circumstances hardly came to a freshmen's class, was at the doorsteps early that Monday morning. It was a surprise that Mr. Maloba came to our class. He was the designated disciplinarian who only made classroom visits when a student was in trouble. To my utter amazement, he called me out of the classroom. I followed him while my classmates mumbled under their breath, thinking that I was in trouble.

8.1 My Elder Brother's Unsuccessful Attempt

He broke the news to me that my elder brother was present at school that morning, a fact that shocked me. He cautioned me to stay in the classroom even during breaks until I would be called to the headmaster's office for a meeting. Students were prohibited from leaving classrooms on a typical weekday except during official parades, meal breaks, and extracurricular activities. Unlike high schools in other countries, the Kenyan system requires students to be in the same classroom all day while teachers visit them teaching various lessons. Students usually segregate during religious education.

Even though the Kenyan public school system had many flaws, I appreciated how trespassers were threatened with prosecution. That effectively forced some visitors to report to the office. However, there were many illegal short-cuts that led to many entrances into the fenced school compound. There would have been a problem had my elder brother sneaked in through one of them.

I nervously waited for the meeting. My elder brother has a very bad temper. It was just seven years earlier that he had ruthlessly beaten my brother Saidi, who eventually died as a result. It was extremely difficult for me to face him that day. The fact that the meeting was at school gave me some solace, however, because there were security guards who escorted unruly visitors out of the compound.

The deputy headmaster came back to get me for the meeting. I walked into the office jittery. My mind was teetering on the verge of despair. To say the least, I was terrified to face my elder brother. I nervously waited for the meeting to commence. My brother was not in the room yet.

I waited for a little while until my brother and a security guard walked into the office. The presence of a security guard assuaged my worries. I stood behind the headmaster's chair for the meeting and my brother stood across from the headmaster with the security guard adjacent to him. He was incensed.

The meeting started and I was once again confronted with false accusations. This time my brother contended that I had not gone home for the April holiday. I could not believe what I was hearing but should not have been too surprised because my family had previously accused me falsely. I thought about my experiences the previous four weeks of dealing with the barrage of false allegations, and I was ready to strike back. I soon realized that he came to school with the sole purpose of taking me home to face more persecution.

I found out a few years later that he had come to school to take me to an Islamic boarding school in Mombasa, Sheikh Khalifa Bin Zayeed Al-Nahyan Secondary School, where I would be disciplined and probably tortured until I converted back to Islam.

I did not know that day that he had been at vigil, lying in wait for me at the landlord's house the previous night. I countered his false accusation by asking the headmaster Mr. Muchilwa to telephone Mr. Muhoro, the District Officer in Garsen, to confirm whether I had been at home during the April holiday. My brother became enraged when I challenged his assertion. He muttered some words.

Then he offered to pay my school fees on the condition that I would go home with him. He reached for his pocket and showed a large sum of money. He was bringing to the bargaining table an amount that seemed to equal all the capital of our cattle-trading business. I refused to accept his offer unless he changed the condition. I argued that there was no reason to pay school fees if I were not to stay behind to learn. I knew what cards he was playing. Had I agreed to him paying the fees but failed to go home with him, war would have broken out. In light of what I had faced the previous many weeks, going home was not an option because I knew what would be in store for me.

My brother was furious. He then attempted to bribe Mr. Muchilwa but to no avail. Then he said arrogantly, "I will see if the Jesus you believe in will come from heaven to pay your school fees." He added that all my cattle would be distributed among my brothers. He dejectedly walked out of the office with the security guard trailing him and was escorted out of the school compound. I was relieved that the meeting was over. I talked with the headmaster for a while and went to class escorted by the deputy headmaster.

That was a rough day for me. It was a day on which my family ties were further severed. But I knew that if I had gone home that day with my elder brother, I would have been subjected to torture. Considering my elder brother's volatile temper, I was grateful when the meeting ended without incident.

8.2 More Persecutions at School

The atmosphere on campus was tense. I was subjected to more scolding, insults, and beatings. Muslim students continued persecuting me. I was jeered, insulted, and tormented. Since my knowledge of the Qur'an was better than most of theirs, I quoted it frequently and exposed to them some of the points in Islam that do not make sense. In one instance I pointed out that contrary to what they accuse Christians of believing, I did not believe that God married the Virgin Mary who later bore Him a Son. However, I maintained that Jesus Christ is the Son of God. I recited Suratul *Al-Ikhlas*, which states, "He [Allah] begetteth not nor was begotten. And there is none comparable unto Him."[1] Since their accusations involved only physical birth, I maintained that Jesus was the Son of God of supernatural birth. They were bewildered.

8.3 God's Providence

My life at school turned out to be very difficult because I did not have any money for my school fees. Mr. Muchilwa let me stay at school without paying until I found someone to help me. He encouraged me to stay strong amidst my hardships. He told me not to worry about my school fees because God would provide for me if it were His will.

The school administration entrusted me with some responsibilities running the school canteen after school. I was given an allowance for working there, which sustained me for a while.

A few months later, a Christian young man who was an engineer with the Ministry of Agriculture visited me. Charles was visiting the Tana River District headquarters for work. He had heard about my plight from other Christians and offered to provide me with some pocket money every term. I was thankful to God that He sent someone my way to alleviate my suffering. What an amazing God who puts strangers in our path when we least expect! I was grateful for the help because that helped me to focus on my studies without spending more time at the school canteen. I split my time there with another student.

I continued to be in school without paying any fees. The fee arrears were mounting. Life was getting tougher and tougher for me. I was getting further in debt and quitting school was in the offing. It wasn't likely the headmaster would indefinitely let me stay in school with the mounting fee arrears. His kind gesture toward me could have cost him his job had my fees gone unpaid and the government auditors discovered that I was still in school.

My elder brother had mockingly said he would see if Jesus Christ would come from heaven to pay my school fees. Muslims believe that Jesus is in heaven and will come back at the end of the world for the final judgment. The Qur'an states:

> And (Jesus) shall be a Sign (for the coming of) the Hour (of Judgment): therefore have no doubt about the (Hour), but follow ye Me: this is a Straight Way. Let not the Evil One hinder you: for he is to you an enemy avowed. When Jesus came with Clear Signs, he said: "Now have I come to you with Wisdom, and in order to make clear to you some of the (points) on which ye dispute: therefore fear Allah and obey me."[2]

They also believe he will come to disown Christians, fight the antichrist, die in Medina, and be buried next to Muhammad's tomb. He will be raised up alive, and that will be the end of the world. Prophet Muhammad said in the Hadith:

> There is no prophet between me and him, that is, Jesus (peace_ be_upon_him). He will descent (to the earth). When you see him, recognise him: a man of medium height, reddish fair, wearing two light yellow garments, looking as if drops were falling down from his head though it will not be wet. He will fight the people for the cause of Islam. He will break the cross, kill swine, and abolish jizyah [tax imposed on non-Muslims in Arabia by Muhammad]. Allah will perish all religions except Islam. He will destroy the Antichrist and will live on the earth for forty years and then he will die. The Muslims will pray over him.[3]

My brother believes Jesus is coming back. I believe that as well even though our expectations of Him are different. Nevertheless,

He would not come back to pay my school fees. If I had to wait that long for the fees that I direly needed, then my elder brother would have won.

Foregoing my education due to lack of funds for the sake of maintaining my faith in Christ was already an option I had contemplated. Had I done so, my family would have rejoiced. I resolved to put my trust in Him who was able to immeasurably sustain me. He was able not only to supply my earthly needs but also to supply them abundantly.

It was a long term at school and my hardships did not abate. The August holiday break was fast approaching, and I had to think of where to go and hide until the new term started in September. In spite of the probable threat on my life, I traveled to the Garsen area. While there I visited with Mr. Buya, who had instigated my transfer to a boarding school at the end of sixth grade. He talked with some leaders from his church denomination about my problem with school fees. I met with them, and they looked into a possibility of helping me. They later agreed to pay for that term. Muslims' animosity toward me somewhat quieted down partly because of my absence while attending secondary school.

Many churches by then had heard about me. One of the church leaders—the one who sent me on a meaningless errand to buy him a soft drink against my objection when I was waiting for a hearing at the D.O.'s office—invited me over for a visit. I decided not to judge him from my first experience, and actually didn't mind visiting him because many Christians had put their lives on the line to identify themselves with me. Many helped me at the expense of their families. It was quite a sacrifice and I did not show any prejudice even though I had a bad experience with him.

We ate lunch together at his house and afterward talked about my financial needs. I was always shy in talking about my problems, especially the ones touching on finances, because I did not want to be anyone's burden. As a result I only talked about them when I was asked and occasionally even declined when I felt uncomfortable or deemed it unnecessary.

The church leader knew what my pressing need was. He told me that he would pay my school fees for the remainder of my high school education if I switched churches and started attending his. I told him that this was not an option. Then he went on to point out to me that I was initially a member of his denomination.

I was taken aback by his bold allegation, but there was some truth to it. He contended that the elders and pastor who had prayed with me when I converted to Christianity were from his denomination; thus I was a member of his church. I told him that although those elders and the pastor had prayed with me, they had deserted me when the persecution started. I also told him that it was not an option for me to join his church because I was content where I was. I told him to keep his money and not to worry about my high school fees because he did not seem to care. And we parted.

8.4 Fleeing Persecutions

Persecutions picked up again, and it was getting hard. One day I was discussing Islam with a Muslim young man who initiated the conversation. Before I knew it, he was rolling up his sleeves ready to fight me. There were some onlookers. Fortunately we were near the mechanic garage belonging to an elder from my church. The mechanics saw what was unfolding and came to my rescue. The young man was glowering with rage. They held him back and escorted him away.

The going got tougher. I was subjected to constant ridicule. *Madrassa* students trailed me, pelting me with stones and worn-out batteries. A church I attended was pelted with stones on numerous occasions while the service was in progress. In spite of that my Christian brethren were quite supportive of me. We collectively endured the suffering.

The situation eventually got out of control. It was later decided that I should spend the rest of the August holiday break in 1990 with a family in Nairobi because by then it was unsafe for me to be in my province. I arrived in Nairobi on the same day that there was a requiem mass for the Bishop Alexander Muge, who had been killed in a mysterious road accident earlier that week. The Kenyan government was allegedly involved because he was its main critic. The city streets were awash with police clad in riot gear in readiness for the University of Nairobi students who were vowing to cause havoc. The traffic swirled through the city center avoiding the All Saints Cathedral where the mass was held. We arrived safely at my temporary residence. I stayed with Charles's family, which had taken responsibilities to care for me. I participated in some evangelistic meetings in Nairobi without any incidents. I kept a low profile and rarely shared my testimony.

My stay in Nairobi was successful. My Christian families and I made the decision to transfer to a school in Nairobi, a bigger city where I hid in the masses and was not subjected to persecution. I got involved in a church and kept my movement restricted. I changed my first name to Zachariah. I also had a few aliases: Abba, Rufa, and Waba. I rarely used Hussein but often used Abbarufa and Wario as first names. I was very careful and kept a low profile in Nairobi, especially when I encountered Muslims.

Even though I was far away from my family and the Muslim community that knew me, I still lived in fear.

I continued with my studies in Nairobi, briefly taking a break for one term because of problems I had encountered. It was hard for me to see families making sacrifices to help me. Some of them were already in financial difficulties. On the other hand, some of my relatives moved to the area. I was concerned for my safety because my school was a day school with lots of commuting during the week. At that time I quit going to school hoping that I could go to a Bible college instead because I wanted to learn more about Scripture.

That decision to drop out of school upset Mr. Buya—my host in Christmas 1988. He advised me to go back to school. The Kenyan missionary pastor also played a role in convincing me to go back. All of this was happening about a year and a half after my relationship with my family was severed. They still did not know of my whereabouts.

8.5 The Transfer to the third High School

Providentially, I met Jane at a conference, and she helped me to transfer to Waa High School in January 1992. She worked for the National Council of Churches of Kenya (NCCK). I repeated a grade as advised by my Christian brethren because I missed so much during my sophomore year due to hardships.

Waa is located about 20 kilometers from Mombasa. This is a Muslim area and the student body was more than 75 percent Muslim, but the school was a boarding school. Even though public boarding schools have a bad reputation in Kenya, I liked the fact that there were security guards who kept out trespassers. It gave me some sense of security to know that my assailants could not just walk in and torture me. My family also did not know that I had transferred there.

The headmaster was a friend of Jane. He was a Christian who was excited about my enrolment and announced it at a Christian Union meeting. That action was ill-advised because it angered Muslims when they learned of my background. It was a joy for Christians, but Muslims did not take it lightly. Even though I was a sophomore, I was subjected to more suffering than typically befell any freshman. I was defiant when I was asked to do menial tasks by ruthless student leaders called prefects. Most of them did that in order to find a reason to write me up.

Muslim students asked me questions about why I converted to Christianity. Some of them were warned against having discussions with me because they had little knowledge of their religion, hence they could easily be influenced to abandon it. Even the leaders who cautioned others to keep away from me could not have a discussion with me because they were simply trying to cover up for Islam's inconsistencies.

Waa High School was unique from other schools I attended in that its students elected their leaders. That was atypical of Kenyan schools. All schools I had previously attended had prefects selected by the teachers. Prefects are indispensable on Kenyan high school campuses, especially those schools that are prone to strikes. They are considered the "eyes of the teachers," writing up their peers who break school rules. They were invested with powers to punish wrongdoers. The most common punishment was digging pits to bury garbage. Some prefects went as far as flogging students. Prefects worked in conjunction with the deputy headmaster, who was the chief disciplinarian.

Prefects generally were students who excelled in studies and were teachers' favorites. The religious groups on campus were also represented. I was barely at Waa High School for two terms, when, to my surprise, I was elected the prefect in charge of the Christian Union in July 1992. What a responsibility to give to a young convert. It was a challenge worth taking.

Muslim students also elected their own religious prefect. They elected Mohamed, who was my biggest critic. I got together with him a number of times to discuss some passages from the Qur'an and the Bible. He was full of ideas about Christianity that he learned from Islamic street preachers who occupied street corners in many coastal cities.

Islamic street preachers in Kenya unabashedly disparage Christianity to the point where if the roles were reversed, such utterances about Islam would result in riots. They were everywhere in Mombasa. I avoided their public debates because of the angry mob that posed a threat to an apostate.

Mohamed and I sat down one Saturday afternoon. He had a New Testament Bible in his hand, ready to challenge me on a verse the street preachers widely used to attack Christianity. He opened 1 Corinthians 15:18, "Then also those who have fallen asleep in Christ have perished."[4] He claimed that according to the verse all Christians who died were lost. He continued to say that those who were alive had a chance at redemption by embracing Islam, Allah's religion. He extended the invitation for me to convert back to Islam because according to the Bible, Christians were supposedly lost.

I read the same verse in my Bible at his insistence, and it had the same meaning. I requested him to read the preceding verses for me. He was hesitant. I went ahead and read from verses 12 to 21, which shed some light on verse 18. I explained to him that the apostle Paul was answering those who claimed that there is no resurrection of the dead at Christ's second coming. I implored Mohamed to read the Bible in context, because unlike the Qur'an, at least one could understand a passage based on its context. He was quite disappointed that he was unable to pull the tricks street preachers normally pulled on unsuspecting audiences. That gave him another reason to hate me.

I was grateful to God for putting a hedge of protection around me, guarding me against the wiles of my enemies. Many devised strategies to silence me, but God thwarted and scuttled their plans. And the weapons they forged against me were rendered powerless. Thus I live to worship Yahweh.

---

[1]   Pickthall, 112:2–3. Bracket mine.
[2]   Yusuf Ali, Suratul Al-Zukhruf, 43:61–63.
[3]   *Sunan Abu Dawud, Volume 3, Book 32, Number 4310.* Bracket mine.
[4]   NKJV.

CHAPTER NINE

Muslims Attempt to Proselytize Me

~~~~~~~~~~~~~~~~~~~~~~~~~~~~~~~~~~~~~~~

School recessed for half term in March 1993, and I went to visit one of my host families in Mombasa. David and Jane's family lived in one of the Mombasa suburbs, Kizingo, in a Kenyan government house that was close to the Indian Ocean. David, my host father, was the provincial director of the Ministry of Livestock Development in the Coast Province.

I left for "home" that morning after most students had deserted the school compound. I cautiously stepped out of my safe haven and boarded a *matatu* (commuter taxi) at the gate for Likoni—a town on the mainland where many commuters to the island catch a ferry. My new home was only a short trek from where the ferry docked. It was adjacent to the State House-Mombasa (Kenya's president's official residence when in the Coast Province), which is located on the famous Mama Ngina Drive. I was home in time for lunch.

Coping with the thought that my own family had disowned me was difficult. There was a time of about a year during this period when I did not see my mother due to the high level of animosity I faced at home. Whenever I did visit my home, I always went unannounced and left within minutes of arrival. I made the effort to visit my mother when I was in the Tana River District during school recesses. She was unfriendly and always denigrated me for being a Christian. It was evident from her tirades that like the majority of Muslims, her views about Christianity were skewed. I often refrained from engaging in polemics with her because whatever I would have said in response to her charges would have fallen on deaf ears. It was difficult to listen to her disparagement, but I did so knowing that my allegiance is to the One greater than even my mother.

My host families tried to help me cope with the problems I was having with my family. I divided my time among David and Jane's family and a few other families. Even though I had known David and Jane's family for a year now, getting used to them was hard. Their family was peculiar in that it represented two distinct cultures. David (now deceased) was a native of the Coast Province, while Jane is from the Western Province. The couple was from two different tribes, with their families living hundreds of miles apart. Their intertribal marriage succeeded, however, because their love for God and each other transcended their allegiance to their tribes.

Adjusting to the presence of the two different cultures in the household was hard for me. The children identified more with their father's side of the family. They had learned the Chonyi language because they had more contact with his side of the family. Jane and her house-helper communicated in Luhya, their native language. At least the presence of the family's two distinct native languages in their household did not present a communication problem for me because they conversed in English or Swahili most of the time. In contrast, other households I stayed with often used their tribal vernaculars. Since some churches I attended held services in languages foreign to me, circumstances compelled me to learn some of these languages so that I could follow the proceedings. As a result, I became fluent in the Pokomo language, which is totally unrelated to the Orma language.

Mombasa is a unique island that serves as the headquarters for the Mombasa District and the Coast Province. It is the second largest city in Kenya after Nairobi, with about a million people. The Indian Ocean's English Channel, the ancient Fort Jesus museum (a fifteenth-century fort built by the Portuguese), and the Old Town were within walking distance from my new "home." Pristine white sandy beaches, Bamburi Natural Trail, and the Kilindini Harbor (Kenya's main seaport) were all a short *matatu* ride away. I was just getting used to going around this historical city.

The most fascinating phenomenon that I observed in Mombasa was the tides. The oceanic water retreats into the deep sea in the morning. People then walk on the dry oceanic floor all the way to the deep sea. Some of them snorkel along the coral reefs where there are assortments of fish, sea creatures, and plants, some embedded in the coral reefs. The natural beauty is sublime. The ocean roars in the afternoon, and the high tide starts with huge waves. The water fills up to the shore with turbulent tides. During high tide the ocean becomes off-limits for swimmers because the chances of drowning are high.

9.1 Physically Assaulted

The weather the day I left school was ideal for venturing into downtown Mombasa. I was concerned, however, at the possibility of running into a Muslim who would recognize me. Even though I was in a sprawling city of about a million people and more than two hundred kilometers away from my native home, I was still concerned for my safety. My brothers and many men from my home area frequented Mombasa. Most of them hauled cattle herds to the Kenya Meat Commission (KMC) slaughterhouse.

In spite of my concerns, I went for a walk that afternoon. Freedom to sightsee was new to me. At school I was confined to a small compound surrounded by a barbed wire fence, and this restricted lifestyle was a routine for me for many months out of the year.

I walked to Nyerere Avenue, across the street from the Pandya Memorial Hospital, and boarded a *matatu* for downtown Mombasa. I alighted at Mwembe Tayari marketplace on Kenyatta Avenue. Surprisingly, I ran into an Orma man who told me that my elder brother Roba was staying in a nearby hotel. It had been three years since I had seen him. Foolhardily, I decided to visit him.

Mombasa is a predominantly conservative Muslim town. As a result even tourists are advised to dress modestly. Since tourism is the backbone of the Kenyan economy, the government ensures that a police presence is on the streets. That makes Mombasa streets some of the safest in Kenya.

I inquired after my brother at the hotel that afternoon. The man at the desk confirmed that some Orma men were at the hotel and asked me to check upstairs for my brother. I found out that Roba had indeed spent the previous night there. He had left that morning to check on the cattle awaiting slaughter in Mazeras (a suburb of Mombasa).

I was a little concerned that my volatile brother was staying less than four kilometers from David and Jane's residence. I talked with the men for a little bit and got up to leave. That was when I ran into Abbas. He was the one who had come all the way from his home to beat me up when I was a freshman because I had converted to Christianity. It had been about three years and I had never thought that encountering him would be an issue. Abbas was in Mombasa pursuing his medical training at the Kenya Medical College-Mombasa.

He asked me a few questions about Islam and Christianity. I answered his questions as I did other Muslims. I was respectful and did not denigrate Prophet Muhammad. I thought he was genuinely inquisitive. On the spur of the moment, he started punching me. The altercation attracted an audience. The hotel proprietor, a Somali refugee, came running. Abbas had me pinned to the wall and was trying to push me down the stairs. An Orma man, Swale, intervened, restraining Abbas. I was shaken.

The hotel proprietor was infuriated. He was a refugee operating a business in Kenya. In case I had needed medical attention, the police would have become involved, creating a scenario in which refugees in Kenya typically get exploited. I hurriedly left the hotel and went home.

I realized that it was unwise of me to have gone to that hotel, and additionally, that I should not have engaged in a discussion about religion. I even regretted my decision to venture downtown.

I was grateful to God that my family and many Muslims, including Abbas, did not know where I was staying or attending high school. There was a security staff at school, but things would have been ugly had they known I was in a school with a predominantly Muslim student body. The fact that my family believed that I was a high school dropout who was involved in a fulltime Christian ministry probably deterred them from scouring area high schools for me. They had heard about me often from other Muslims who had seen me address public evangelistic meetings. Moreover, my elder brother had refused to pay my school fees, and they perhaps thought I dropped out due to the lack of funds. They were oblivious to the fact that God was providing for my education.

9.2 Tension at the New School

The half term ended, and I went back to school. Muslim students did not give up on me. They relentlessly tried to convince me to abandon Christianity. They were harsh toward me. These engagements gave me opportunities to raise more questions about Islam. Some of them shoved me, attempting to provoke a fight. I didn't flinch because they were trying to scare me from sharing what was true even by Islam's account. Notwithstanding their anger toward me, I continued questioning Islam.

I tried to distract myself from persecution by participating in various Christian activities. Thus I became involved with the Kenya Students Christian Fellowship (KSCF) in the Coast Province, which provides pastoral services and also organizes retreats during holiday breaks for high school students. While attending these retreats I sharpened my personal evangelism skills. I was the chairman of the Christian Union and worked in collaboration with area high schools in organizing "weekend challenges." These meetings are mass gatherings of Christian students on weekends. I visited various schools, among them Shimba Hills Secondary School, Kwale High School, Matuga Girls' Secondary School, Khamisi Secondary School, and Mivumoni Secondary School. Muslim students from these schools were angry that I was on their campus.

The atmosphere on my high school campus became more tense because Muslim students were angrier toward me. They must have heard from their counterparts at other schools that I was making some progress in proselytizing Muslims. They spurned me and stopped conversing with me even during discussions in class. Mohamed, their leader, was different in that he continued discussing with me various religious topics, hoping to win me back to Islam. However, as with the majority of Muslims, his views about Christianity were skewed, and as a result he did not fare well in some of our discussions.

9.3 Inconsistent Messages of the Qur'an

Mohamed was willing to answer any questions I had about Islam. He was hoping that in the end I would reconsider and convert back to Islam. He was a sophomore in high school but was a budding Islamic scholar who had studied Islam at a higher level at the Mahd-Ul-Tawhid Maganyakulo Islamic School. It is common for young adults to enroll in a second school in Kenya. Therefore Mohamed's level of education in Islam qualified him not only to answer my questions, but also to instruct Muslim students.

Since he previously had challenged the infallibility of the Torah and Gospel during our discussion, I wanted my question about Islam to revisit the subject from a slightly different perspective. I began by showing Mohamed a verse in the Qur'an about Prophet Muhammad. In this text Allah urges his doubting Prophet to ask Jews and Christians about the authenticity of messages he was receiving during Islam's preliminary stage. Suratul Al-Yunus (10) verse 94 states:

> And if thou (Muhammad) art in doubt concerning that which We reveal unto thee, then question those who read the Scripture (that was) before thee. Verily the Truth from thy Lord hath come unto thee. So be not thou of the waverers.[1]

Prophet Muhammad boasted in the Qur'an and in the Hadith (on numerous occasions) that the Angel Gabriel came to him with Allah's message sometimes while in the presence of his family, followers, and foes. They supposedly were able to see the angel on occasion because sometimes he appeared in the form of a man.[2]

I asked Mohamed, "If the Torah and the Gospel were indeed corrupted, why would the supposedly all-knowing Allah—who due to his attributes should know the alleged corruption—urge his prophet to ask Christians and Jews about its authentic message?" He refused to answer my question. I told him this verse put an end not only to his question but also to his quest of finding a contradiction in the Bible consistent with Islam's allegations. I added that if these allegations were true, what an oxymoron that the supposedly all-knowing Allah would ask his beloved Prophet to have a corrupt source as a reference.

This verse is just one of the many blunders in Islam on the subject of Christians and Jews who are featured both as good and evil people. In one instance the Qur'an states, "Lo! Those who believe, and those who are Jews, and Sabaeans, and Christians— Whosoever believeth in Allah and the Last Day and doeth right— there shall no fear come upon them neither shall they grieve."[3] In this case both Christians and Jews would enjoy paradise like faithful Muslims. This verse does not set the condition that Jews and Christians must accept Muhammad as a prophet in order to enjoy paradise. Elsewhere the Qur'an states, "Lo! Those who disbelieve, among the People of the Scripture and the idolaters, will abide in fire of hell. They are the worst of created beings."[4] This verse refers to Jews and Christians who refused to accept Muhammad as a prophet in Medina during Islam's final push for converts. These two Qur'anic verses came from the same source—Allah—and are diametrically opposite on the fate of Jews and Christians.

The cases these two verses pose are a drop in the ocean if compared with other contradictions in Islam. The only reason given by some Islamic scholars to justify the divergent views in the Qur'an regarding the fate of Christians and Jews is the rule of abrogation. They believe that some latter verses of the Qur'an annulled the ones revealed earlier, hence there is no contradiction. This strategy is effective because, "The practical application of this principle [abrogation] is that when there is a contradiction between two verses in the Quran, the newer revelation overrides the previous revelation."[5] Therefore the rule of abrogation is employed to absolve Allah and the Qur'an of inconsistencies. I have wondered how the all-knowing and all-wise Allah needs this rule to excuse himself after giving contradictory messages without any plausible explanation. The need for transparency in Islam should have started with Allah.

There are some Muslims who, like Mohamed, do not believe that there is abrogation in the Qur'an. In fact, that notion contradicts Allah, who said, "None of Our revelations do We abrogate or cause to be forgotten, but We substitute something better or similar: Knowest thou not that Allah Hath power over all things?"[6] Yes, indeed. Allah had the power to flip-flop at will on his decrees without giving any plausible reason and got away with it. The Hadith makes the rule of abrogation in Islam even clearer in stating that Allah revealed (to Muhammad), "A verse that was among the cancelled ones later on."[7]

Islamic scholars, including Mohamed, need to be candid and point out which verses in the Qur'an were "cancelled" so that the world can accurately understand Islam. I do know that their hesitance has to do with the latter verses that essentially justify violence against the infidels and Muslims who collaborate with them. A good example of them is, "the Verse of the Sword abrogated the Qur'an's peace treaties."[8] The Verse of the Sword is the fifth verse of Suratul Al-Tawba (9), which states:

> Then, when the sacred months have passed, slay the idolaters
> wherever ye find them, and take them (captive), and besiege
> them, and prepare for them each ambush. But if they repent
> and establish worship and pay the poor-due, then leave their
> way free. Lo! Allah is Forgiving, Merciful.[9]

("Idolaters" in the Qur'an also refers to Christians and Jews— Suratul A-Baqara, 2:135.) Some medieval Muslim "jurists declared that a single Qur'anic verse, which advocated fighting the unbelievers, abrogated 124 verses which called for tolerance and peace."[10] Apparently Islamic scholars' sparring over the abrogated verses is not new but "most Muslim authorities agree that the ninth sura [sic] [Al-Tawba] of the Qur'an was the very last section of the Qur'an to be revealed."[11] This Surah in actual fact annulled everything previously revealed in the Qur'an that remotely suggests peace with those who resist embracing Islam. Therefore, it can be extrapolated from reading the Qur'an that Islam is synonymous with terrorism.

Suratul Al-Tawba leaves no stone unturned when it comes to ordering Muslims to fight non-Muslims and Muslims who collaborate with them. No wonder its title means "repentance" in Arabic, which in this case means turning to Islam against one's own will and at all cost.

Islamic scholars prevaricate when dealing with the latter verses of the Qur'an because these verses essentially prove that Osama bin Laden is indeed Allah's darling because he understands the Qur'an and lives in accordance with what Allah has decreed. For the same reason ardent Muslims fail to take a stand against what some Muslims like bin Laden preach and practice.

9.4 Ranks of Muslims

The world labels bin Laden as fundamentalist and terrorist, but in essence he is a *Mu'min* (true believer). The Qur'an mentions three different *darajat* (ranks) of Muslims, namely, Muslim, *Mu'min*, and *Muhsin*. One Islamic scholar states, "Not everyone who is a *Muslim* is a *mu'min* and not everyone one who is a *mu'min* is a *muhsin*, but a *muhsin* must also be a *mu'min* and a *mu'min* a *Muslim*." He adds, "In any case, throughout Islamic history there have been the ordinary believers, or M*uslims*, or those of intense piety, *m'umins*, and those who have sought God here and now, or *muhsins*."[12] Allah envisaged each ordinary Muslim to strive at least "to become a *mumin* [sic], whose attitude is reflected in his actions."[13] This clarifies that ordinary Muslim masses are not true believers, *Mu'mins*.

The Qur'an called the "monotheists" Muslims. For example, it refers to Jesus's disciples and Abraham as Muslims[14] because a Muslim is anyone who submits to the will of one God. According to the earlier Islamic teachings, any monotheist would pass for a Muslim. (The condition changed later to requiring monotheists to embrace Muhammad as a prophet. Therefore, anyone who recites the creed "There is no god but Allah and Muhammad is his messenger" is also considered a Muslim.)

On the other hand are *Mu'mins* who are characterized by their piety. Osama and the other Muslims the world hates are at least *Mu'mins* according to the *darajat* prescribed in the Qur'an. The world would become a scarier place if every Muslim becomes at least a *Mu'min*. The Qur'an states, "The (true) believers [*Mu'mins*] are those only who believe in Allah and His messenger and afterward doubt not, but strive with their wealth and their lives for the cause of Allah. Such are the sincere."[15] The Qur'an is clear that a *Mu'min* has to believe, without any doubt, in the Qur'an and the Hadith and his or her calling is to spend his or her life and possessions for *jihad*. A *Mu'min* graduates into a *Muhsin*.

Now, let us consider *Muhsins*. *Muhsins* are the doers of good in Islam. Good in this case includes fighting for the cause of Allah. Their lives are characterized by excellence in obedience to Allah and his Prophet. The Qur'an further states, "And Allah gave them a reward in this world, and the excellent reward of the Hereafter. For Allah Loveth *those who do good* [*Muhsins*]."[16] The *Muhsins* in this verse are those who fought alongside Prophet Muhammad in the Battle of Uhud. This was the battle that was waged against the infidels who refused to accept Islam. The fighters en masse were called *Muhsins* in the Qur'an because they fought in Allah's cause.

Mainstream Muslims argue that Islamic terrorists are lunatics who have hijacked their religion. That argument, however, is a charade because it does not comport with the later teachings of the Qur'an that call for violence against non-Muslims who resist conversion to Islam. Such Muslims are merely pandering to the whims of the politically correct and peace-loving non-Muslims who long for peace in this world beleaguered by terrorism.

The Qur'an clearly shows that Allah lucidly intended the latter revelations of the Qur'an to replace the earlier ones that were more passive. Rather than arguing, mainstream Muslims would be wise to devote their time in studying the Qur'an. Perhaps then they would learn the correlation between Islam and terrorism. It is inappropriate that they hurl blanket criticism at bin Laden when he indeed properly understands and practices the authentic Islamic teachings.

The fact that there are classifications of Muslims in Islam is new to a lot of ordinary Muslims, because many Islamic scholars resort to diversionary tactics of attacking other religions, instead of clearly articulating Islamic teachings. I wonder how long this tactic will last.

Because the plethora of inconsistencies in the Qur'an was just too conspicuous to ignore, Mohamed refused to have any further discussion with me because he was not making any progress with his attempts to convert me back to Islam. He was definitely in a quandary when presenting his case. These inconsistencies were irrefutable and beyond any plausible explanation without him validating the rule of abrogation. By the same token, any Muslim who will not accept that some verses in the Qur'an were abrogated has zero chance of defending Islam.

The rift between Muslim students and me widened that term. Although they treated me like scum, God enabled me to stand firm. Their animosity toward me did not deter me from being who I am—a Christian. In fact the persecutions helped me to grow deeper in my knowledge of God in His Word. I am thankful to God for leading me through all of my adversities. I was ridiculed, rejected, and beaten, but He saw me through.

The first term of my junior year of high school concluded.

1   Pickthall.
2   *Sahih Muslim, Book 1, Number 331; Book 19, Number 4370;* and Qur'an, Suratul An-Nahl, 16:102–103.
3   Pickthall, Suratul Al-Maida, 5:69.
4   Pickthall, Suratul Al-Bayyina, 98:6.
5   Mark A. Gabriel, *Islam and Jews: The Unfinished Battle* (Lake Mary, FL: Charisma House, 2003), 47. Bracket mine.
6   Yusuf Ali, Al-Baqara, 2:106.
7   *Sahih Bukhari, Volume 5, Book 59, Number 417.*
8   Robert Spencer, *Onward Muslim Soldiers: How Jihad Still Threatens America and the West* (Washington, DC: Regnery Publishing, 2003), 135.
9   Pickthall.
10 Khalid Abou El Fadl, *The Place of Tolerance in Islam,* ed. Joshua Cohen and Ian Lague (Boston: Beacon Press, 2002), 101.

[11]   Robert Spencer, *The Politically Incorrect Guide to Islam (And the Crusades)* (Washington, DC: Regnery Publishing, 2005), 25. Bracket mine.

[12]   Seyyed Hossein Nasr, *The Heart of Islam: Enduring Values for Humanity* (San Francisco: Harper Collins, 2004), 62.

[13]   Arshad Khan, *Islam 101: Principles and Practice* (Lincoln, NE: iUniverse, 2003), 37.

[14]   Al-Imran, 3:52, 67.

[15]   Pickthall, Al-Hujraat, 49:15. Second bracket mine.

[16]   Pickthall, Al-Imran, 3:148. Bracket and emphasis mine.

CHAPTER TEN

A Lugubrious Year

A t the conclusion of the first term of my junior year of high school in April 1993, I visited my host families and friends in the Tana River district. It was a difficult decision to go to the area considering I had to deal with a lot of persecutions, but I did not let that deter me from having a normal life. Although there were difficulties, I tried to rejoice in my hardships because that is my calling as a Christian. After all, Scripture does not state in vain that "all who desire to live godly in Christ Jesus will suffer persecution."[1]

The storm that my conversion had brought onto the area three years earlier had calmed partly because I was away for most of the time. On this visit I moved around rather cautiously and even attended a convention my church had organized in a Pokomo village, which is predominantly Christian.

10.1 My Sister Gets Sick

While in this village I stumbled across my sister Halima. She was the one who had planned for my food to be poisoned. It was strange to see her in Idsowe. She must have heard from the word going around that I would be in town.

Halima had a different attitude about me this time. She neither disparaged me for being a Christian nor approved of my conversion. Her noncommittal tendency was a departure from her rigid disposition the previous few years. She told me that she was sick and requested that I take her to the hospital. She said that she felt abnormally nauseous and that the symptoms had been persistent. She looked very pale.

I thought about her request. Kenya had socialized health care with a government-instituted cost-sharing program that was affordable. She was a businesswoman and could afford it. Since some of the medical doctors and clinical officers (the equivalent of physicians' assistants in the United States) were Christian, she probably thought my position as a Christian would help her get the urgent treatment she needed.

It had been a few years since Halima and I were at loggerheads; however, I was still concerned that she was plotting to turn me in to be persecuted. She had a fanatical zeal for Islam, and I thought she could have faked being sick to get to me. Nevertheless, giving her the benefit of the doubt, I agreed to meet with her the following day so that we could plan a trip to a hospital in Malindi or Mombasa. She went home to consult with her husband.

Halima came back the following day and informed me that her husband had refused to let her go to the hospital. His refusal perhaps was due to my willingness to accompany her, which he probably interpreted as a ploy to convert his wife to Christianity.

Halima's husband, Dokota, even told her that she would be treated with medicine from Muslim clerics. The clerics hand copy passages of the Qur'an on paper then immerse them in water. The eventual solution is locally called *tallishi*, which is drunk by the sick after the ink has dissolved. This sounds unpleasant to some people, but it is palatable if compared with the oral medicine Prophet Muhammad prescribed for some ailing Muslims. The Hadith mentions more than half a dozen instances in which he commanded the sick to drink camel urine, which remarkably made them feel better.[2]

Halima probably drank some *tallishi*. Even though she was visibly suffering, Dokota overruled her desire to get medical treatment. He was definitely indifferent to her paleness and must have thought his wife was not intelligent enough to arrive at that conclusion. Islamic teachings clearly portray that women are deficient in intelligence. Prophet Muhammad said, "'Is not the evidence of two women equal to the witness of one man?' They [women] replied in

the affirmative. He said, 'This is the deficiency in her intelligence.'"[3]
Therefore, among Muslims the story of two women carries as much
weight as that of one man. My sister had almost no chance of her
desire for medical treatment being honored because her husband
thought she was not smart enough to decide on her own medical
treatment.

Halima complied with her husband's decision that she should
not go to the hospital because she was trying to be the good Muslim
woman she always was. The Qur'an states:

> Men are in charge of women, because Allah hath made the
> one of them to excel the other, and because they spend of
> their property (for the support of women). So good women
> are the obedient, guarding in secret that which Allah hath
> guarded. As for those from whom ye fear rebellion, admonish
> them and banish them to beds apart, and scourge them. Then
> if they obey you, seek not a way against them. Lo! Allah is
> ever High, Exalted, Great.[4]

Allah's message on how women should be treated in Islam is
explicit. Halima had to obey her husband, or she would suffer the
consequences. Islamic teachings forbade Halima to leave her home
even to seek treatment without her husband's permission. Had she
attempted, she would have suffered severe implications. It must have
been a difficult decision for her, considering she was gambling on
her life, but she was abiding with the Muslim belief that a Muslim
woman will enter paradise only if her Muslim husband is pleased
with her.

I went back to school for the second term with Halima
constantly on my mind. I was concerned for my sister's wellbeing.
She had persecuted me three years previously, but I held no grudge
against her because she had simply been fulfilling her duty as
a Muslim. If there were any blame, it would rest squarely on the
Islamic ideology.

10.2 Events at School

Life at school continued to be challenging for me because Muslim
students attempted to make it horrendous. And they were successful.

My Muslim teachers were also involved in the tussle. My biology teacher always frowned when I asked questions in class or brought up an issue as simple as a mark down on a test for which I should have been given credit.

The second term progressed. I participated in Christian Union events, attending "weekend challenges." Meanwhile, I did not get any information about my ailing sister because no one in my family knew my whereabouts. It was difficult to go three months without knowing her prognosis.

10.3 The Election of Prefects

I kept up with my schoolwork, anticipating the upcoming end-of-term examinations, which were two weeks away. At the same time I was keen on the outcome of the election of prefects. Students who were interested in being prefects were all campaigning. I was interested in becoming one of the top prefects (I was already the Christian Union chairman, who was considered a prefect), but the majority of the student body was Muslim. Hence it was impossible for me to get elected.

As previously stated, prefects are indispensable on Kenyan high school campuses, especially those schools that are prone to strikes. Teachers only punish those culprits who refuse to comply with the punishments levied by the prefects. Those who repeatedly break the school rules have their names entered into the black book. Records in a black book adversely affect the quality of a leaving certificate.

Unlike their counterparts in some countries, Kenyan employers generally ask for a high school "leaving certificate" as a reference when one applies for a job. A leaving certificate is an official government document endorsed by high school administrators, which lists, among other merits, a student's conduct in school. Employers reference this document because a summary of a student's behavior during four years of high school is recorded. Even a university graduate has to produce his or her high school leaving certificate when applying for a job. Therefore, it is a crucial document, and a prefect plays a role in developing a record of a student's behavior.

Some high school graduates who are notorious in school become angry when their leaving certificates render them unable to get a job. I once heard the deputy headmaster of a school I attended say that some leaving certificates are inscribed with the words "employ him at your own risk." The power of these words would doom any employment prospect for the bearer of the leaving certificate. Such an alumnus' struggle to land employment in a bleak job market can easily result in holding a grudge against his or her alma mater.

Students know the importance of maintaining good conduct in school. Those who know their behaviors are detrimental and will likely render them jobless after graduation resort to destructive behavior. They sometimes advocate for strikes with the intention of burning down the buildings that house the students' records. (It was for this reason that the administration building at Waa High School was petrol bombed a few years after I graduated.)

Illicit activities abounded on campus particularly during my junior year (1993). Drugs were used openly. Stemming these activities was the school administration's main priority. Given that most prefects colluded with the culprits, there was a need for electing effective leaders.

There were a few candidates who campaigned to become the head boy. This position is the most powerful and with many benefits. Lower classmen cater to the head boy. He oversees students' behavior and is accorded various privileges, including that of leaving the school compound anytime he wants because no teacher would deny him a leave-out (permission slip).

10.4 Our School Water Supply Shut Off

The campaign for the election of prefects was in high gear in July that year when without notice our school water supply was shut off, apparently due to bill arrears. This was a shock to students and staff alike. The water shortage hit our school two weeks before the August recess.

The deputy headmaster convened an emergency meeting with the top prefects, including the two religious leaders. I attended the emergency meeting. He told us to tell the students to remain calm. He added that the water problem was there to stay. The school administration was apparently trying to avert a strike.

Kenyan secondary school students are known to go on strike sometimes without even an excuse. A committee appointed by the government found that "between 1986 and 1991 ... at least 567 schools had strikes."[5] That is a staggering number of schools within only a five-year span.

The prefects asked the deputy headmaster to send the students home that week for three weeks (the length of the August recess) and have them report back to school early for the third term. He rebuffed our idea. Instead he instructed us to encourage the students to remain calm. The meeting ended without a solution.

We went one whole weekend with dry taps. The school organized for a water tanker, which supplied water twice a day. Students fetched water for quick baths.

Many students were frustrated. Their parents had paid for them to learn, not to worry about a trivial thing like a water shortage brought upon them due to someone's unscrupulous handling of funds. Having no water was too much to ask of them on top of a school curriculum that was already taxing.

High school students habitually causing chaos in most Kenyan schools shows how impatient they became with some unprincipled school administrations. Most often they perceive the school administration as oppressive. It was atypical of Kenyan high school students that the Waa students waited that long without causing mayhem.

It was Monday night. The prefects went to another meeting with the deputy headmaster. We revisited some of our previous discussions. The school administration once again was reluctant to send students home. We were again asked to tell the students to remain calm and the water would be restored. The situation was already getting out of control.

Students congregated at the head boy's office later that night to discuss our second meeting with the school administration. The head boy talked about the risks of going on a strike. He was concerned that some students would use that opportunity to destroy school property.

10.5 Students Go on Strike

Although students' striking in Kenyan schools was a norm, we did not want to be a part of that despicable legacy. Most school strikes resulted in the burning of buildings, including offices, kitchens, teachers' houses, and dormitories—sometimes with students trapped inside. Waa High School students resolved that night to go home en masse peacefully at 3 a.m.

I went to bed that Monday night wondering what I would do. I did not advocate for students to strike, but at the same time the administration was refusing any ideas the prefects presented to avert the imminent strike. I thought about the school water supply that had been disconnected for failure to pay the outstanding bills. It was the fifth day of dry taps.

Rumors had begun to circulate that the headmaster had borrowed the money from the school's contingency account for his business. Students had pressed him for an explanation, but he refused to take responsibility, which would have cost him his job.

I was worried about my detractors, who could use the strike as an opportunity to settle scores. The bell rang at 3 a.m., and I took a friend of mine along to the teacher in charge of the Christian Union's house. Paul and I were privileged to shower at the house during the water shortage. The teacher let us into his house, which was within the school compound and adjacent to the Mombasa-Lunga Lunga main road. We spent the night there.

In the meantime, infuriated students flattened the barbed wire fence surrounding the school compound and went to the bus stop. Someone must have tipped off the *matatu* drivers. It was just after 3 a.m. and the road was abuzz with buses and minibuses. Paul and I left the teacher's quarters in the morning. We went home awaiting the announcement of when school would reopen.

While on the way home, I heard from one of my friends that some students had been looking for me during the night. The hedge in the form of stringent school rules that had protected me was broken, and now it was time for them to harm me because they hated me for my religious convictions. By God's grace, they looked for me in vain that night. Many students have been killed during school strikes in Kenya. I was grateful to have been in a safe haven that night.

10.6 The Sad News

In the days that followed, I went to visit my Christian friends near my home area in the Tana River district. Upon my arrival in Garsen I was shocked by the news that my sister Halima had passed away. She died on Thursday, July 22, 1993, two days after the Waa students went on strike. I was grief-stricken. I went to an elder from my church's house. He dispatched his son to inform the missionary pastor what had happened.

I was angry that my sister died so young. I wondered if she would have survived if I had taken her to the hospital against her husband's directives. Halima was the biggest opposition I had faced within my family since my conversion to Christianity became evident. She was pragmatic and had used her possessions to restrict my activities as a Christian. She had used her brilliance to argue in the Chief's Court when I appeared there to answer the charges that I had left home without my mother's consent while I was still a minor. Halima had attempted to "save" me from Christianity, a religion she thought led people to doom.

The missionary pastor came to the elder's house to comfort me. He offered to take me to see my mother the following day. I was concerned for our safety; however, at the same time I was very sad and just wanted to see my mother. I knew it was precarious for us to visit my home when my extended family was still around. The funeral had already taken place (Muslim burial normally takes place within hours of death), and the prescribed three days of Muslim mourning had elapsed.

The missionary and I embarked on the trip to visit my grieving mother the following morning. It was the first time I took a Christian along for a visit since the Kenyan government official (District Officer) separated me from my family. The chances were high that we would run into my volatile elder brother. Since he had not met Christians I associated with, I was concerned that the presence of the missionary pastor would elicit retaliation.

We rode the missionary pastor's motorcycle to my home. We arrived when the men were escorting the cattle—a daily routine— to the grazing land. We took advantage of that opportunity to visit with my mother and my brother-in-law Dokota. We cried together. That was one of the saddest days of my life. My mother narrated to me how she had accompanied Halima to a hospital in Lamu and to various Muslim clerics to no avail.

My mother did not bring up any religion in our conversation. She had lost a son (me) to Christianity and three years later was dealing with the natural death of her daughter.

She could not outwardly mourn (by wailing) the demise of her daughter Halima because Islamic teachings prohibit it. Prophet Muhammad banned wailing due to the fact that "the deceased is punished for the wailing of his relatives."[6] My family was reeling from the shock of Halima's death but was not allowed to express their grief.

There was nothing I could do to help them deal with the grief because of our difference in beliefs. I was in shock that I would not see my sister again, but life had to go on. I have wondered why God terminated her life so young. She left behind three children. It was hard for us to fathom, but God had to execute His will regardless of our protest.

Our visit was brief. Grief had brought my family and I together, but I was still concerned for my safety. The missionary pastor and I left for Garsen a short while later.

10.7 Muslim Students Plot Against Me

I stayed in Garsen for about a week and left for Mombasa to find out when school would reopen. I received a letter telling me to report to school in company of my guardian one week prior to its scheduled opening for the third term. My host mother, Jane, along with some women from my church in Mombasa, escorted me to school.

When we arrived on campus, there were people everywhere. Students were meeting one-on-one with teachers who were gathering information about the perpetrators of the strike.

All students were arbitrarily found guilty of leaving the school compound without permission. Each student was slated to receive ten strokes of the cane. Boys were beaten on their buttocks, girls on their palms. The school administration charged each of us to pay one hundred shillings for flattening a small section of the barbed wire fence.

It was my turn to be quizzed on what had transpired the night of the strike. I was accused of being the mastermind before I was even given a chance to tell my version of the story. I protested. When it came to my turn to receive strokes of the cane, I flat-out refused.

The school administration concluded that I was the ringleader of the strike. They had heard false testimonies from Muslim students that I had ordered students to leave the school compound at 3 a.m. In addition, they claimed that I gave bus fare to those in need from the Christian Union's Sunday offerings. By virtue of being the Christian Union chairman, I had access to the funds collected. They did not know that the money I had allegedly distributed to the students was intact. It was deposited weekly with the school's bursar office for safekeeping. My accusers and the administration were oblivious to the policy that the Christian Union committee had to approve each spending.

On these flimsy accounts the school administration suspended me for two weeks. My host mothers and I were shocked at the turn of events. I was confident, however, that I would be exculpated.

I went home that day furious with the Muslim students. They probably were rejoicing that I was suspended. I was scheduled for a hearing before the Board of Governors. I looked forward to that day because I knew I would be accorded the privilege of exposing the lies of their allegations. They did not know that I had an alibi that night.

It was really hard trying to explain to people what had befallen me. A suspension from school carries a certain stigma that is difficult to remove. My host mothers had only known me for a year and a half. They were concerned. My name was on its way into the black book.

My host mothers and I went back to school after my two-week suspension had ended. We met with the Board of Governors. The meeting started with the headmaster reading the charges against me. I requested for the witnesses to be produced to no avail. I told the board that the money I allegedly distributed to students was intact and with the bursar's office.

Then I requested for the teacher at whose house I spent that night to testify. Mr. Ziro talked about how Paul and I came to his house around the same time the students began to strike. Then my host mother Jane took over. She talked to the board about how Muslim students hated me. She insisted that it was a case of a witch-hunt.

The Board of Governors deliberated behind closed doors for a while. It ruled that I was innocent of all the charges and should not pay the hundred-shilling fine or get the ten strokes of the cane. My mothers and I rejoiced at the verdict. I was instructed, however, not to discuss the proceedings of the meeting and the ensuing verdict with the students. We went home.

I thought about transferring to another school but decided against it because it would have been the fourth high school in as many years for me. Besides, the level of persecution at Waa was not as severe compared to what I had faced at Mau Mau Memorial Secondary School. I reported to school at the end of my suspension when the third term was already in progress. I borrowed notes from Christian students and played catch-up for a while.

10.8 I Am Selected as a Prefect

It was already the third week of the third term, and the school did not have new prefects because of the strike. In a departure from the school tradition, the teachers selected new prefects. To my surprise, I was selected to be the compound prefect in charge of the cleanliness of the entire school compound. I turned down the appointment because it was a very tough position. I thought the position would foster more hatred, especially from Muslim students. Besides, I was upset with the administration for suspending me on flimsy grounds.

The school administration convinced me to become the compound prefect. Some teachers told me that if I failed to take up the position, Muslim students who were prefects would persecute me. That reasoning led me to accept being the compound prefect.

The head boy and I, along with some students of our choice, were given a house in which to live through our senior year. It was a small colonial-era house furnished with bunk beds and desks. We used it also as an office.

10.9 1993 Christmas Holiday

The chaotic third term of my junior year came to an end. I looked forward to the six-week break when I would visit various Christian friends around the province and also participate in church activities. A quick unannounced visit with my mother was also in the plans.

My church was involved in church planting. Our missionary pastor traversed the Coast Province preaching the Gospel in various towns. He organized large evangelistic meetings that lasted about two weeks during school recess in December. I also participated in church conventions.

Our church applied for a permit to have an evangelistic outreach in Lamu District, which was predominantly Muslim, in December 1993. Lamu is another port city in the Coast Province and is also the capital of the district. The town, which is a part of the Lamu Archipelago, was established in the fourteenth century A.D. Its inhabitants are mostly Arab of Omani descent. It is a hub of Kenyan tourism and fishing industries, which is only accessible by air and sea. The only vehicle on the entire island is for the official use of the District Commissioner. Donkeys and bicycles are the means of transportation.

Two highly regarded Islamic institutions of higher learning in East Africa, as well as the sacred graves of Prophet Muhammad's descendants, make Lamu a popular place for religious tourists all year round. There are a few Christian churches on the island that were established during the British colonial rule. Nevertheless, Christians were not allowed event permits from the government to hold open-air evangelistic meetings in Lamu town.

The only Christians who reside in Lamu are natives of other parts of Kenya, and their tribes are considered mainly Christian. For that reason, it is impossible for local Muslims who convert to Christianity to be tolerated.

The island is very active during the Islamic month of *Rabi al-Awwal* when revelers come to celebrate the birth of Prophet Muhammad. Muslims converge "for the week-long competitions in Qur'an recitation drawing participants and spectators from near and far."[7] They come in droves via tour buses from throughout the Islamic world to celebrate the birth of their prophet. Bus companies allocate extra fleets of buses to ply the Lamu route during the festivities.

Some Muslims in the Coast Province believe that making six trips in their lifetime to Lamu for *ziara* (visiting the Prophet's descendants' gravesite during the weeklong commemoration of his birthday) is equivalent to making a pilgrimage to Mecca. I do not know if this is a ploy used by Arabs—the majority of the business owners in Lamu—to sustain the influx of tourists and keep business booming, or whether the belief has a backing of some sort in some surreptitious Islamic tenets. Whatever the case, thousands of faithfuls descend on the city annually.

Our church did not even attempt to apply for an open-air evangelistic meeting permit from the city of Lamu because the government officials would have turned down our request for security reasons. It was obvious that the presence of former Muslims with the evangelistic team would have sparked riots. Instead, we settled for a venue on the mainland. The church rented the Mpeketoni Secondary School dormitories for lodging and a local church provided a building for our meetings. It was an easy decision for me to go to Mpeketoni because we would have escaped rather easily in the event of a Muslim riot.

There were teaching sessions early in the morning and witnessing in the mid-morning. We had discussions and debates with Muslims in the afternoon and public evangelistic meetings at the marketplace in the evening. The day ended with devotions.

Most of us trekked to various places doing evangelism. Unlike in some countries where people hardly talk to strangers, most people in Kenya are quite engaging even when it is their first encounter. We used *The Four Spiritual Laws*, an evangelism pamphlet written by Bill Bright, founder of Campus Crusade for Christ International. It was a good start-up tool for personal evangelism and gave us opportunities to formulate conversation starters.

It was the final day of the two-week outreach, the day I was slated to address the public evangelistic meeting. We went back to our base and rested for the afternoon. The choir practiced some songs. The missionary pastor went over the program with me. Then we set off for the evangelistic meeting downtown.

The meeting started with the choir singing various tunes. After the singing had ended, one of our elders prayed and introduced the speaker. No sooner did the missionary pastor take the dais than he announced that I would give a testimony. There were hundreds in attendance. Most of the attendees had never heard about me. Many Muslims clad in robes watched from a distance. They were afraid of attending our meetings out of fear of being rebuked. It was a norm for local *imams* to warn Muslims against attending Christian events.

I shared my conversion to Christianity. The preaching of the Gospel followed. An altar call was made, and some people came forward to be prayed for. I left for our station in company of others as soon as the meeting concluded.

10.10 A Threat

We did not hear until the following day how my presence at the evangelistic meeting had especially infuriated one Muslim young man. The story was that he had been determined to blow up our meeting place with a petrol bomb that night. His family, who owned various businesses in town, apparently locked him up in one of their stores when he threatened to come after me. We had police presence at our meetings. Had he carried out his threat, he would have been apprehended.

Even though some Muslims do not outwardly show their resentment, inherently every ex-Muslim exasperates them. Their attitude is derived from the austere teachings of Islam, which prescribe death for an apostate. Islamic teachings in the Qur'an and the Hadith are lucid that death is the ultimate punishment for apostasy. I have heard some Muslims in the West argue that Islam does not call for the killing of an ex-Muslim. Nevertheless that argument is misleading because it does not comport with what Allah and Prophet Muhammad said in the Qur'an and the Hadith respectively.

I wondered how the supposedly sovereign and omnipotent Allah needs Muslims' help in dealing with me. His command for Muslims to kill an apostate is nefarious. I wonder why he is too impatient to wait until the Day of Judgment to avenge my disobedience. Why would he urge Muslims to retaliate for him? Does he really need their help? These questions lingered in my mind that day. I left Mpeketoni town and have not been back except for passing through a couple of times without disembarking from the vehicle.

We were grateful to God that our base was not burned down that night and that I was safe. Muslims were to continue making similar threats against Christians. Unfortunately, some of them materialized. In one instance, reported by the *East African Standard*, "Five churches were burnt down in Bura Division of Tana River District."[8] This incident took place not very far from my home. When that wave of violence broke out, however, I was already attending college overseas. I have constantly wondered what it would have been like had I still been in Kenya during this violence and the tribal clashes pitting Pokomos (Christians) against Ormas (Muslims) in which my former third-grade teacher, a Christian, was killed in 2001.

The six-week holiday break concluded. I returned to school for a new term. It was a brand-new year (1994), and I hoped for ease in my persecutions as well as excellence in school. I shared what had happened during my break with the members of the Christian Union and continued debating Muslim students.

The unexpected death of my sister, suspension from school, and constant threats from Muslims were emotionally and mentally draining for me. The end did not seem in sight for my sufferings. Nevertheless I always found solace in God's Word, which contains the experiences some believers before me had faced. King David said, "All who hate me whisper together against me; against me they devise my hurt." He added, "My enemy does not triumph over me" because "You [LORD] uphold me in my integrity, and set me before Your face forever."[9] I knew that my detractors and foes would get the better part of me if and only if my Heavenly Father so willed.

1 NKJV, 2nd Timothy 3:12.

2 *Sahih Bukhari, Volume 7, Book 71, Number 590.*

3 *Sahih Bukhari, Volume 1, Book 6, Number 301.* Bracket mine.

4 Pickthall, Suratul An-Nisa, 4:34.

5 Bethwell A. Ogot, *My Footprints in the Sands of Time: An Autobiography* (Victoria, BC: Trafford Publishing, 2003), 488.

6 *Sahih Bukhari, Volume 2, Book 23, Number 391.*

7 Bill Musk, *The Unseen Faces of Islam: Sharing the Gospel with Ordinary Muslims at Street Level* (Grand Rapids: Kregel Publications, 2004), 79.

8 Philip Mwakio and Jesse Masai, "Five Churches torched in Tana River District," *The East African Standard*, June 13, 2003. Retrieved from http://216.185.134.103/archives/june/fri20062003/headlines/news20062003003.htm on May 11, 2006.

9 NKJV, Psalm 41:7, 11b and 12b. Bracket mine.

CHAPTER ELEVEN

Success Amid Adversities

It was the second term of my senior year of high school, and I was getting ready for the final examinations. High school students in the Kenya's infamous 8-4-4-education system take mock examinations in the second term to gauge how they might do in the final exam—the Kenya Certificate of Secondary Education (KCSE). This system was introduced in 1985 and requires students to be in primary school for eight years, four years in secondary school, and four years in college or university. The Kenya National Examination Council administers the KCSE nationwide. Every form-four (an equivalent of twelfth grade) student dreads the KCSE exam because it amasses everything that a student has learned during the four years of high school.

My host mothers bought topnotch preparatory books for me for the KCSE. I diligently studied for the mock KCSE exam while keeping up with my duties as a prefect and also participating in the Christian Union events. The persecutions on the school campus had abated.

11.1 Attempts to Derail My Hope for Excellence

It was Sunday morning, June 12, 1994. I went to my classroom just before the Sunday church service. The Kenyan school curriculum was strenuous, so I had to study seven days a week. When I got to my desk that morning, I was shocked to discover that the locked drawer was open and all my textbooks and notebooks were missing. The padlock was still intact, but the drawer had visibly been tampered with. I notified the school administration, which launched an investigation.

My five years of painstakingly preparing for the KCSE exam were partly wasted. I was thankful to God, however, that the vandal struck four months before the start of the KCSE. The perpetrator(s) perhaps hoped that stealing my books would sabotage my performance on the exam.

All my coursework was gone. I indiscriminately scrambled for reading materials and tried not to be disheartened. The inadequacy of relevant course materials made it quite difficult to prepare for the exam that covered four years of schooling.

A men's fellowship group from one of the churches that had adopted me bought some textbooks for me. These men (among them a lawyer who is now a Kenya High Court judge) mentored me. Some of my teachers also helped me with their respective subjects. I made progress within a few weeks.

Then in July, almost a month to the day of the first vandalism, another vandal struck. This time again my locked drawer was broken into but very little was stolen. Fortunately I had started the habit of carrying my books back and forth from my assigned house on a daily basis.

The school administration's investigating into the vandalisms did not yield any results, but made it obvious that I was the only one targeted. Since Muslim students had been unsuccessful at getting me expelled from school the previous year, they tried to derail my hopes of passing the KCSE examination by vandalizing my books.

The second term examinations started. The form-four students sat for the mock KCSE examination, which I passed. I went to Mombasa during the August holiday with a lot of schoolwork to do. I also spent part of the break helping my friend Del and his wife, Debbie, to relocate to the Coast province. They were missionaries among my tribe in a different part of the Tana River district, but had to evacuate after being targeted by frequent bandit attacks. We had met for the first time at a Muslim evangelism conference at Word of Life Kenya in Diani (near Mombasa) in July 1992.

11.2 My Graduation from High School

The August holiday break ended and I went back to school preparing for the KCSE exam. I was able to sit for the exam that spanned over four weeks—covering nine subjects—without a setback. Each subject had two exams. Geography was the only subject with 25 multiple-choice questions, which accounted for a paltry 1.5 points toward the overall grade for the subject based on a 12-point scale. As always, writing short answers and essays was the hard part.

It was Wednesday, November 16, 1994. I had just finished my high school final exam. The education policy required that each student who accomplished the KCSE exam be issued with the Kenya Secondary School Leaving Certificate. The school administration gave me a flattering leaving certificate. My certificate in part reads, "He was industrious, responsible and honest student of excellent academic ability. He was an active prefect.... His conduct is excellent."[1] After all that took place in high school, leaving high school on a high note armed with a promising leaving certificate was a moment to savor! Just the previous year, I had been teetering on the verge of being declared of the worst conduct when I was suspended from school. But on this November day in 1994 there was cause for celebration.

I was ecstatic to be finished with high school after five years riddled with various forms of persecutions and hardships. My family had thought that I would not accomplish this feat without their help, but they were wrong. I succeeded because God provided for my financial needs.

But leaving Waa High School that Wednesday afternoon was bittersweet. I was sad to leave the boarding school system that had protected me from outside Muslim threats since my conversion to Christianity became public five years earlier. I stayed with one of my host families, bracing myself for a new and difficult life outside the school compound.

Most graduates looked for jobs while awaiting their KCSE exam results, which the cabinet minister for education officially announced. They waited for at least a year after the results to get into undergraduate programs because admissions to the four public universities were backlogged. Constant university student strikes and an inadequate number of universities contributed to the delay in admission. There were about three private universities in Kenya in the 1990s, which lacked diversified courses and enrolment space.

Therefore, there was not much I could do but to wait for the KCSE results and afterward look forward to admission to a university if I passed the exam. In the meantime I was involved in various church activities.

11.3 The 1994 Christmas Holiday

My church had organized another convention and evangelistic meeting. It was held in Witu, Lamu District. The town was predominantly Muslim but was fairly safe for me to visit. Our church obtained an event permit from the government, and we embarked on our weeklong convention and evangelistic meetings. Due to the previous year's firebomb threat involving the young Muslim man, we asked the government for extra security. Thus plainclothes policemen mingled with the masses at our meetings.

We followed our convention routine of teachings, witnessing, and evangelistic meetings. The missionary pastor and I met. He advised that I should share my testimony on the last day of the evangelistic meetings. I realized later that this was a brilliant idea because had I addressed the meeting earlier in the week, Muslims would have rioted, and the government would have cancelled the rest of our evangelistic meetings.

Some of the conventioneers witnessed in Muslim-populated areas, but I avoided these areas. Instead, I went to an area whose inhabitants were mostly animists. We traversed Witu and its environs sharing the Good News. We trekked for many kilometers encouraging some Christians in remote areas.

I skipped debating Muslim leaders that year because I was known in the area. Witu is close to where my elder brother Roba resides and is about forty kilometers from my home. I thought he would probably be in town. His neighbors also came to town on a regular basis. Since they knew me from days when I was a Muslim, I thought that entering town for debates might be a problem.

All was going well at the convention. So far no unusual events had occurred. Then I went to the downtown with some friends one afternoon, and a Muslim man approached me with some questions. Within minutes, a crowd had gathered around us.

Witu was an idle town. Its unemployment rate must have been higher than the Kenyan national average of 40 percent because many people roamed the streets doing nothing.[2]

Witu has many villages on its outskirts without mosques. Some Muslims come to town for prayers at the grand mosque because Islamic teachings encourage performing the five daily prayers together. Prophet Muhammad instructed that the Friday prayers must be performed in a large mosque with a quorum of forty men. For these reasons, the town is always abuzz, especially on Fridays. Many men from my tribe, which was considered to be 100 percent Muslim, came to town for business and to observe the prayers.

The crowd gathered around me that afternoon waiting for answers. They wondered how Allah could have a Son, why Christians ascribe partners to him, and why I had left Islam. No sooner did I commence talking about the Trinity than one of them slapped me. I was stunned.

Muslims believe Christians have three gods, namely, god the father, god the mother, and god the son. Their belief is derived from the Qur'an and the Hadith, which lucidly portray the alleged Christian trinity as tantamount to associating partners with Allah—the most heinous sin in Islam. Muslims I knew generally asked questions about Christianity from what they knew. If the answer to their questions contradicted what they knew, some of them would fight.

I was shaken by the man's attack. But I was soon surprised when plainclothes police officers promptly arrested my assailant. He was bundled into a waiting police Mahindra Jeep and taken to the police station. His arrest perhaps sent a strong message to the angry crowd against attacking me. They dispersed. I hurriedly retreated to our station.

It was good to see justice prevailing. Kenyan police officers were known for inefficiency and complacency. They were notorious for taking bribes and letting lawlessness be the order of the day. Nonetheless, they were different that day.

The incident necessitated that the police beef up security on the last day of the evangelistic meeting, when I was slotted to give my testimony. The Officer Commanding Police Division (O.C.P.D.) guaranteed that hooligans would not disrupt our meetings. Accordingly many plainclothes officers were at our evangelistic meetings, which were held at a public showground. It was easier to mobilize them because most of them were Christian.

In spite of the police presence, I was quite nervous that day because I did not know if Muslim youth would cause mayhem. The evangelistic meeting started with the choir singing a few numbers. When the singing was finished, the speaker introduced me. I talked about my conversion to Christianity. I finished my testimony reciting Suratul Al-Maryam (chapter 19 of the Qur'an) verses 19 and 21, which state:

> He said: 'Nay, I am only a messenger from thy Lord, (to announce) to thee the gift of a holy son.'... He said: 'So (it will be): Thy Lord saith, 'that is easy for Me: and (We wish) to appoint him as a Sign unto men and a Mercy from Us.' It is a matter (so) decreed.[3]

I explained a little bit about these verses of the Qur'an that supposedly prophesy the birth of the "Jesus of Islam."[4]

Many Muslims drew near to the venue as I was speaking. They looked quite furious. At that time I turned over the meeting to the missionary pastor who briefly preached the Gospel.

11.4 Muslim Youth in Hot Pursuit

This pastor was a discerning man. He had anticipated that there would be a problem with me addressing the meeting. For this reason he had parked his motorcycle at the meeting beforehand. He prayed for the people. As soon as the "amen" sounded, he started the motorcycle and asked me to leave with him. We put on our helmets and left from the center of the meeting heading toward Garsen.

I thought we were out of danger, but suddenly a Land Rover was trailing us. To our amazement, it was full of enraged Muslim youth, who began to chase us. The missionary pastor accelerated his Suzuki motorcycle around potholes that were as huge as bathtubs. Thankfully the Land Rover could not keep up with us because of the humongous holes in the road.

The twenty-five-minute journey turned into an ordeal. It was also frightening because the road passed through the Lango la Simba (meaning "the gate of lions" in Swahili) National Forest where wild animals roamed. Lions, hyenas, buffaloes, hippopotamuses, leopards, elephants, and many other animals called the forest home. We could not know when an animal might enter the road in front of us. Some animals, like hippos and elephants, may have kept us from driving past them for a time. It was before dusk, and the Land Rover was not in sight. We were grateful that we had lost them on the treacherous road. They were out to avenge for Allah but were unsuccessful.

We nervously rode through the forest but thankfully were not held back by any animals and made it home safely. We gave our gratitude to God for saving us from that danger. We prayed for the safe trip home of those we left behind. We found solace in God, who works in extraordinary ways. I live to thank Him even for the less-maintained roads that slowed our pursuers.

11.5 A New Job

I stayed in Garsen for about a week. The high school national examinations results were still pending. In the meantime, I went back to Mombasa to help Del and Debbie with a translation project. I worked on the "People of God study course," a series of four books that was geared toward introducing Muslims to Christianity. Since an Orma man had translated them, my task was to proofread them. I also worked with George, who was affiliated with the Summer Institute of Linguistics (SIL) and had an assignment with a local Bible translation agency that worked on the Orma Bible.

The examination results were around the corner. I stayed tuned to the national media, which carried the announcement. The results were normally sent to respective schools after the official announcement. Examinees obtained the official transcripts, commonly known as "result slips," and then waited for at least a year before admission to undergraduate programs. The Joint Admission Board (JAB) is the body that oversees the Kenya public universities admission program. It is mandated to assign qualified students what university to attend and what field to study. Private universities were scarce and they had their own admission criteria, admitting mostly students who were not qualified to join public universities.

11.6 My Examination Results

When the KCSE results were announced for the 1994 school year, I was the best student in the Orma tribe. My family was humiliated by the examination results. The rumors they had spread for three years about how I was a high school dropout were overthrown.

The JAB assigned me to the Nairobi University in 1995 to pursue Bachelor of Science in Agriculture. This was to my surprise because agriculture was not among the four fields I had chosen to pursue. Even though my grades warranted me to be invited to study at least one of my four choices (law, medicine, nursing or pharmacy), I was relegated to a field that was of least interest to me.

Many a high school graduate encountered a similar predicament because corruption was rampant. Most slots for professional fields were filled with less-qualified students who found their way there because of nepotism, tribalism, or corruption. The JAB assignment disappointed me.

One of my relatives had connections with the big shots in President Daniel Arap Moi's government. He tried to fix things up for me to study medicine, but I declined his offer. I reasoned with him that it was unfair for someone more qualified than me to be kicked off a program to accommodate me.

I suspected my relative's offer to help was meant to slow me down because he, like others, resented how I crisscrossed the country witnessing of what God had done in my life. He once advised me not to waste my mind on studying theology. His comments were offensive to me. I understood that if I had accepted his offer, I had to pledge allegiance to him like the rest of my relatives he had helped, thus impeding my witness for Christ among Muslims. Had I given in to his offer to help me to get into pursuing medicine, he would have used his connections to keep tabs on me at the university. He would have frustrated my academics with all sorts of impediments.

My family had unsuccessfully tried to convert me back to Islam. They were desperate and had resorted to other ways that did not look quite as obvious to me. They brought up an idea that I was getting old—when I was only twenty—and should get married to a girl they chose for me. I heard she was very beautiful. Nevertheless I was taken aback by their desperate move that even contravened Islamic teachings, which forbid Muslim women to marry non-Muslim men. Conversely, Muslim men are called upon to marry unbelieving women so that through their rule in the home they can coerce their unbelieving wives into conversion to Islam. Double standard.

I had been a pariah for the five years I was in high school, but now everyone wanted the best for me. I wondered why all of a sudden I was a sought-after man. I suspect the offers to help me to get into medical school and get married were genuine because it all started when they realized that I had the good grades. I knew they now dreaded that I would be a Christian witness in Ormaland. It wouldn't take long and their worst fear would be confirmed. I was unwilling for my own tribe and family to remain ignorant of the Gospel or repressed by the lies of Islam.

11.7 Pioneering the Writing of the Orma Language

I embarked on a project underwritten by Literacy and Evangelism International, headquartered in Tulsa, Oklahoma, to have the Orma language written for the first time. The workshop was held in Mombasa. There were Orma men and women drawn from various villages. My tribesmen take a keen interest and pride in their language and culture. For this reason various village elders appointed some qualified individuals to attend the workshop.

While at the workshop, we learned some rules of the Orma language that George, a linguist with SIL, had documented and commenced on developing the language structure. It took us only a week to produce the language primer. We agreed on the entire alphabet chart, thirty-three letters in total, which lacked the letter "v" because there is no sound for it in the Orma language. At that workshop I connected with a lot of Christians who worked for various multinational organizations.

While I was waiting for the date to report to the University of Nairobi, I got a job with one of the organizations as one of the Orma language specialists, working on translating various evangelistic and medical outreach materials into Orma. I was equipped with a computer that had several translated books on it. Since the books had been translated before the Orma language was officially written, I was assigned the task of editing the books. A font was specifically modified to accommodate some elements of the Orma language that were incompatible with ordinary word processing.

I lived in a gated compound away from the city life with Del and Debbie. I did not worry much about Muslims coming after me because there were two guards who alternated manning the compound, especially at night. A big dog, Yogi, barked at strangers. Occupants of gated houses in Kenya keep dogs that are ferocious. Most gates bear signs "Mbwa Kali" and "Beware of Dog," which mean the same thing to a thief but the former means "ferocious dog" in Swahili. There are a few odd gates that bear "Mbwa si Kali" which means the opposite of a ferocious dog. In that case, a large dog visibly roams the yard, barking violently at strangers. It would be ill-advised to walk into that compound without being accompanied by the owner.

I worked Monday through Friday on translations, occasionally meeting with my colleagues, Del and Debbie, to go over the progress of the project. We had lunch breaks together, which mostly were dominated by discussions on hurdles facing the project. They had a house helper who cooked meals for lunch and dinner.

As part of an outreach to Muslims, a few guests frequented our weekday lunch breaks that lasted at least an hour. Various topics in Islam and Christianity were discussed. I missed some of the outreach opportunities because I was "on loan" to a team that was affiliated with Wycliffe Bible Translators in Nairobi. I wasn't missed as such because most Muslim guests preferred my absence at the discussions.

11.8 Debating Muslims

The word spread about our lunchtime meetings. During one of my absences, Ismail, a Somali Muslim, came over for lunch. I had heard he was an avid debater but frequently got angry when things went against his expectations.

One day around lunchtime the telephone rang, and it was Ismail. He confirmed that he was coming over but did not apprise us of his friend who was accompanying him. It is normal in the Kenyan cultures for extra visitors to be at meals. Those who go home for lunch take along their friends who live out of town.

Yogi barked, and there were Ismail and a friend who was clad in a long white robe standing at the gate. Ismail introduced his friend to us as a former Christian evangelist who had converted to Islam. The introduction raised some eyebrows. We ushered them in while keeping the dog at bay since Muslims detest being touched by dogs. Yogi stayed in a doghouse and was not allowed into the house.

We talked about our daily happenings while waiting for lunch. No sooner did we finish lunch than Ismail suggested some topics we should cover. He was confident that the former Christian would help him cover some ground with us.

Ismail and the former evangelist tried to discredit Jesus by using what was written about Him in the New and Old Testaments. The deity of Jesus, the prophecies about His virgin birth, and His sacrifice on the cross were under attack that afternoon. In one instance the former evangelist asked us to open our Bibles to John 1:18, which reads, "No one has seen God at any time. The only begotten Son, who is in the bosom of the Father, He has declared *Him*."[5] He was contending that, since according to the verse no one has seen God, our claim of Jesus being the Begotten Son of God was unfounded.

People often read and misinterpret passages in Scripture. I have encountered many Muslims who raised questions from what they read in the Bible, but then those questions backfired on them. The former evangelist was no exception. He was proved inept and regretfully admitted his mistake.

The former evangelist was as misguided as Ismail, who argued but never grasped what was being conveyed. Anyone who reads the abovementioned verse should think twice before raising an allegation of that magnitude. Del and I went over the verse with them. Del reread it before we explained to them what was meant by the entire verse. We went back to the preceding verses to prove that it was talking about Christ's mission of coming to earth to make the Father known. Also, the latter part of the verse that reads "who is at the Father's side, has made Him known," refers to Jesus.

It was not a surprise to us that Ismail and the former evangelist had not bothered checking the immediate context of those verses in the Gospel of John. Muslims normally try to read and understand the Bible thinking that it was written like the Qur'an. The Qur'an has many random verses in a chapter. This randomness gives credence to the teachings that individual verses were revealed at different times, leading to differing topics in some immediate verses. Some Muslims believe that this randomness is an aspect peculiar to the Qur'an—an advantage over other sacred books—because when one reads ten of its verses in a row, he or she amasses varying valuable lessons during a short reading. (Instead the varying lessons turn out to be haphazard.) By the same token, unfortunately, some Muslims read the Bible expecting the same format.

Del and I were agape at how little the former evangelist knew the Scriptures. I have wondered if we were duped so that we would believe what he was saying about Jesus.

Even without going into the exegesis of the aforementioned verse, anyone who reads it could see its true meaning. I went on quoting passages from the Qur'an—not that I believe in its authority on Christianity—to help Ismail and the "former evangelist" understand that since Jesus is in heaven with God, which even the Islamic teachings allude, he sees God the Father and is waiting for the command to come back for the Judgment Day.[6] The Hadith also reiterates the same sentiment about Jesus being in heaven and his imminent second coming.[7]

Ismail and the "former evangelist" were dumbfounded. Del and I waited for their next move. Since it was made evident to them that John 1:18 shows a lot more about Jesus than they initially had thought, they asked us to open the Old Testament book of Deuteronomy.

Muslims believe in the Torah, but they contend that Jews corrupted the Torah of the biblical Old Testament. They claim that the Qur'an contains the unaltered Torah, Psalms, and Gospel. I have wondered why they raise such a claim, because the Qur'an is full of haphazard verses, purportedly of Old and New Testaments in nature. If it indeed contained the abovementioned sacred books, it would have at least had them in order, but that is not the case.

They asked us to open to Deuteronomy 23:2 which reads, "One of illegitimate birth shall not enter the assembly of the LORD; even to the tenth generation none of his *descendants* shall enter the assembly of the LORD."[8] We wondered what questions they would bring forth this time.

We were taken aback when the "former evangelist" contended that since Jesus was born out of wedlock, making Him an illegitimate child, He was unfit to be anyone's savior. He added that the sacrifice through His death for the forgiveness of sins as claimed by Christians would be forfeited because He could not have gone into the Holy of Holies like the blood that the high priests in the Old Testament took with them. The "former evangelist" continued to show that since Jesus was banished from the tabernacle of God per the Mosaic Law, He could not be an appropriation for any sin. We did not see that coming.

Del and I hesitated for a little bit, perusing through the Bible and the Qur'an. It was quite a challenging afternoon. The duo not only tried to show how Jesus was unfit for sacrifice but also called on us to shun Him. Since they wholeheartedly believed in the Qur'an, we showed them passages that showed Jesus' virgin birth, His superiority to all prophets mentioned in the Qur'an, including Muhammad, and also His ascension and subsequent return at the end of the world. The proof of the virgin birth from the Qur'an dismissed their assertion that he was an illegitimate child.

We continued to show them that the Qur'an and the Hadith both highly spoke of Jesus and His mother. Among other mentions of them in the Qur'an and the Hadith, it is stated that they were the only two at whose births Satan was absent.[9]

They ceded the debate. It had been a tough afternoon for both camps. We then inquired about the background of the "former evangelist." It turned out he was without a seminary education or church affiliation and had been converted by Islamic street preachers after he had failed to answer some questions about Christianity.

Knowing the Scriptures is imperative for Christians. Many I have met at various churches insist in learning about Islam. This is a good idea. Nevertheless, being grounded in what the Bible teaches is beneficial not only for our spiritual walk but also when dealing with those Muslims who intentionally manipulate its meaning.

The "former evangelist" was a prize in whom many Muslims took pride. He appeared at many gatherings and private engagements. But he failed to convince us that afternoon. He was quite unhappy that his tactic did not work on us. We urged him to repent of his sins.

The lunch hour passed. The afternoon concluded with two sad people leaving for their abode. We praised God that despite their striving to discredit Jesus Christ as the Savior of the world, God gave us wisdom and knowledge to confound their onslaught.

This duo avoided us from that time on. Other Muslims with whom we debated always looked for other Christians to ask similar questions. Even those whose questions were satisfactorily answered continued to ask similar questions. I wondered if that was a tactic to confuse Christians.

Life right after my graduation from high school was a challenging period of seclusion. I stayed out of the spotlight most of the time, making only one appearance at the evangelistic meeting in Witu. I was concerned that if I kept up with making appearances, Muslims would make life more miserable for me. So I kept to myself most of the time, staying indoors working on translations. I was grateful to God for His protection and dreamed of a day when my family would tolerate me enough for me to see them again.

1   These remarks appear on the "Headmaster's report on the pupil's ability, industry and conduct" section of my high school leaving certificate.

2   Central Intelligence Agency World Fact Book http://www.cia.gov/cia/publications/factbook/geos/ke.html Retrieved on June 23, 2006.

3   Yusuf Ali.

4   This topic is covered in chapter 15. I prefer referring to the Jesus mentioned in the Qur'an and the Hadith as "the Jesus of Islam."

5   NKJV.

6   Suratul Al-Zukhruf, 43:61.

7   *Sahih Bukhari, Volume 4, Book 55, Number 657–8.*

8   NKJV.

9   This topic is covered in chapter 15.

Chapter Twelve

My First Overnight Visit to My Home since April 1990

My family and I were still at loggerheads toward the end of 1995, even after I had attained excellent Kenya Certificate of Secondary Education (KCSE) examination results. Their animosity toward me was entrenched, transcending an educational accomplishment that typically would have guaranteed a family celebration of some sort. It was a grave matter to them that I was a Christian. (They still firmly believe that since I discarded Allah and the rhetoric of his Prophet, I am hell-bound.) Nevertheless, I tried to establish some contact with them in 1995, hoping that a reconciliation would allow me to be a Christian witness among them.

My efforts to secure a visit with them were fruitless for a while. I figured it was perhaps a payback for my dismissal of their advice to study medicine at the university—a program that I was not initially selected to pursue by the Joint Admission Board—and an early proposal to marry a girl of their choice. To my amazement, my younger brother changed gradually and became friendly toward me. He kept me up-to-date on my family's wellbeing.

12.1 My Elder Brother Becomes Less Hostile

After eleven months of relentless attempts to secure a planned visit with my family, word came through my younger brother that it was all right for me to go home, and even to spend the night, for the first time since April 1990. The only condition was that I had to eschew religious polemics. I was excited about going home but was also anxious because of what had transpired. Even though it had been more than five and a half years since I was severely persecuted, my past freshly lingered in my mind. I was hopeful that this visit would go well provided I went during the absence of my elder brother, although even he had gradually become less hostile toward me.

My elder brother's gradual change was partly due to two trage-dies. The first one was the collapse of the Kenya Meat Commission (KMC) in the early 1990s. He had been a successful businessman up until the liquidation of the parastatal (state owned) corporation. The man who had mocked me when I was in high school saying he would see whether Jesus would pay my school fees was humbled. Most of the capital for his livestock marketing business was lost. The collapse of the KMC took a toll on him. The harder tragedy, however, was that crocodiles killed his ten-year-old daughter on October 11, 1995. He was devastated. I too was very sad that my niece Saria had died such an atrocious death so young. All that was left of her was an arm.

My elder brother and I were still at an impasse while he was going through these traumatic times. When I got the sad news about my niece, I consulted with my pastor. Despite the concern for my safety, the pastor encouraged me to go while my family was still observing the three days of mourning. He was hopeful that this visit would somewhat improve my relationship with my brother. I left the following morning for my elder brother's home in Lamu District. The pastor had lent me his motorbike as a quick way out in case the visit went awry. My elder brother was distraught, sobbing most of the time.

That trip changed some of my relatives' perception of me. They wondered how I could get the sad news and in less than twenty-four hours travel such a great distance to be with them. I was grateful that I had heeded my pastor's advice to visit my grieving brother.

Those two events, coupled with the sudden death of my sister Halima in July 1993, partly stymied my family's efforts to convert me to Islam. They were not approving of my conversion to Christi-anity, and yet they allowed me to visit them.

My elder brother was out of town visiting his family in Lamu District the week that my younger brother relayed the message that I should visit my home. Thus I seized the moment to visit my family.

12.2 Going Home

My host families and friends were concerned for my safety when I shared with them the news of my impending overnight visit to my home. That was to be expected considering they had seen me suffer the previous five and a half years. One of my friends was on his way to a veterinary outreach and was passing through a town near my hometown. He offered to give me a ride close to my home and let me go the rest of the way. We were concerned that a ride all the way to my home would garner unwarranted attention.

I anxiously prepared for the trip not knowing what would come of it. Having prayed for guidance, I was at peace about going home. We commenced our journey at dawn on Wednesday, November 29, 1995, in time to catch a police convoy.

Highway travels were dangerous in some parts of Kenya at that time due to the situation in war-torn Somalia. Bandits, commonly known as *shifta*, frequently ambushed motorists, especially in the Coast Province. The government had decreed that armed policemen should escort all vehicles. It was a three-hour drive to Kanagoni, where we joined the police convoy.

I was quite nervous that day. The vehicle convoy left for Garsen. We arrived in Garsen around 11 a.m. I disembarked from the vehicle at a shop owned by an elder from my church. My friend proceeded on his journey to do some animal husbandry work in the interior part of the district.

It was still too early to go home. I did not want to walk home at the same time that most people would be coming to Garsen for shopping. Instead, I went to the missionary pastor's house and talked to him about what I was going to do. He was supportive. He thought the thawing of my family's relationship with me would open up opportunities for evangelism.

Nevertheless my mind was saturated with thoughts about my past. I thought about my contingency plans in case the visit with my family went awry. My Christian friend Raphael lived about seven kilometers away and would harbor me. I prayed for God's will to be done.

Having plucked up some courage, I left for my home that afternoon with another ride taking me very close to my home. My old neighbor Shora joined me in the trip home. He was a moderate Muslim and did not have a problem with my conversion to Christianity. The vehicle passed close to where an attempt was made to force me to denounce my faith in Christ five and a half years earlier. Seeing the place when I was going home for the first overnight visit since that incident was melancholic.

We disembarked from the vehicle at the bus stop and trudged on slowly toward our homes. We passed some herdsmen with their enormous herds of cattle, sheep, and goats devouring the pasture. The ravine southwest of town that drained floodwaters was coming into view. The tall African palm trees graced the distant eastern horizon. What I had longed for during the previous five and a half years was steadily becoming a reality.

12.3 Arriving at Home

I arrived in my hometown and went straight to my mother's house. A "new" sister-in-law who had married one of my brothers a few years after I was separated from my family greeted me. She had since had a son who was three years old. I also shared some sad moments with my family about my sister who had died two years earlier. What an emotional rollercoaster.

The call to the *Maghrib* (dusk) prayer blared, and the faithful thronged into the mosque for the prayer. I was invited to join them but declined their offer. It was common for them to invite non-Muslims to join them in prayer. That was one way they tried to recruit new converts or in this case try to win back an apostate. Instead I went to my favorite place by the cow corral to spend some time there.

My old friends joined me a little bit later after the evening prayer. We exchanged a few pleasantries. One of them, Mustafa, was attending an Islamic school of higher education to become a Muslim cleric and was home on recess.

12.4 The Question

The evening was going well. Then Mustafa asked me why I left Islam. Islam teaches that every child is born a Muslim. Prophet Muhammad said, "No child is born except on *Al-Fitra* (Islam) and then his parents make him Jewish, Christian or Magian, as an animal produces a perfect young animal: do you see any part of its body amputated?"[1] He added, "Had his parents been Muslim he would have also remained a Muslim."[2] Muslims believe that Allah predestined every child to be a Muslim. Those who are born to non-Muslim parents end up non-Muslims because of their parents' influence. It seems that Allah, with all his sovereign power mentioned throughout the Qur'an and the Hadith, does not have the power over his creation (babies) that he predestined to be Muslim. Non-Muslim parents seem to wield greater power over him because they convert children he supposedly made Muslims to be non-Muslims, resulting in non-Muslims outnumbering Muslims in the world.

Islamic teachings give unbelieving parents as the only valid reason behind the proliferation of non-Muslims. Because children born to Muslim parents are expected to comply with Allah and Prophet Muhammad's decrees, it is considered inconceivable for them to leave Islam. For this reason, Muslims kill apostates, especially those born to Muslim parents because they are expected to remain Muslims.

I thought that Mustafa's question was a good question, but I was ambivalent as to how I should answer it. My past experiences with Muslims who deliberately asked questions to provoke fights, especially when the answers were offensive to them made me hesitant. Any answer that I would give that evening would upset my old friends because I would be justifying my rejection of Islam. I wanted to give a short answer that would put being a Muslim into perspective. In case a fight broke out as a result of my answer, I was outnumbered. Nevertheless it was an auspicious opportunity for me to instill provocative questions about Islam—ones that Muslims hardly tackle—in my friends' minds.

12.5 The Answer

That evening I told my old Muslim friends that I left Islam because the Qur'an clearly states that all Muslims would go to hell, and I reiterated that there is no exception to even one who lived a purely pious life. My answer astonished them, but I did not know that I had opened Pandora's box.

My conversion to Christianity was not of my own. I believe it was the Almighty God who fashioned it in my heart through the work of the Holy Spirit to show me His truth that is found only through Jesus Christ His Son. But to answer Mustafa's question the way I would a Christian's question would have been a mistake, because it would not have made any sense to him or his fellow Muslims and would have exceedingly exacerbated their confusion about Christianity.

Ardent Muslims only look at things from the perspectives of the Qur'an and the Hadith. Thus they do not expect anyone to give a "plausible" reason for a Muslim to leave Islam. On the other hand, I was sick of repetitious and shallow questions some Muslims often asked about Christianity. Whatever explanation I would have given that evening, regardless of its judiciousness, would have been ignored.

Steering Muslims to think beyond what they hear from the *imams* and clerics is hard. Most of my old friends often sought advice from these religious leaders, who cautioned them against asking questions that would lead them to sin. That strategy discourages ordinary Muslims from exploring a lot of controversial topics in Islam that are rendered as enigmas even though there is a plethora of references in the Qur'an and the Hadith.

I loved my old Muslim friends and wanted them to think for themselves about their religion. Therefore I answered Mustafa's question in a way that would make my friends more curious about some esoteric aspects of their religion.

My answer highlighted a mystery mostly known only to Islamic scholars about the punishment of every Muslim on the Day of Judgment. The Qur'an's teaching in Suratul Al-Maryam, 19:71, that every Muslim is going to hell is indeed uncharted territory in Islam because Islamic scholars gloss over this topic, perhaps for fear that it will render Islam null and void. Their tight grip on this topic, coupled with their misleading commentaries, fail to raise the eyebrows of most Muslims and hence contribute to further ignorance.

The few Muslims who persistently and defiantly ask questions that could expose the weak points of Islamic ideology are not appreciated. Some Islamic scholars know details of some tenets in Islam like the punishment in hell that were borrowed from other sources without giving credit. The answer I gave Mustafa that evening poses a dilemma for Islam that the scholars would not admit, but proves that Islam borrowed from the Zoroastrian religion the idea of the punishment in hell.

12.6 Muslims Subdue Me

No sooner did I finish answering the question than my friends pounced on me, forcing me to go in the direction of the local mosque. I was petrified. My mind started racing. Thoughts of that botched forced conversion a few years before engulfed my mind. I thought of the close calls and wondered if it had taken them more than five and a half years to finally catch me. I thought that was the end of me. I was at a loss for words and prayed, anticipating the worst. I regretted answering Mustafa's question.

I gathered myself and inquired where they were taking me. They told me they were taking me to the Muslim cleric to ascertain my claim about all Muslims going to hell. They promised that they would convert to Christianity if the cleric concurred with me. And if he dissented, then I should be forced to convert back to Islam.

A crowd followed us. We met the cleric between the mosque and his house. He had just finished with the *Maghrib* prayer. My accusers told him about how I claimed that according to the Qur'an all Muslims would go to hell. They wanted to know if my claim was true.

12.7 A Meeting to Discuss My Answer

The cleric did not know me very well. He had heard of me but did not know to what extent I had studied Islam before converting to

Christianity. He urged the crowd to calm down and promised to answer their question at a meeting to be held at his house after the noon prayers the following day.

I promised to attend the meeting, and he asked them to let me go. He boasted that it would be a successful meeting because he was determined to do what many Muslims had failed to accomplish, that is, to convince me about the plausibility of Islam.

Dreading the impending meeting, I went straight to my mother's house and retired for the night, sleeping intermittently. So many wild scenarios flooded my mind when I was awake. What if the teacher differed with my answer? It was very frightening to me that we were meeting in broad daylight. There was no darkness like during the past meetings to slip into in case the outcome was unfavorable to me.

When dawn broke, I got out of bed and went to the cow corral for a while, a daily routine for the males in the Orma tribe. I cherished some of our cultural practices. Then I went back to my mother's house for breakfast, eating and drinking only what was also served to others. I did not take any chances because I thought my family's kind invitation to visit their home could as well be a ploy to kill me.

When breakfast was over, I stayed in the house, researching some answers to the possible questions the Muslim audience would ask. I knew from experience what some of them would be.

Since I was concerned for my safety that day, I did not venture out of my family compound until it was time for the meeting. The Muslim community was aggravated because they had always believed that they were spared from hell.

The noon hour drew near, and I could sense that the ambiance was tense. My mother gave me a piece of her mind about my stance on Islam. It was quite unpleasant. The Muslim community considered me an "evil" person who relentlessly challenged the status quo, not sparing even the shrewd Islamic cleric.

The call to the noon prayer blared, and I went over my tentative answers. When the prayer ended, the faithful filed out of the mosque. I walked over to the cleric's house after the crowd had dispersed. I resolved that afternoon to not answer any other questions until the Islamic cleric gave an answer to the question that had necessitated an audience with him.

Having arrived at his house, I sat on a special leather carpet that he used for prayers. I noticed he had invited some elders and Islamic leaders in the area to the meeting. There were also many young men in attendance, with some of them listening to the proceedings from the outside. Mustafa and my other friends were also in attendance.

The scene was reminiscent of a momentous occasion, a ceremony of converting a non-Muslim to Islam. I sat nervously waiting for the cleric to start the meeting. I was confident, however, that the shrewd Islamic cleric would concur with me on the correct interpretation of the verse from which I had drawn my answer.

He showed us a Qur'an that was in Swahili. It had the correct translation of the verse but with a conflicting commentary. Suratul Al-Maryam verse 71 wreaks havoc for Islamic scholars; hence they dread writing commentaries on it. Even the widely respected translation of Abdullah Yusuf Ali is indecisive with its commentary, giving a few confusing scenarios as possible meanings.

The teacher started the meeting with a word of caution. He urged us to use restraint and debate in a dignified manner. Since I was outnumbered, I thought his advice was playing to my advantage.

Then he turned toward me with a question that was totally unrelated to the topic at hand. I insisted that I would not answer his question until he dealt with the one that gathered us together that afternoon. It was evident that he did not want to tackle the topic touching on all Muslims going to hell. He shrugged off my response and asked defiantly, "How can one plus one plus one equals one?" I guessed he did not want to rile up the audience with an unpleasant answer to a question about all Muslims going to hell.

The heated exchange took a few minutes. Then I realized the only way the cleric would address the topic of all Muslims going to hell would be to answer his question. I told him that the numbers did not sum up to one and urged him to proceed to my claim that the Qur'an clearly states all Muslims would go to hell.

12.8 Islamic Teachings on Muslims and Hell

The Muslim audience was attentive. It was their first glimpse of a religious debate right in their backyard pitting a Muslim against a Christian. Perhaps it was an uncomfortable situation for them. Since the inhabitants of my village are 100 percent Muslim, Christians or other non-Muslims hardly ever come and engage them in conversations about religion. No adherents of other religions are allowed to hold religious events in my village. The community is unwelcoming toward non-Muslims.

The Islamic cleric ended the impasse and read Suratul Al-Maryam verses 70–72:

> And certainly We know best those who are most worthy of being burned therein. Not one of you but will pass over it: this is, with thy Lord, a Decree which must be accomplished. But We shall save those who guarded against evil, and We shall leave the wrong-doers therein, (humbled) to their knees.[3]

He then answered the question "Will all Muslims go to hell?" in the affirmative. The answer made me shout with exultation while the Muslim audience sat somberly.

I rose to my feet and demanded that those who had promised to abandon Islam do so. No one came forward, and I sat down to answer some of their questions, which were similar to the ones Islamic street preachers put forth on a regular basis. I savored that moment, one of a kind in my own hometown.

The seventy-first verse of Suratul Al-Maryam that the Islamic cleric read lucidly portrays that all Muslims will go to hell even if it would be for a short while. It adds that Allah had decreed that Muslims must go to hell, which seems like evidence that no Muslim could challenge. However clear this verse is, Islamic scholars still use diversionary tactics of bringing many topics into the discussion when commenting on it. A good example is a widely used commentary written by Abdullah Yusuf Ali. He stated that, "Three interpretations are possible"[4] for this verse. His argument takes into account many Islamic scholars' interpretations, which mostly try to divert attention from the only meaning of the verse. Islamic teachings clearly portray that both Muslims and non-Muslims alike will go to hell. Although Muslims will supposedly be in hell only a short while "it must inevitably come to pass, and there is no avoiding it."[5] In order to grasp how Abdullah Yusuf Ali arrived at his three possible interpretations, it is imperative to look at them individually.

First of all, Ali started with:

> The general interpretation is that every soul must pass through or by or over the Fire. It may be the fire of temptation or anxiety or distress; but they must see Hell. Those who have had *Taqwa* will be saved by God's Mercy, while unrepentant sinners will suffer the torments in ignominy.[6]

(One Islamic scholar defines *taqwa* as "consciousness or aware-ness of God in your [Muslim's] life.... The more *taqwa* you have in your heart, the closer you are to God."[7])

Ali's interpretation of verse 71 diverts the attention from hell to fire. The Arabic word in verse 68, which is referred by the pronoun "it" also in verse 71, is *jahannam*, which means "hell." "Fire" in Arabic is *nar*. His argument about "hell" being the "fire of temptation or anxiety or distress" diverts the attention from hell itself. Ali is trying to downplay "hell" in this context the same way many Islamic scholars try to divert the attention from the real meaning of *jihad*.

Islamic scholars have been successful at assuaging the meaning of verse 71 of Suratul Al-Maryam. Nevertheless, Prophet Muhammad clearly showed that Muslims would go to hell because he himself—though the closest to Allah among Muslims—was not sure if he was going to hell or paradise. He was asked whether a Muslim man who had died would go to paradise. His response was, "As to him, by Allah, death has overtaken him, and I hope the best for him. By Allah, though I am the Apostle of Allah, yet I do not know what Allah will do to me."[8] If Prophet Muhammad himself did not know if Allah would have mercy on him and send him to paradise, who are ordinary Muslims in Allah's sight? It seems that Islamic scholars are in damage-control mode.

Ali's next possible interpretation of the verse states, "If we refer the pronoun 'you' to those 'obstinate rebellion' in verse 69 above, both leaders and followers in sin, this verse only applies to the wicked."

Ali is masterful at diverting attention. One thing that is worthy of noting: he talks about a pronoun "you" here that supposedly carries over from verse 69 to correctly interpret verse 71, but fails to use the pronoun "it" that all along was for hell in verse 68 through verse 71. Verse 69 is totally unrelated to verse 71 because the former is about the wicked in hell and the latter is about Muslims in hell.

The Hadith shows that Prophet Muhammad and his wife Hafsa recited verses 72 and 71 respectively during a discussion about hell.[9] The issue at hand that necessitated the duo to recite these verses was whether some Muslims would go to hell. The Hadith corroborates that in verse 71 Muslims would go to hell and in verse 72 the wicked would be left in hell after Muslims are rescued. Evidently, the extensively used Abdullah Yusuf Ali Translation and Commentary that took many Islamic scholars' views into consideration, is misleading in claiming that verse 71 is about the wicked.

The pronoun "you" in verse 71 could not refer to those "obstinate rebellion" in verse 69 because the ones in verse 71 had some among them who "guarded against evil" as mentioned in verse 72. What is baffling is how the wicked would suddenly be the ones who guarded against evil, implying that they are the ones without sin. Ali is diverting the attention yet again.

Prophet Muhammad said, "The believers, after being saved from the (Hell) Fire, will be stopped at a bridge between Paradise and Hell."[10] Here again, the "believers" are the ones who are saved from hell after being there for a while. Then they proceed to the next stage. This just proves that Islamic teachings, which include verse 71 of Suratul Al-Maryam, state that Muslims will go to hell even if it will be for a short while.

Third, Ali concluded his possible interpretations for verse 71 with, "Some refer this verse to the Bridge over Hell, the Bridge *Sirat*, over which all must pass to their final Destiny. This Bridge is not mentioned in the Qur'an." He was frank in bringing to his readers' attention that the bridge Muslims widely believe would stretch over hell is not mentioned in the Qur'an.

Islamic scholars do not admit it, but the bridge over hell is a doctrine that never originated from Allah. Allah communicated his decrees to Prophet Muhammad using only these two means: the

Qur'an and the Hadith Qudsi. Hadith Qudsi is "divine communication direct from Allah to the Prophet, which was other than a revealed verse of the Quran [sic]."[11] There are forty of this type of Hadith, and they are considered sacred. Since the bridge over hell is not mentioned in the Qur'an and the Hadith Qudsi, one can categorically claim that the bridge is an idea foreign to Islam that was borrowed from Zoroastrianism.

The idea stated in the Qur'an and the Hadith that Muslims will go to hell is quite similar to that of Zoroastrianism where "hell, for the Zoroastrian, is not eternal."[12] There are staggering similarities in descriptions of hell in these two religions.

Tenets that Islam borrowed from religions preceding it are randomly mentioned throughout the Qur'an and are closely guarded. The only way the faithful can know what Islam teaches is if they read for themselves the context of these tenets. However, this is discouraged, with the justification that the Qur'an contains all the information they need. If "Indeed, the Qur'an's miracle lies in its ability to offer at least something to non-believers and everything to believers,"[13] ordinary Muslims need to know its content. Otherwise they will continue to live with blind prejudice because they leave Islamic scholars to read and interpret Islamic tenets for them.

The call to *Asr* (midafternoon) prayer sounded, and the faithful left for prayer. And I retreated to my mother's house for fear that they would come after me. No one came to attack me that day or night, probably because the issue I brought up perplexed the Muslim community. They had all along thought that Christians, Jews, and other non-Muslims would fuel the fire of hell. It was probably a very bitter pill for them to swallow learning that Allah had decreed that they would go to hell.

I was thankful to God for the first night at home since April 1990 and for the opportunity to have a discussion on a sensitive issue in a hostile environment and get away without any injuries.

One of my friends who had seen me go through some persecutions in Kenya was quite excited about how my relationship with my family was changing for the better. Debbie is quoted in a 1998 book as saying, "With God's help, Hussein and his family are reconciled to the point where he is welcome in the family home."[14] I do not quite say we are reconciled yet, because my family members do not tolerate my beliefs. I only get along with my younger brother, who equally does not approve that I am a Christian. But I have to be grateful and take the little that has improved because this relationship has come a long way.

[1]   *Sahih Bukhari, Volume 6, Book 60, Number 298.*
[2]   *Sahih Muslim, Book 33, Number 6429.*
[3]   Yusuf Ali.
[4]   Abdullah Yusuf Ali, *The Holy Qur'an: Text, Translation and Commentary* (Beirut: Dar Al Arabia, 1968), 782. Commentary Number 2518.
[5]   Muhammad Saed Abdul-Rahman, *Islam: Questions and Answers: Basic Tenets of Faith (Belief) Part 2* (London: MSA Publication, 2003), 342.
[6]   Yusuf Ali, Commentary Number 2518.
[7]   Yahiya Emerick and Quasim Najar, *The Complete Idiot's Guide to Understanding Islam* (Indianapolis: Alpha Books, 2001), 45. Bracket mine.
[8]   *Sahih Bukhari, Volume 5, Book 58, Number 266.*
[9]   *Sahih Muslim, Book 31, Number 6090.*
[10] *Sahih Bukhari, Volume 8, Book 76, Number 542.*
[11] Hajjah Amina Adil, *Muhammad: The Prophet of Islam* (Washington, DC: Islamic Supreme Council of America, 2002), 578.
[12] Satguru Sivaya Subramuniyaswami, *Dancing With Siva: Hinduism's Contemporary Catechism*, 4th ed. (Concord, CA: Himalayan Academy, 1993), 559.
[13] Muhammad Habib Shakir, *The Qur'an*, 7th ed. (Elmhurst, NY: Tahrike Tarsile Qur'an, Inc., 1999), paper rack size outside back cover.
[14] Morrell F. Swart, *The Call of Africa: The Reformed Church in America Mission in Sub-Sahara, 1948–1998* (Grand Rapids: Eerdmans, 1998), 479.

CHAPTER THIRTEEN

Leaving Kenya

The first overnight visit with my family was going better than I had expected. Area Muslims, however, were angry with me for charging that the Qur'an teaches that all Muslims must go to hell, even though my accusation was admitted to be true by the Muslim cleric. Hajj Guyole—the man who had offered me some financial incentives to convert back to Islam in April 1990—was especially enraged. He insulted me whenever our paths crossed, saying among other things, "Laanatu Allah alaika!" which means, "Curse from Allah upon you!" in Arabic. The barrage of disparagements was difficult to ignore, but I was grateful considering I had faced worse persecution the previous years. I stayed in the Garsen area for a few days visiting my Christian friends.

13.1 The Myth about the "Stamp" Unravels

Meanwhile, I thought of ways in which I would restore my fractured relationships with my old Muslim friends. The best opportunity I had while I was home this time was to spend time with them escorting our livestock and swimming afterward.

The missionary pastor from my church had always challenged me as to when I would show to my Muslim friends the alleged stamp that I got on my buttocks. We laughed hysterically every time we revisited the subject. He had been waiting for the day that I would show off the "stamp."

Every time I passed through Garsen, Muslim children followed me, with some of them giving me funny looks. Many area Muslims had all along believed that my rear end was stamped. The fact that the "stamp" was a myth made it harder for me to put up with the stigma.

The missionary pastor had posed a challenge and I followed through. I thought the only way that I would stop that propaganda and myth was to go swimming with my Muslim friends who were equally curious. One morning I escorted the cows and afterward went swimming with them.

My old friends were surprised that the stamp was nonexistent. I proved that the stamp was a deceptive scheme that Arab Islamic missionaries had used to keep area Muslims from exploring other religions as a viable option to Islam. Their scare tactic had once been effective, but that day marked its demise in my home area. Mission accomplished!

The missionary pastor was glad that I had helped to unravel the myth behind the stamp. The losers that day were the Arab Islamic missionaries who had all along duped the local Muslims. Allah seems to hate what happens in a Christian church.

One wonders how anyone could fall for a ruse of that stature. The answer is that local Muslims were not as educated as the majority of Kenyans and hence would easily be deluded. In fact, some of them still believe their religious leaders' lies about other religions.

Their ignorance is also partly to be blamed on the Arab Islamic missionaries who had advised them against sending their children to secular schools, where they were supposedly taught Christianity. On the other hand, the Islamic missionaries did not practice what they preached because they sent their children to boarding schools. As a result, their descendants are among the most educated Muslims in the Coast Province, holding high paying secular jobs.

13.2 Orma Muslims Exploited

The Arab Islamic missionaries did not end their propaganda campaign with the myths about the stamp and secular education. They took it up a notch, advising the local Muslims against depositing money in commercial banks where it would accrue interest. (Islam teaches against earning money from interest.) Instead, they advised them to deposit their money with businessmen who were Arabs, where the money accrued no interest.

I remember very well how my family would sell cattle and put the money with an Arab trader. My mother and father would then take goods from that trader's shop until the money was used up. There were cases where not enough goods were bought and the money was depleted. This is one of the instances of Arab traders' exploitation.

Arab traders tremendously benefited from such exploitation. Some of them ended up putting up commercial buildings in upscale markets in major towns in the Coast Province. For example, I knew of two families who came to the Tana River District very poor, and within a few years they had established themselves with fleets of buses and semi trailers plying international routes.

Islamic teachings on interest were to blame for the exploitation of the local Muslims who adhered to the teachings with blind agreement. The five daily prayers sensitize Muslims about the torment of hell. Local Muslims definitely wanted nothing to do with earning interest, a nefarious act they believe is punishable in hell. Nevertheless some of them now regret that they were slumbering while the Arabs, who masqueraded as genuine missionaries, were reaping.

Muslims with whom I have talked argue that Christianity also teaches against charging interest on money lent, a contention that tries to bolster Islam's position. On the contrary, that argument is a mere generalization and is not true because in the Bible "interest may be charged [by Jews] when lending money to a non-Israelite."[1] The command forbidding the charging of interest was given in the Old Testament and explicitly applied to loans between Jews.

13.3 Preparing for College

The visit with my family ended, and I went back to work in Mombasa. My Christian friends were relieved that I returned to them safely. I was optimistic that my relationship with my family was headed in a better direction.

There was so much to do for the Orma translation project. I occasionally met with some Orma men who proofread my translation work. Some of them were interested in Christianity. A few of them met with a missionary on a regular basis. Most of them had families and were reluctant to embrace Christianity when it was certain that their spouses would not support their decisions.

I continued working on the translation project. One of my friends bought some Christian song sheets in Borana, a language that has many similarities to Orma. We tried to sing them during our devotions, but they were quite hard because the Borana alphabet is different from the Orma alphabet. At that point, I realized that if the songs were translated into Orma, they might be less confusing. I translated them and the singing became much easier.

During my free time, I sent out applications to various colleges and universities in Africa and around the world, including Hope College in Holland, Michigan. Some of my friends had a friend who was a member of the Board of Trustees at the college. Doris, a member of the board, had heard that I had applied to Hope College and she advised me to apply for a scholarship for African students.

In the meantime, I started my application for some vital legal documents. Kenya allows late registration for birth certificates. Since I did not have mine in my possession, I was concerned that my family would use it as a tool to jeopardize my chances of studying overseas. (A birth certificate is required in Kenya when applying for a passport.) In spite of my first overnight visit to my family home in more than five years, our relationship was still sour.

I picked up an application form for a new birth certificate and went over the requirements with a registration official. I learned that I could not get one without my parents' identity cards. My father was deceased, but my younger brother knew that one of my sisters-in-law had his identity card. He collected it for me. He also went to my mother to collect hers, but it was lost. The registration officer told me since I had my father's identity card, I should get at least one of my siblings' identity cards. The Chief of Bilisa Location had to endorse the application form.

It had been more than five and a half years since I had visited the Chief's office. He was the same Chief who had ordered me to appear before his court because I had allegedly left my home without my mother's consent. He was also the one whom my family had used to obtain an order to scour Christians' homes in search of my belongings and me in May 1990. I thought about attempting to obtain his signature but was quite pessimistic, thinking that he would refuse to sign my application form, which would dash my hopes of obtaining a new birth certificate and studying abroad, where I hoped I would get a reprieve from persecution. I prayed for God's will to be done.

I plucked up some courage and went to the Chief's office but he was out of the office due to an illness. The Assistant Chief was the one in charge. He was also a Muslim and my expectation of him was the same. He knew my family and me very well. I used to frequent his home during the *Maulid* celebration. His eldest son, Hamisi, and I had been good friends. Getting the Assistant Chief's signature proved quite a nightmare for me. Had he signed my papers as expected, perhaps I would have attended college overseas in 1995.

He harangued me every time I went to his office requesting his signature. Then, after several months of unsuccessful attempts, he finally signed my forms. I got my birth certificate the following day.

I was overjoyed to have my new birth certificate, which was a preliminary step to acquiring a new passport. The passport process promised to be even tougher, and I hesitated to start it because most applications were denied for lack of sufficient reason to travel abroad. Instead, I waited to hear from Hope College about the status of my application.

13.4 Orma Seekers

Meanwhile, I started getting involved with some Ormas who were interested in Christianity. Typically referred to as "seekers," they numbered about eighteen men and two women. The missionary pastor organized a gathering for them. We had retreats a few times that year, which most of them attended in secret. At the retreats, we sang songs I had translated. A 1998 book sums up the events:

> One of the highlights was hearing of the group of twenty Ormas singing Christian songs in their own tongue, songs that a Christian named Hussein had helped the Braaksmas to put together. These were not translations of Western hymns; rather, they were Orma words put to genuine Orma tunes.[2]

We spent weekends together singing and learning from various teachers. Out of concern for our safety, our meetings were held at undisclosed locations.

The missionary pastor is with a Pentecostal church and believes in instant baptism of new believers. These Orma "seekers" were not strong in their faith and were afraid of repercussions in case their conversion became known. The pastor baptized them in spite of some concerns.

Unfortunately, none of them at the moment professes to be Christian even thirteen years after their baptism. Having retreats at which we had fellowship with one another was beneficial; however, it was discouraging to see these "seekers" not willing to count the cost and follow Jesus Christ.

They had genuine fears. Making their conversion to Christianity public was a matter of life and death for them. They knew very well that the punishment of apostasy in Islam is death. Most of these "seekers" were married. Publicly making a commitment to follow Christ meant they would lose everything. Their wives, children, and cattle would be taken away, in addition to the beatings they would endure. I encouraged some of them to take a step forward but my advice fell on deaf ears. Perhaps it wasn't the Lord's time yet for them to become Christian.

13.5 News from Hope College

The good news from Hope College came via email on Wednesday, March 20, 1996. One of my friends logged onto his computer to dial up to Nairobi for emails around nine o'clock that night. The short message came through from the director of admissions. It was a euphoric moment. The college offered me the Geneva Scholarship. This scholarship is given annually to one student from Africa who has a strong Christian commitment.

To have been selected for the scholarship was a blessing. I was quite joyful that my college education, which had once been only a dream, was going to become a reality. I was grateful to God for the opportunity to study at one of the most prestigious Christian liberal arts colleges.

My friends, their children, and I celebrated that night. I went to the missionary pastor's home the following day to share with them the news. My family also learned that I was accepted at the college. They were excited but at the same time were concerned that I would probably be studying Christianity. They had all along advised me against the idea.

13.6 Final Preparation to Leave for College

The preparation to go to college in the United States was underway. I worked first on my passport application. The presence in Kenya of many foreigners from neighboring countries makes it harder even for Kenyans to get legal documents. The government had a vetting system for members of some people groups that identified passport applicants through tribal elders who conferred with the local chiefs. The presence in Kenya of many Oromo refugees from Ethiopia gave credence to members of my tribe, Orma, being vetted. The system put me at a disadvantage because the Orma elders and Chief were opposed to me on account of my religious affiliation.

Thankfully, I had the birth certificate that I had obtained several months earlier. I talked with a lawyer from my church (now a Kenyan High Court Judge) who advised me. He, along with an elder from my church, endorsed my passport application. I then went to a few government offices to get signatures. The application was complete within a week.

Since I was already twenty-one years old, my mother was not required to approve my application for a passport, which was quite a relief. I filed my application, along with the email I had received from Hope College, with the immigration office in Mombasa, paid the fees, and was interviewed. Since I lived near the Coast Provincial Headquarters, where the immigration office was located, I made frequent trips to check on the status of my application.

I went through a few more interviews. One time I was told my file was on the sixth floor of the building and it needed to come down to the first floor for it to be checked, which implied paying someone to bring my file to the ground floor. I did not understand at first and when I realized what that entailed, I talked about how bribery was incompatible with my Christian faith.

Weeks went by without a new passport. I made more frequent trips to the immigration office. The immigration officers probably got tired of my constant visits. They issued me a new passport a month after I had filed for it. I was excited. I knew that I was one step closer to attending Hope College that August.

I went home and prepared for the overnight trip to Nairobi to visit the United States embassy to apply for a student visa. Hope College had sent me an elaborate I-20 (a student visa document). I did not even have to produce a bank statement to get my visa. I was impressed that my visa application was approved on the spot.

13.7 A New Muslim Organization

I was excited to leave Kenya because persecution was still the order of the day for me. My home area was especially becoming unwelcoming to me. A new Muslim organization, the African Muslim Agency (AMA), mostly bankrolled by the Kuwaiti government was becoming established in Kenya.

The AMA had a presence in almost all eight Kenyan provinces, building *madrassas* and mosques. It sponsored a lot of children, even some from Christian homes to study Islam in *madrassa*.

This agency was rumored to be behind armed attacks on Christian missionaries and their stations in some predominantly Muslim areas in Kenya in 1992. The AMA possibly sponsored those attacks because it was conducting religious educational "activities" in some African countries that were actually fronts to illicit activities. A former visiting professor at Yale University, Abdou Maliq Simone, has studied various Islamic agencies' student sponsorship activities in Africa. He has discovered that:

> Agencies such as the African Muslim Agency (AMA), which is largely funded by Kuwait, were established to disseminate religious materials and support religious education in each African country. While much of the effort of this agency is indeed focused on such pedagogical activities, it also has developed substantial business interests in many countries. Even some of the scholarships it offers for advanced religious and secular studies are "sold" on the open market, and many

Christian students attempt to access such scholarships by pretending to be Muslim. On the other hand, such "converts" are frequently sought out by the various Muslim agencies themselves... Many of the students from Nigeria and Ghana in particular are "converts" who are provided these opportunities in exchange for their participation in *a wide variety of illicit business ventures* by entrepreneurs in the Gulf States.[3]

I was surprised to read that the AMA abets criminal activities in some countries. Now I can see how it could be true that they were involved in the attacks and ousting of Christian missionaries in Kenya. I traveled with a friend one time to a place where he was once a missionary and was appalled to see the devastation "bandits" had caused. The walls of his house were covered with bullet holes. Some of his appliances were sprayed with bullets such that they could not function again. The attack on his mission station was not a mere act of thuggery.

13.8 Face to Face with My Foe

In July 1996, I offered to help a group with Youth With A Mission (YWAM) to go on an outreach in some parts of the Tana River District where people knew very little about me. One of my friends was supposed to accompany them, but he was out of the country. I took over some of his responsibilities.

The group was participating in a medical outreach program. They were trained to render basic medical services such as immunizations. Their campaign that month was in remote areas. Since their base was in Shimba Hills, about an hour out of the way, I asked them to stay with me in Mombasa the night before the trip. We left early the following morning in order to catch the police escort at Kanagoni.

Bus companies plying the route were on strike that week, protesting a government directive that required them to pay for the police escort. Our vehicle was one of the few that were heading toward Hola. There had also been tribal clashes in the area pitting the Ormas against the Pokomos the previous week. Some young men who perpetrated the attacks were arrested and among them was the son of the Assistant Chief.

There were a lot of passengers on the road that day looking for transportation to Hola, the Tana River District headquarters. Some of them were offering twice the amount of money for the normal bus fare to get a ride. The YWAM group was new to the area. They delegated to me the responsibility to choose who would ride with us free of charge.

The Assistant Chief happened to be one of the stranded passengers. He asked me for a ride, and I did not know how to respond. Thoughts of how he had mistreated me flooded my mind. Then I recalled a passage in the Book of Romans:

> Beloved, do not avenge yourselves, but rather give place to wrath; for it is written, "Vengeance is Mine, I will repay," says the Lord. Therefore If your enemy is hungry, feed him; If he is thirsty, give him a drink; for in so doing you will heap coals of fire on his head. Do not be overcome by evil, but overcome evil with good.[4]

I realized it was not worth the retaliation. I offered him a ride along with my cousin Algi.

The Assistant Chief had caused a lot of problems for me. He also had publicly insulted, ridiculed, and scolded me. He had often called me *kafir* (infidel). He had also refused on numerous occasions to sign my application for a new birth certificate. That day I had the power in my hands to leave him stranded. He direly needed a ride to Hola in order to report to the jail in time to secure his son's release. He pleaded with me to give him a ride and I came to his aid without asking for anything. He was at a loss for words.

The whole trip for the medical outreach went well. The YWAM group planned more trips because there were a lot of medical needs. I was grateful to God for the opportunity to go on that outreach. I learned a lot from the group, but at the same time God crossed my path with one of my foes to whom I learned to do good. I came across the Assistant Chief a few weeks later, and he acknowledged my presence and expressed his gratitude. His perception of me had certainly changed.

13.9 Departure for the United States

It was the day to depart for the United States. My younger brother made the trip with me to the Jomo Kenyatta International Airport in Nairobi. I flew out on a KLM flight to Amsterdam on Saturday, August 17, 1996. I was scared to fly that day because the Trans World Airlines Flight 800 had crushed just a month to the date.

The flight from Amsterdam to Detroit was delayed for several hours due to the extreme security measures occasioned by the TWA Flight 800 crash. Passengers were screened multiple times. Some of us were selectively interrogated. The flight that was supposed to take off at 10 a.m. did not depart until after 3 p.m. I sat next to Akbar, a U.S.-educated engineer from Kuwait, who was coming to Michigan to visit some of his college friends. An opportunity came up, and I talked with him about Jesus Christ using *The Four Spiritual Laws* booklet.

A short time into the flight, he found out that I was a former Muslim. We discussed various issues in Islam and Christianity the rest of the nine-hour trip. We were separated at customs. His parting shot that Sunday afternoon was that I would revert to Islam in the United States, where according to him a lot of Christians were converting to Islam. I wondered if that was true.

Going through customs was fast. I boarded a connecting flight and arrived in Grand Rapids. A representative from Hope College who was supposed to pick me up was not at the airport because my arrival was delayed. Waiting for a ride that night was hard because I did not know whether someone from the college would come after hours to pick me up. However, an agent of Northwest Airlines called the college and an international student picked me up later that night and took me to my dorm room. I went to bed right away.

Thousands of miles now separated me from the Muslims who had persecuted me the last six and a half years in Kenya. I did not expect that I would be spared from any persecution now that I left Kenya, because I knew very well that suffering for the sake of Christ is not limited to certain geographical locations. The Scripture lucidly states, "All who desire to live godly in Christ Jesus will suffer persecution."[5] Nevertheless, I was upbeat at the prospect of a possible reprieve during the four years I would study in the United States, a bastion for those deprived of freedom elsewhere. I looked forward to starting a new chapter of my life. Barring any threats to my life, I was determined to return to Kenya after my studies to be a witness among my own people.

---

[1]   Alfred J. Kolatch, *Inside Judaism: The Concepts, Customs, and Celebrations of the Jewish People* (New York: Jonathan David Company, 2006), 352. Bracket mine.

[2]   Swart, *The Call of Africa*, 479.

[3]   Abdou Maliq Simone, *For the City Yet to Come: Changing African Life in Four Cities* (Durham, NC: Duke University Press, 2004), 127. Emphasis mine.

[4]   Romans 12:19–21, NKJV.

[5]   2nd Timothy 3:12, NKJV.

Chapter Fourteen

A Cocktail of Events

~~~~~~~~

S tarting a new chapter of my life thousands of miles away from those who had persecuted me the previous six and a half years gave me a new sense of freedom. The fear of persecution that had subjected me to using different names and traveling routes in Kenya had abated. However, thoughts of Akbar's comments about Christians in the United States converting in droves to Islam were fresh in my mind. From his comments I gathered that there were some Muslims in this country who would proselytize. Nevertheless I had doubts that they would be so uncompromising as to persecute an ex-Muslim. I was optimistic that I would be safe in a predominantly Christian town.

14.1 My First Semester in College

The new student orientation started a few days after I arrived at Hope College. My orientation group was comprised of students from diverse backgrounds. Every international student was paired up with a host family. My host family did a phenomenal job of helping me to adjust to the new culture.

Debbie, my missionary friend from Kenya, and her family visited me at the end of the orientation week. They came to Holland to speak at the Maplewood Reformed Church. I went with them to my first Sunday church service in the United States. The worship service was quite formal compared to the one I was accustomed to. My friends and I addressed the congregation during the service.

Classes started. Even though I was just a freshman, I thought a lot about my future vocation. My aspiration was to reach out to the Orma people with the Gospel. Many Christian missionaries I had known who had worked among Muslims had professions that allowed them to do evangelism indirectly. Barring any threats to my life, I thought that working in a medical field in order to proselytize my tribe, which is predominantly Muslim, was the ideal plan. I looked forward to how the first semester of my college experience would pan out.

Meanwhile, the staff at the Paul G. Fried International Center at Hope College organized trips to the malls and area social events for international students representing over twenty countries and territories. Two Palestinian Muslim students learned that I was a former Muslim. They called me *murtad*, Arabic for "apostate," many times when our paths crossed. When I asked them the reason they were calling me by a different name, they told me it was their new nickname for me. They had assumed I did not know the meaning of *murtad*, but I had been called *murtad* many times in Kenya. I came across them one morning going toward the international office. They greeted me using the nickname, and I confronted them. They were shocked and had no idea that all along I knew they were calling me an apostate. They were embarrassed and apologized profusely. Like the majority of Muslims I meet, they assumed that I had converted to Christianity without having proper knowledge of Islam.

Word spread quickly among Muslim students that I was an apostate. One Muslim American of Pakistani descent was especially incensed. He always was rude to me and tried to pick a fight. He often spat when our paths crossed. I did not budge even when he was insolent toward me. Other Muslim students at Hope College also disrespected me, with the exception of one who was from an Islamic sect, Ahmadiyya, whom Sunnis persecute in his native Pakistan. He was very friendly toward me.

Life on campus was going well in spite of the conflict with Muslim students. I connected with many Christians in the Holland area. One of them, Bill, worked for the Worldwide Christian Schools, which was giving financial assistance to Kenyan high school students attending Christian schools. One day he approached me about doing an interview for his organization's newsletter, to which I consented.

On Wednesday, October 23, 1996, Bill, along with a freelance journalist and a photographer from the Grand Rapids Press, met me at the Dewitt Cultural Center on the campus of Hope College. The interview lasted about two hours. Surprisingly, the article ended up being featured in the Press the following day. I learned about it when my English professor brought the newspaper to class.

Afterward, I went to the international office to pick up my mail and discovered that an intern had already put the article on the bulletin board. I requested it be removed because I did not want it to exacerbate my strained relationship with Muslim students.

The first semester of my freshman year ended. I visited some missionary friends in Randolph, Wisconsin, who had invited me to spend the Christmas holiday with them. While I was there, a former member of the board of trustees at Hope College, Doris De Young, introduced me to her family. I was also introduced to the Green Bay Packers football that dominated the local airwaves. My break culminated with the InterVarsity Christian Fellowship's Urbana96 Convention held at the University of Illinois at Champaign. While at this conference, I met Matt. He and I shared a passion for proselytizing non-Christians.

14.2 My Younger Brother Enrolls in a Secular School

I continued to keep in touch with some of my friends in Kenya via email. My younger brother Ali was attending an Islamic school in Lamu. One of my Christian friends was working in the same town. Eddie and I communicated often. My intention was to have him contact Ali and possibly convince him to drop out of the Islamic school. Six years had elapsed since Ali was forcefully taken out of a secular school to study Islam exclusively. I was determined to ensure that he quit the Islamic school. I called Ali often, but the school officials were concerned that he was getting calls from overseas. In addition, our frequent calls always lasted long. The fact that we conversed in our native Orma language, on which the Arab officials couldn't eavesdrop, was helpful. They were aware that Ali had a brother who had converted to Christianity.

Ali and Eddie continued meeting. Within weeks, Eddie invited him over for dinner. I continued praying for the situation and was optimistic that one day Ali would leave the Islamic school for a secular school, which would bring to fruition what I had envisioned over those six years. He made his decision to quit the Islamic school in 1997, a decision that enraged my family and the local Muslim community. He reported to the Taita Academy as a seventh grader in January 1998. I was grateful that Ali was going back to school after seven long agonizing years. He started where he left off in 1991. Providentially he would graduate from eighth grade, after stints at a few schools, and proceed to high school.

14.3 The Sad News

In the meantime, the news in the United States in 1997 was sad. Doris died suddenly of a heart attack. She had written often and visited me on campus during the first semester of my freshman year. Her children also visited me during homecoming and class reunions. Her sudden death saddened me. An email message I had received upon returning from a spring break mission trip to South Dakota conveyed the troubling news.

My sophomore year was a better year because my relationship with Muslim students had thawed. I also had a new roommate. Matt, the friend I had met at Urbana96, ended up being my roommate. He was very diligent in his studies and was aspiring to become a Catholic priest. Our friendship flourished to the point where even after he transferred to Aquinas College, we stayed in touch.

14.4 An Encounter with Baha'i Believers

Life on campus was going well. On the other hand, I missed the close-knit Christian fellowship in Kenya who would go together to witness. The cultural difference deterred me from effectively witnessing in the United States.

While witnessing, I became friends with my fellow student Sara, who was from the Baha'i faith. One evening she invited me to a Baha'i study, and I went with her to the meeting. The leader of the group discovered that I did not subscribe to the Baha'i faith, and began to proselytize me.

The Baha'i faith teaches that the Promised Comforter, whom Jesus Christ promised his disciples would come (see the Gospel of John chapters 14 and 16), is their Prophet, Bahaullah, a nine-teenth-century Persian who was born Mirza Husayn Ali. Para-doxically, Muslims claim that the Promised Comforter is Prophet Muhammad. (The subject of Muslims' claim is addressed in chapter 16.) I inquired about Bahaullah that evening. Within a short time, I started to disprove their claim using mostly the same argument I use when debating with Muslims about the Promised Comforter being Muhammad. The debate intensified. One lady wondered if I was the ex-Muslim who had been featured in the Grand Rapids Press the previous fall. I answered in the affirmative, and that marked the end of our discussion.

14.5 A Trip to Kenya

The spring semester of my sophomore year was going well. Then I learned that one of my nieces had died suddenly of cerebral malaria in Kenya. My family and I were still at an impasse. They were even more upset with me by this time because my younger brother had dropped out of the Islamic school. However, since I still loved my family, I made an arrangement to travel to Kenya in the summer of 1998 for a visit.

Plans for the trip to Kenya were underway. My travel plans were shrouded in secrecy. My brother Ali was among a handful of people who knew I was coming home. At my request, Hope College gave me a new I-20 to change my names legally while in Kenya.

On Monday, June 29, 1998, my journey home did not begin well. My flight from Chicago to London was delayed due to a hail-storm, which resulted in me missing a connecting flight to Nairobi. The revised itinerary from London to Nairobi was long and odious, with the worst part being a layover at the Cairo Interna-tional Airport, where my passport was confiscated. Many passen-gers had similar ordeals in Egypt, with some of them missing their connecting flights, leading them to stay in the airport for a few days. Thankfully I arrived in Nairobi on Wednesday, July 1, but without my checked-in luggage.

My host brother Charles had planned to meet me at the airport, but he left when I failed to arrive on the original flight. No one else knew my itinerary to plan to meet me at the airport. Ali was in school and could not make the trip to Nairobi. I called him to let him know that I had arrived safely. I stayed in Nairobi for a few days awaiting my luggage. Once I got my luggage, I traveled to Mombasa to visit my host parents, David and Jane. While there I traveled to the Taita Academy to visit Ali, who was in seventh grade. The school administration gave him permission to go home for a few days.

Ali and I traveled to Malindi. We came across our brother-in-law Daalle, who was in town to take his expectant wife to the Tawfiq Hospital, which is run by an Islamic organization. He had chosen this hospital over the Malindi District Hospital because Tawfiq follows strict Islamic rules pertaining to obstetric medicine. My half-sister Hashoni was in labor and battling acute pregnancy-induced hypertension but had to wait for hours because doctors had refused to see her. Apparently the hospital administrator wanted a large sum of money to be deposited—an equivalent of a week's worth of hospitalization—before even her vital signs would be checked. Daalle was frustrated and asked me for help. I talked him out of having his wife treated at this hospital. We got a cab and took her to the Malindi District Hospital, where she received help, delivering a healthy baby girl. He was grateful that I helped her. The sudden death of my niece had necessitated my trip to Kenya; however, I was thankful that I could help my half-sister along the way.

Ali and I traveled to my home in the Tana River District. People were surprised to see me back in the country. My foes were not happy. The month of July 1998 coincided with the month of *Rabi Al-Awaal* of the Islamic calendar, which marks the commemoration of the birth of Prophet Muhammad. Fiery speeches were hallmarks of such gatherings. Muslim leaders in my home area gave speeches during the *Maulid* celebrations condemning my conversion to Christianity. I had hoped that being overseas would at least allow them to forget about me. Even though I had been out of Kenya for two years, and my conversion had become public eight years earlier, there was still some animosity toward me.

The visit to my home area, however, turned out better than I had expected. I spent some time with my bereaved sister Fatuma, who was the one who had slashed my neck. One of my cousins, Boneyo, traveled with me often because he thought it was too dangerous for me to move around alone.

One Saturday afternoon my brother-in-law Daalle stopped me as I was going to Garsen unaccompanied. He was sympathetic toward me because I faced constant threats. In spite of the ugly depictions Muslim leaders had presented of me, he knew my character and was uninfluenced. I had helped him just a few weeks earlier when his wife required hospitalization. Although Daalle was opposed to my conversion to Christianity, he cared for my well-being and thus suggested a few safe routes that I should take. He told me that it was not safe for me to travel alone because he knew some people along the way who would attack me. He walked with me, and we reached my destination without an incident.

My struggle in Kenya continued. I was concerned for my safety everywhere I went. My younger brother returned to school after one week. Boneyo, who is now a police officer, accompanied me to most places.

Hope College had given me a new I-20 to change my name. Since my stay in Kenya was already challenging, I abandoned the quest to have my names changed. I was grateful that I did not pursue it because the U.S. embassy in Nairobi was bombed on August 7, 1998. Had I pursued changing names, I would not have obtained my visa or returned to Hope College in time for the fall semester. Visa seekers were diverted to the U.S. embassy in South Africa. I knew that remaining in Kenya for an extended period of time would have given my detractors more time to devise my harm.

The embassy-bombing aftermath devastated many Kenyan families. Our family friend Jarso Soka was in the Ufundi Cooperative Building adjacent to the embassy. The blast demolished the building, killing him. His death sent the local Muslim community into mourning. My friend Mutua narrowly escaped death.

Staying in Kenya was challenging for me. My mother constantly denigrated me. Some of my relatives were harsh toward me. Although I stayed out of religious polemics, I was not spared criticism. My elder brother Roba had changed a little bit from his volatile self. He was callous but did not attack me.

One time I traveled to Tarasaa—a town between Malindi and Garsen—to visit my oldest sister. I met a sheikh, an employee of the African Muslim Agency, who implored me to convert back to Islam. When I rebuffed his gesture, he got upset. He requested to meet with me at a later date to have a religious discussion. Due to his insistence, I agreed to the meeting only to cancel it later because I felt unsafe. Rumors I had heard about his organization's alleged illegal activities in Kenya game me second thoughts about the scheduled meeting.

I exercised extra caution when I traveled, especially in the Coast Province. The best reprieve was visiting my friends in other parts of the country, which were predominantly Christian, while maintaining a low profile.

I returned to the United States at the end of August. My friends who had prayed for me when I was in Kenya were relieved that I made it back safely.

14.6 The Daunting Task of Choosing a Major

The fall semester of my junior year started. I began my major in nursing with the intention of going back to Kenya to do medical missions after graduation. In spite of the persecution I had experienced, I was still determined to do an outreach among my tribe. I felt that if I didn't, who would? Although I was concerned for my safety should I return home, that did not deter me from thinking about the enormous need. Nonetheless, thoughts lingered concerning foreseeable danger to my life.

Since I was interested in doing missions, I tried ways I could fit my future vocation into what I had envisioned of helping the Orma people. Then I recalled a daily devotional I had read when I was a freshman. Scottish minister Oswald Chambers once said:

> In missionary work the great danger is that God's call will be replaced by the needs of the people, to the point human sympathy for those needs will absolutely overwhelm the meaning of being sent by Jesus. The needs are so enormous, the conditions so difficult, that every power of the mind falters and fails. We tend to forget that the one great reason

underneath all missionary work is not primarily the elevation of the people, their education, nor their needs, but is first and foremost the command of Jesus Christ—"Go therefore and make disciples of all the nations... (Matthew 28:19)."[1]

Rereading this devotional changed my attitude toward missions. There were times when I thought I was obliged to do medical outreach or community development work among the Orma people. I still feel that way sometimes. Nevertheless, I believe Muslims need to hear the Gospel of Jesus Christ openly proclaimed because all they know about him is from the Qur'an and the Hadith, which is skewed. I felt that if I returned to Kenya after graduation, aside from my safety being greatly compromised, I would not be effective reaching Muslims with the Gospel. Attending to the physical needs of people is not wrong per se; however, it should not take precedence over the preaching of the Gospel message.

Thoughts about my career goals persisted. Mark, a student at Western Theological Seminary, surprised me at JP's Coffee Shop in downtown Holland one evening in December 1998 with a new book he found at the seminary library. This book contains information about me. *The Call of Africa* also gives graphic details about how bandits ambushed missionaries who worked among my tribe in Kenya. It does not aver, however, that the African Muslim Agency (AMA) allegedly sponsored these attacks. Reading the firsthand accounts of these events made me realize that it would be too dangerous for me to do outreach in Kenya on the scale that I had envisioned. Had I followed through and moved back to Kenya after graduation, if I were still alive, I would not have had an opportunity to share overtly my conversion story or comment on Islam.

Doubts about becoming a nurse mounted. I talked with my Christian friends, and some of them encouraged me to hang in there. Then in April of 1999, I knew I had had enough of pursuing what I had no interest in. I handed in a letter to the chairperson of the Hope-Calvin nursing program stating that I was quitting. That decision was really tough for me, but I had no other choice than to quit. I felt some of my missionary friends were biased in how they advised me. They seemed to care more about what I would do for their organization in Kenya.

Quitting the nursing program ended my pandering to my family and friends. Switching my major to religion to study theology was easier than I had thought. My professors were supportive. Since I already had a few religion credits, I crammed the rest of the credits (twenty-eight) and a few prerequisites into a year and one summer and graduated on time in May 2000. My new major upset my family and friends, but life had to go on.

14.7 Life after College

My first job after graduation from Hope College in May 2000 was working with troubled youth at Pine Rest Christian Mental Health Services. My assignment was mentoring teenage boys who were wards of the state.

It was while working at Pine Rest in 2000 that I received an email from my younger brother Ali telling me that some people in my home area in Kenya were sending to their enemies armed bandits. Since I had many enemies on account of my conversion, he advised that I should not visit Kenya. There were prevailing tribal clashes pitting my Orma tribe (Muslim) against the Pokomo tribe (Christian) in 2000 that must have also heightened his concern. He called me often to update me on the situation.

The security situation in Kenya was getting direr in 2001. The intertribal fighting was going into its second year and was not abating. My student visa was about to expire and I did not want to return to Kenya, especially during the conflict. I had experienced enough trouble on my visit in 1998. I knew that some Muslims would target me.

I had an option of getting a new kind of visa through my employer. However, I did not pursue it because if the petition were denied, I would have no option but to return to Kenya. Although I had a job offer from an international not-for-profit organization to work in Kenya, I knew the threats to my life were immense; hence I declined the offer. The only option I had to continue staying in the U.S. legally was to go back to school.

Without any financial backing from my family, graduate school was out of reach for me. With my meager savings I enrolled at Grand Rapids Community College not knowing what field to pursue. I took various classes and was determined to become a professional student in order to maintain my student visa status so that I would not be forced to return to Kenya where my security would be in jeopardy. I enrolled in a twelve-credit minimum that the now-defunct Immigration and Naturalization Service (I.N.S.) required international students to take to maintain legal immigration status. I had to resign from my position at Pine Rest because U.S. immigration law prohibited me from working off-campus.

I continued taking classes at the community college while trying to keep busy with various activities at my church. I also made a lot of friends in the local immigrant community. Some of them had immigrated to the U.S. as refugees. Their backgrounds were unique and fascinating. I learned from them in 2002 that I could file for asylum.

Afterward, I read on the I.N.S. website about asylum in the United States. The information I found corroborated what my immigrant friends had told me. I could file for asylum if I could prove that I had a well-founded fear of persecution should I return to Kenya. I filed for asylum in August 2002 and thereafter received my legal authorization to work. I returned to work in the behavioral health field. I worked with patients who suffered from a myriad of psychiatric diseases and also with federal inmates who served the final phase of their sentences in a program that tried to stem recidivism.

14.8 The Situation in Kenya

The reports from Kenya had not been favorable. Ardent Muslims seemed comfortable waging *jihad* in a country that is widely believed to have a meager Muslim population. The Central Intelligence Agency (CIA) estimates Kenya is ten percent Muslim,[2] while the U.S. State Department states twenty percent.[3] There is a huge disparity between these estimates; however, the bottom line is that avowed Muslims are causing anarchy in Kenya. I was out of the country for barely two years when the 1998 terrorist attack occurred on Kenyan soil. Then in 2002 a tourist hotel was bombed, and in 2003 a Muslim mob burnt five Christian churches in the Tana River District.

The culmination of these events was on Friday, May 12, 2006, when a Christian radio station owned and operated by a denomination I was affiliated with was firebombed, with the night guard killed and two other people injured. The Associated Press reported, "Gunmen attacked a Pentecostal church radio station during a program that compared teachings of the Bible and the Quran [sic], killing one person and setting the building on fire."[4] The *Daily Nation* added, "At the time of the attack, the station was airing a program *Yesu ni Njia* (Jesus is the Way) where Muslims who have converted to Christianity were talking about their past experiences."[5] The gunmen escaped and have not been arrested nor charged with the crime even after more than two years of investigation.

I was concerned about the most current incident because Radio Bible Class (RBC) Ministries once taped and aired my conversion story nationwide in the United States and in some select countries around the world on its program *Words to Live By*. The program aired on October 11 and 12, 2003. Based on news reports, at the time of the attack on the Kenyan radio station, the Muslim converts were not present in the studio. That was a relief because the attackers would have killed them. I still do not know if my taped testimony was the one airing on the station at the time of the attack because RBC Ministries could not confirm whether its affiliate station in South Africa had distributed the program to radio stations in Kenya.

14.9 The Strange Emails

A lot had transpired in Kenya since my visit in 1998. The fact that I was overseas did not deter some Kenyan Muslims from contacting me about converting back to Islam. Some of them were concerned that my conversion to Christianity would not bode well for Islam. A Muslim man wrote to me an email on December 16, 2005, threatening me with Allah's punishment if I failed to heed his advice to convert back to Islam. I had never heard of Hussein Abdulkadir, and out of the blue he sent me an email urging me to convert back to Islam. Upon failure to heed his advice, he said I would be a great loser in this world and hereafter.

I was quite shaken when I first read it because of its language, especially the part about being "a greatest loser." I looked up his name in the online telephone directories and background-check websites, and two hits came up with different birthdates. One of the people was in North Carolina, and the other one was in Massachusetts. Then I looked up the time the message was sent, and it wasn't one of the United States' six time zones.

The website that provided Hussein Abdulkadir's email account was an Islamic website. I looked up the Uniform Resource Locator (URL) and landed on a website that fanatically promoted Islam. The website, http://www.road-to-heaven.org, provided email accounts and chat rooms. I was concerned that Hussein would share my personal information with other Muslims through chats or emails.

The following day I talked with my friends about the strange email. Some of them urged me to call the police. They argued that my past persecution gave credence to taking action against the strange emails. I waited and eventually replied to Hussein Abdulkadir's message because I was more interested in how he got my email address. One of my friends was an FBI agent, and his advice not to reply to this email came a little too late.

Hussein Abdulkadir was unwilling to disclose the name of the person who gave him my email address. I was concerned. At this time I sent emails to my younger brother and some friends in Kenya, Uganda, and Tanzania, inquiring if they had inadvertently given him my email address. When they denied any knowledge of him, I became more concerned.

My friends continued urging me to call the police. The origin of the emails was uncertain. I also knew there were at least two people with similar names in the United States. On December 24, 2005, I finally called the police. A police officer came to my residence around 7 a.m. He printed the emails off my computer and took them to a detective with the Kent County Sheriff Department, who carried out the investigation. The detective "attempted to further identify Hussein Abdul Kadir [sic] through public and

FBI databases... received several possible hits for the name, however, was unable to obtain an [sic] further identifiers on the suspect."[6] The police report added that the emails originated from overseas. I was relieved to know that Hussein Abdulkadir was not in the United States.

Ten years had elapsed since I left Kenya. I wondered what it would have been like had I still lived in Kenya when Hussein Abdulkadir heard about my conversion. The website that provided his email account clearly quoted the Qur'an, 33:36:

> It is not fitting for a Believer, man or woman, when a matter
> has been decided by Allah and His Messenger to have any
> option about their decision: if any one disobeys Allah and
> His Messenger, he is indeed on a clearly wrong Path.[7]

Islam does not give provision for a Muslim to change religions. Allah and Prophet Muhammad both prescribed death as the punishment for apostasy, and any Muslim who does not heed the call to kill an apostate disobeys both Allah and his Prophet.

14.10 Conclusion

Muslims in Kenya seem to have their way in either forcing Islamic apostates back to Islam or killing them. I know a Kenyan Somali Muslim who converted to Christianity in December 1992. Muslim youths attacked him in 1995 and beat him very severely, breaking his left hand. The hand healed, but bits of broken bones still protruded from his wrist when I visited Kenya in 1998. The Orma "seekers" (see chapter thirteen) who were interested in Christianity in 1995 have yet to come forward as professing Christians because they are afraid of ominous repercussions.

The plight of some Kenyan Muslim apostates is summed up in the words of Paul Marshall, a senior fellow at Freedom House in Washington, DC: "Vigilantes have killed, beaten, and threatened converts in Pakistan, the Palestinian areas, Turkey, Nigeria, Indonesia, Somalia, and *Kenya*."[8] Having read this account, I concluded that there is no way as a former Muslim I would be able to return to Kenya to live and practice Christianity without being harmed.

The situation in Kenya looks bleak for me, but I am grateful that my younger brother Ali has gained his formal education and has become a very prominent person among my tribe. I savor his accomplishment whenever I read about him in the Kenyan newspapers. Ali rubs shoulders with elite Kenyan politicians and knows very well that had he not accomplished his secular education, he would have had no chance of realizing his success. Perhaps someday his knowledge will spur him to seek clarification on esoteric doctrines of Islam, which, if exposed, would be earthshaking and result in the ideological bankruptcy of Islam.

The rest of my family and I are still at loggerheads. However, our relationship has not been as sour as it used to be. This relative stability would end if they became aware of this book.

I wrote a guest article about Islam for the press in October 2006, and inadvertently emailed it to Ali when I sent it to people in my address book. That unpublished article was about the rule of abrogation in Islam, which, if properly understood, is the main key toward understanding why austere Islam justifies violence especially against non-Muslims. Ali was incensed to read it but at the same time was concerned for my safety. He succinctly advised, "Stay out of religious polemics because it will just proliferate your enemies."[9]

The article urged the audience to strive to understand the rule of abrogation in Islam, which could "assuage the confusion about Islam."[10] I did not apologize to Ali and refused to heed his advice to eschew writing on Islam. If our fragile—and at times acrimonious—relationship has to collapse on account of my frankness, I will have no regrets. After all, I have not converted to Christianity to be silent. Dealing with persecution the past nineteen years has prepared me to stand by my convictions.

---

[1] Oswald Chambers, *My Utmost for His Highest* (Grand Rapids: Discovery House Publishing, 1992), October 26.

[2] CIA -The World Factbook --Kenya, Retrieved from https://www.cia. gov/cia/publications/factbook/geos/ke.html on June 28, 2006.

[3] U.S. State Department's Bureau of African Affairs, May 2006, Background Note: Kenya, Retrieved from https://www.state.gov/r/ pa/ei/bgn/2962.htm on May 15, 2006.

[4] Rodrique Ngowi, "1 Dead in Kenya Religious Station Attack," *Washington Post*, May 13, 2006, Retrieved from http://www. washingtonpost.com/wp-dyn/content/article/2006/05/13/ AR2006051301107_pf.html on September 21, 2006.

[5] Beatrice Hongo and Mike Mugwan'ga, "Radio Station Under Attack," *The Daily Nation*, May 13, 2006.

[6] Kent County Sheriff Department, *Complaint 80115-05,* January 17, 2006.

[7] Yusuf Ali.

[8] Paul Marshall, "Apostates from Islam: The Case of the Afghan Convert is Not Unique," *The Weekly Standard*, April 10, 2006, Volume 011, Issue 28. Emphasis mine.

[9] Ali Ibbe, Wednesday, October 18, 2006.

[10] Hussein Hajji Wario, *One Key Toward Understanding Islam*, October 11, 2006.

PART II

The Confusion in Islam

Muslims generally are confused about Islam because it has many conflicting teachings. Most of them do not admit it, but evidences in the Qur'an and the Hadith prove that Islam heavily borrowed tenets from pre-Islamic Arabian idol worship, Judaism, Christianity, and Zoroastrianism. Indiscriminate borrowing and unsystematic adoption from eclectic sources have led to the plethora of inconsistencies that renders Islamic teachings deficient in consensus, thus betraying Prophet Muhammad's claims that he received revelations from God. These insurmountable contradictions render Islam ineffective, with no authority even to discuss its own teachings.

A lot would have been understood about Islam had Prophet Muhammad devoted his time at least to articulating Allah's message. Instead, he was initially more interested in being accepted and jumped on the bandwagon of pre-Islamic teachings, only to realize that he could not corroborate them—perhaps because of his illiteracy or obstinacy.

A good example of a colossal blunder in Islam is its account of Jesus Christ. Some Islamic teachings widely tout Jesus as a mere prophet. The following chapter discusses his depiction in Islam, showing how he is by far superior to all the prophets mentioned in Islam including Prophet Muhammad. This chapter proves how, at the outset of Islam, Muhammad tried to impress Christian Jews in Arabia by commenting on Christian doctrines—only to end up in grotesque errors. And he did not stop there.

Prophet Muhammad claimed that he was predicted in the Gospel as a prophet to come after Jesus. Chapter 16 discusses Islam's contention that Prophet Muhammad is the Promised Comforter mentioned in the Gospel of John chapters 14 and 16. It debunks that claim using the Islamic "arsenal" of the Qur'an and the Hadith. "Arsenal," I would call these two sources, because they bring out Muhammad's nature and behavior, which are atypical of the Promised Comforter portrayed in the Gospel. Had Prophet Muhammad properly understood the teachings of Jesus Christ on the Holy Spirit, perhaps Islam would be nonexistent today.

My hope and prayer is that the following two chapters will expose some of the gross flaws that abound in Islam. The cracks in Islam are far-reaching. Exposing them will perhaps give recourse to Muslims and non-Muslims who are seeking answers.

CHAPTER FIFTEEN

Islamic Depiction of Jesus Christ

Confusion and controversies abound in Islam. The Qur'an, Islam's supposedly infallible scripture, is awash with banal, outrageous, conflicting, and mostly negative statements about Christianity and Judaism that hinder Muslims from grasping Islamic teachings. There are also huge amounts of ipse dixits—assertions lacking proof—posing tremendous difficulties even for Islamic scholars to interpret. Had the author of the Qur'an carefully formulated the Islamic doctrine and left out issues touching on other religions, perhaps less confusion would have resulted. Moreover, ordinary Muslims are generally the victims as they are left rummaging through the morass in search of guidance.

The Qur'an contains more information derived from Christianity and Judaism than from Islam. The excuse is that Muslims claim "their religion to be a continuation and culmination of Judeo-Christian traditions, Islam being the third and last cycle of a divine plan and abrogating Christianity in the same manner the latter was revealed to abrogate Judaism."[1] Thus they claim it is justified to have excerpts of the Torah, Psalms, and Gospel included in the Qur'an.

It is ludicrous that Muslims claim Islam came to abrogate Christianity because most of its information about Christianity is either exaggerated or false. We will look at one example, its account of Jesus Christ.

15.1 The Jesus of Islam

The accounts of the Qur'an and the Hadith on Jesus Christ are absurd, abstruse, and aloof, tantamount to ridicule. For these reasons, it would be fair to refer to Jesus as He is mentioned in Islam as the "Jesus of Islam." Even though the Qur'an and the Hadith depict the Jesus of Islam with a wide range of travesty, they inadvertently accord him tremendous attributes that by far show his superiority to all the prophets mentioned in the Qur'an, including Prophet Muhammad. One would wonder how God would send Islam as a religion to abrogate Christianity, when even by Islam's own account, the prophet who brought Christianity is supreme in every aspect. Ideally, it would make more sense to follow a leader who is superior.

Muslims stumble whenever I bring up passages from the Qur'an and the Hadith that show the Jesus of Islam's superiority to all the prophets mentioned in Islam. They believe that "God sent 124,000 prophets to the world and 313 messengers who also received an organized body of laws to pass on."[2] However, only twenty-five of them are mentioned by name. The last three were John the Baptist, Jesus son of Mary, and Muhammad. They claim that just as John the Baptist had prepared the way for Jesus Christ, Jesus did the same for Muhammad in the Gospel. They go further to assert that the Holy Spirit, who Jesus Christ prophesied would come to comfort the disciples, is Muhammad. This doctrine is rather confusing and will be dealt with in the subsequent chapter.

15.2 The Announcement of Jesus' Birth

The Qur'an and the Hadith unintentionally show the Jesus of Islam's superiority to Prophet Muhammad in every aspect, from the announcement of his virgin birth and early childhood through his public ministry. Muslims would be upset to hear of it, but even by Islam's own account, Prophet Muhammad is inferior. The Qur'an gives an account of the virgin birth of its Jesus as follows:

> And make mention of Mary in the Scripture, when she had withdrawn from her people to a chamber looking East, And had chosen seclusion from them. Then We sent unto her Our Spirit and it assumed for her the likeness of a perfect man. She said: Lo! I seek refuge in the Beneficent One from thee, if thou art Allah-fearing. He said: I am only a messenger

of thy Lord, that I may bestow on thee a faultless son. She
said: How can I have a son when no mortal hath touched me,
neither have I been unchaste? He said: So (it will be). Thy
Lord saith: It is easy for Me. And (it will be) that We may
make of him a revelation for mankind and a mercy from Us,
and it is a thing ordained. And she conceived him, and she
withdrew with him to a far place.[3]

According to the Qur'an, the angel Gabriel appeared to Mary
and announced to her that she would have a son. Just as is recorded
in the Bible, Mary was surprised by the announcement because she
was a virgin and did not know how she could have a son since she
was not married and had not been sexually unchaste. She protested
but later accepted Allah's decree.

The angel continued to tell Mary that her son would be a revelation and mercy to mankind. He would also be sinless. The Jesus
of Islam is the only prophet mentioned in Islamic teaching who was
born without sin.

The Qur'an refers to Allah by plural pronouns in the account of
the angel Gabriel delivering the revelations. Muslims—refuting the
idea of the trinity—claim that those pronouns were used in order
to show Allah's immense power. Whatever the case, the news the
angel brought to Mary was unprecedented; nothing of its sort had
ever been told in Islam.

15.3 He Is Protected from Satan at Birth

The Qur'an goes as far as saying that Mary and her offspring (Jesus)
were protected from Satan because Allah granted Mary's mother's
prayer.[4] It was in reiterating this point that Prophet Muhammad
said in the Hadith, "There is none born among the off-spring of
Adam, but Satan touches it. A child therefore, cries loudly at the
time of birth because of the touch of Satan, except Mary and her
child."[5] Some of Muhammad's proclamations are mind-boggling.
He associated a baby's first cry with the touch of Satan.

Science has proven that a baby initially cries in order to breathe
deeper as air rushes into the lungs. An internationally renowned
obstetrician, Dr. Gro Nylander, states that, "Outside the mother's
body, the baby's chest expands, drawing air into the lungs for the

first time." He adds, "This action is prerequisite for the first cry, and that is how it is meant to work."[6] Science confounds Prophet Muhammad. It is a scientific fact that a baby does not cry because of Satan's touch.

Mary, the mother of Jesus, was chosen and exalted above all women even by Islam's standard. The Qur'an states, "O Mary! Allah hath chosen thee and purified thee- chosen thee above the women of all nations."[7] She is not only one of the only two people whom Satan did not touch at birth because of Allah's protection. She is also the only woman who is purified, and far honored above all women, including Prophet Muhammad's nine (some aHadith say eleven) wives, his mother, and the wives of his companions. It was probably necessary for her to be purified because she was going to conceive and deliver a sinless son. The Jesus of Islam is unique because he was born through a purified and blessed woman.

15.4 His Birth

Furthermore, the Qur'an teaches that Jesus is a word of Allah and a spirit from him.[8] Muslims believe that that word became flesh through the power of the Holy Spirit (the angel Gabriel in Islam), resulting in Mary's pregnancy. It was then that she went away to a solitary place because she was ashamed of what her family would say about her pregnancy.[9] The time came for her to deliver her child, and an angel appeared and encouraged her. She was provided with food in the form of dates and drink. When the baby was born, she brought him to her family, who was shocked by the news. They thought she had the child out of wedlock. They were hostile toward her and accused her of being a harlot.

The Qur'an goes on record to show how the baby, who was only a few hours old, spoke to the family in his mother's defense. In contrast, there is no statement in either the Qur'an or the Hadith that shows Prophet Muhammad addressing his family when he was a newborn. Bizarre as it sounds, this is one of the many statements in the Qur'an and the Hadith that shows the Jesus of Islam's superiority to all the prophets, which Muslims fail to grasp. Even by Islam's account, Muhammad is pedestrian.

Allah, the alleged author of the Qur'an, was probably confused when it comes to this story. The Hagar and Ishmael story in Genesis 21 is quite similar to it except for a change in characters and the "illegitimate" talking baby. Aspects such as the family feud and the angel appearing with the provision of food and water are probably derived from this story. However, in the case of Hagar and Ishmael, the angel spoke from heaven and asked Hagar to get water from the well but did not provide food.

15.5 His Maternal Uncles

It is also probable that Allah was capricious in relaying the following story to Muhammad in the Qur'an. He stated in Suratul Al-Maryam, 19:28, that the Virgin Mary was a sister to Aaron, a brother of Moses, who lived many centuries earlier. It is quite confusing because Suratul At-Tahrim, 66:12, states:

> And Mary, daughter of Imran, whose body was chaste, therefore We breathed therein something of Our Spirit. And she put faith in the words of her Lord and His scriptures, and was of the obedient.[10]

How could the Virgin Mary be a daughter of Imran, who was the father of Moses and Aaron in Islam? The Moses and Aaron in Islam's account of Jesus' birth are the same people mentioned in the Old Testament. Miriam was a sister to this duo, and the all-knowing Allah mistook her for the Virgin Mary. So according to Islam, Moses and Aaron are actually Jesus' uncles!

Moreover, the Hadith slams the door on Islamic scholars who try to downplay the contradictions because Prophet Muhammad said, "On the night of my night journey I passed by Moses bin Imran."[11] Mary the mother of Jesus and Moses are siblings not only in the Qur'an but also in the Hadith—an interesting combination considering they lived many centuries apart.

Prophet Muhammad's contemporaries believed that the Virgin Mary and Aaron (Moses' brother) were siblings. The Hadith shows that Christians in Arabia heard this controversial assertion that they actually were siblings, though they lived centuries apart. They were shocked and so approached a Muslim by the name of Mughira bin

Shu'ba, asking him why Muslims recite the Qur'an that way. He had no answer for how the duo was believed to be siblings all along. At that time he approached Prophet Muhammad, who told him, "The (people of the old age) used to give names (to their persons) after the names of Apostles and pious persons who had gone before them."[12] Unfortunately for Islam, this explanation is implausible. The Islamic version of the Virgin Mary, Aaron, and Moses sharing a surname is believable. However, how the Virgin Mary and Aaron end up being siblings in Suratul Al-Imran is incongruent.

15.6 His Public Ministry

Most Muslims do not know or understand what the Qur'an and the Hadith teach about Jesus. They are sold out on him being a mere prophet—what the Qur'an and the Hadith also say—but do not get a chance to compare him with Prophet Muhammad. The Qur'an and the Hadith make staggering assertions about him that quite vividly contradict the Gospel's account of his public life. These accounts are far-fetched and confusing but have the ability to educe some questions about Islam that could lead Muslims toward knowing the truth about Islam.

Islam teaches that the Jesus of Islam was sent in the footsteps of the prophets to confirm the Law and he was given the Gospel, which is light and guidance.[13] He was sent to the Israelites and performed many miracles.

One of the most bizarre cases not mentioned in Christianity is the Qur'an's claim that Jesus created a bird from clay and breathed into it, and it flew away by Allah's permission. Suratul Al-Maida, 5:110, states:

> When Allah saith: O Jesus, son of Mary! Remember My favour unto thee and unto thy mother; how I strengthened thee with the holy Spirit, so that thou spakest unto mankind in the cradle as in maturity; and how I taught thee the Scripture and Wisdom and the Torah and the Gospel; and how thou didst shape of clay as it were the likeness of a bird by My permission, and didst blow upon it and it was a bird by My permission, and thou didst heal him who was born blind

and the leper by My permission; and how thou didst raise the dead by My permission; and how I restrained the Children of Israel from (harming) thee when thou camest unto them with clear proofs, and those of them who disbelieved exclaimed: This is naught else than mere magic.[14]

This verse also shows other miracles attributed to Jesus. He healed those born blind and deaf and also raised the dead to life. It is phenomenal that the Qur'an mentions his creating power and in the same context his ability to give back life. Thus the Jesus of Islam had the power to create and also give back the life that left the body.

The Qur'an in Al-Maida, 5:112–115, also shows how the Jesus of Islam asked Allah to send down a table full of food from heaven. And Allah granted that request. That significant miracle in Islam led to the naming of chapter five of the Qur'an—Al-Maida, which means "The Table Spread." These miracles lucidly portray how the Qur'an, however unintentionally, depicts the Jesus of Islam as superior to all the prophets in Islam, including Muhammad.

Prophet Muhammad is mentioned in the Hadith as having performed a miracle of splitting the moon. The Hadith notes, "The people of Mecca asked Allah's Apostle to show them a miracle. So he showed them the moon split in two halves between which they saw the Hiram' mountain."[15] This cannot pass as a miracle performed by Prophet Muhammad because he recited in Suratul Al-Qamar (54), "The hour drew nigh and the moon was rent in twain."[16] If he had performed this miracle, he would have mentioned it. What the unbelieving audience saw could have happened due to a lunar eclipse. How they could see the mountain due to the splitting of the moon in the sky is baffling. It must have been a huge moon to conceal a mountain in the first place.

The only miracle that could be credited to Prophet Muhammad is what the Hadith states:

Anas bin Malik said, "The Prophet used to visit all his wives in a round, during the day and night and they were eleven in number." I asked Anas, "Had the Prophet the strength for it?" "Anas replied, 'We used to say that the Prophet was given the strength of thirty (men).' And Said said on the authority of Qatada that Anas had told him about nine wives only (not eleven).[17]

It is clearly shown that Prophet Muhammad had sexual relations with all his wives every day and night, a feat that no ordinary man can accomplish without a miracle. Mark you, this happened when he was advanced in age. Prophet Muhammad did it because the Hadith quotes him several times saying that Prophet Solomon had sexual relations on different nights with one hundred,[18] ninety-nine,[19] ninety,[20] seventy,[21] and sixty[22] of his wives.

While the Jesus of Islam performed many miracles, including the creation of the bird, Prophet Muhammad did no such thing. Most Muslims argue that since Muhammad was illiterate, his miracle was the Qur'an because:

> The Qur'anic revelations cannot be equaled or surpassed by any human power in its eloquence and its contents acquired a more precise form in the teaching that each Prophet was given a verifying miracle and that the Prophet Muhammad's miracle was the Qur'an. Muslims maintain that the Prophet was illiterate and, therefore, incapable of producing any literary work, at least of all such "exquisite literary perfection" as the Qur'an.[23]

It is not a surprise that even Islamic scholars admit that Prophet Muhammad did not perform miracles.

The Qur'an's account that Jesus created a bird from clay does not belong to the Gospel narratives in the New Testament. It was perhaps borrowed from the non-canonical Gospel of Thomas where Jesus supposedly "took clay and formed the images of twelve sparrows."[24]

The Qur'an goes further to state that Jesus had power to make lawful certain things Moses forbade in the Torah (Law). It quoted Jesus saying, "(I have come to you), to attest the Law which was before me. And to make lawful to you part of what was (Before) forbidden to you; I have come to you with a Sign from your Lord. So fear Allah, and obey me."[25] If Moses prohibited Israelites the things in the Law as directed by Allah, I wonder how the Jesus of

Islam—a mere prophet—could reverse what the all-knowing Allah supposedly decreed. This contradicts what Jesus Christ said in the Gospel:

> Do not think that I came to destroy the Law or the Prophets.
> I did not come to destroy but to fulfill. For assuredly, I say to
> you, till heaven and earth pass away, one jot or one tittle will
> by no means pass from the law till all is fulfilled.[26]

The mission of Jesus Christ was never about changing the Law. He came to fulfill it. The only law He abolished in His suffering and death was the ceremonial law. As a result, Christians do not have to cleanse themselves outwardly to be accepted of God because:

> The ceremonies and figures of the law ceased at the coming of
> Christ, and that all the shadows are accomplished; so that the
> use of them must be abolished amongst Christians; yet the
> truth and substance of them remain with us in Jesus Christ,
> in whom they have their completion.[27]

It is not surprising that Prophet Muhammad misinterpreted Jesus' teachings again. All rituals in the Old Testament—for example, the ablution before prayers, sin offerings, etcetera—that Muslims still perform were fulfilled in Christ and are not required anymore. Muslims still observe the ceremonial law because Prophet Muhammad did not understand the teachings of Jesus Christ. If he had gotten it right from the outset, a few billion people would be less confused today.

15.7 Did He Die?

This brings us to the biggest miracle in history that Islamic teachings vehemently oppose. Islam teaches that the crucifixion, death, and resurrection of Jesus Christ did not even happen. Unlike Christians, Muslims believe that Jesus ascended into heaven before dying and resurrecting because Allah provided someone else to die in his place. Allah supposedly protected the Jesus of Islam because he "cannot be so humiliated or die such shameful death; [because] God would never allow His honored prophets to end like that."[28] What a contrast with the biblical message of prophets suffering!

The Qur'an quotes the Jews, six hundred years after the death and resurrection of Jesus Christ, boastfully saying, "Surely we have killed the Messiah, Isa son of Marium, the messenger of Allah." In the same breath it refutes their claim:

> They did not kill him nor did they crucify him, but it appeared to them so (like Isa) and most surely those who differ therein are only in a doubt about it; they have no knowledge respecting it, but only follow a conjecture, and they killed him not for sure. Nay! Allah took him up to Himself; and Allah is Mighty, Wise.[29]

It is ludicrous that Prophet Muhammad recited the Qur'an claiming to quote Jews who witnessed the crucifixion and death of Jesus. I wonder how this could be possible when Moses was quoted saying, "The days of our lives *are* seventy years; And if by reason of strength *they are* eighty years, Yet their boast *is* only labor and sorrow; For it is soon cut off, and we fly away."[30] Human beings have had shorter life spans since the days of Moses. The Qur'an's account has little ground to stand on claiming that Jesus' contemporaries lived more than six hundred years in order to recount their accomplishment.

It is very difficult to decipher some of Muhammad's ipse dixits. He claimed to have heard what happened in graves after burial. The Hadith states, "Once the Prophet went out after sunset and heard a dreadful voice, and said, 'The Jews are being punished in their graves.'"[31] Prophet Muhammad dismissed the crucifixion and death of Jesus Christ, claiming to quote the Jews who had been dead for a few centuries. He was wrong even after allegedly contacting the dead because according to the Gospel, it was the Romans who killed Jesus.

Prophet Muhammad was a self-proclaimed illiterate man. Taking him at his word as being illiterate, I am led to deduce that he got the idea of the Jews attempting to kill Jesus from the Gospel, which states:

> So all those in the synagogue, when they heard these things, were filled with wrath, and rose up and thrust Him out of the city; and they led Him to the brow of the hill on which

their city was built, that they might throw Him down over the cliff. Then passing through the midst of them, He went His way.[32]

Prophet Muhammad probably heard the story because, "Jews and Christians [in Arabia] were in the habit of elucidating their scripture in Arabic, whether for missionary, apologetic, or internal purpose, some time before the emergence of Islam."[33]

Another possibility is that when Prophet Muhammad learned to read, he read the beginning of Jesus' ministry in the New Testament in Arabic. It is written in the Hadith that his first wife, Khadija, had a cousin, Waraqa, "who was a Christian convert and used to read the Gospels in Arabic."[34] Khadija took Muhammad to him to consult on the first revelations he received. Waraqa probably read the Gospels to Muhammad who ended up presuming that Jesus Christ escaped from the mob and went to heaven.

The aforementioned verse in the Gospel does not show that the Jews had attempted to crucify Jesus, but Muhammad could have learned later about the crucifixion and pieced together the attempt to kill with the crucifixion and made his own conclusion. It is written in three places in the Gospel that the Son of Man would be betrayed to the chief priests and teachers of the law. They would then condemn him to death and would hand him over to the Gentiles (Romans) who would mock him, spit on him, flog him, and kill him.[35]

The Old Testament clearly shows how Jesus Christ would be born, suffer, and die for the sins of His people. The Book of Isaiah chapter 53 is one of the prophecies that clearly show the suffering and death of Jesus Christ. It starts out, "Who has believed our report? And to whom has the arm of the LORD been revealed?"[36] Seemingly, Muhammad failed to understand the prophecy concerning Jesus and therefore failed to believe the "report." And the revelation he received did not originate from God, because God sent this prophecy about eight hundred years before the birth of Jesus Christ, more than one thousand three hundred years before Muhammad.

The Qur'an intensifies Muslims' confusion surrounding the death and resurrection of the Jesus of Islam in Suratul Al-Imran, 3:55. The Arabic word used in this verse means "death" according to some Islamic scholars. Thus some translations of the Qur'an tremendously differ on the subject of Jesus' death as well. For instance, the Yusuf Ali translation, a translation of the Qur'an geared toward Western readers, states:

> Behold! Allah said: "O Jesus! I will take thee and raise thee to Myself and clear thee (of the falsehoods) of those who blaspheme; I will make those who follow thee superior to those who reject faith, to the Day of Resurrection: Then shall ye all return unto me, and I will judge between you of the matters wherein ye dispute."[37]

Whereas the Maulawi Sher Ali translation states, "When Allah said, 'O Jesus, I will cause thee to die *a natural death* and will exalt thee to Myself"[38], the Pickthall and Shakir translations state, "I am gathering thee"[39] and "I am going to terminate the period of your stay (on earth)"[40] respectively. I wonder why Islam, a religion that boasts of having the infallible word of God in the Qur'an, has its scholars sparring over the meaning of a single Arabic word. The divergent interpretations of this verse give a glimpse of their propensities to cover up the careless words Prophet Muhammad uttered in the name of revelations from God.

Evidently Prophet Muhammad claimed to know everything about Jesus—hair color, stature, and life's details. Nevertheless, when it became clear to him that Islam cannot abrogate Christianity as he preached, because the foundation of Christianity solely rests on the death and resurrection of Jesus Christ, he claimed to have received "divine" revelations refuting them.

It is farcical that the all-knowing God waited six hundred years to disprove the Jews, who had claimed that the Messiah was crucified, dead, and buried, and on the third day He rose again from the dead. Allah ostensibly took that long only to reveal a verse that wreaks havoc among Muslims. Sadly, even after the revelation of the verse the subject of the Jesus of Islam's death is still unclear.

That leaves Islamic scholars scampering for words to interpret what Muhammad attributed to God.

The Islamic scholars' efforts to disguise the real meaning of the suffering, crucifixion, death, and resurrection of the Jesus of Islam plummet because the Qur'an also states:

> Certainly We made a covenant with the children of Israel and We sent to them messengers; whenever there came to them an messenger with what that their souls did not desire, some (of them) did they call liars and *some they slew*.[41]

> We gave Moses the Book and followed him up with a succession of messengers; We gave Jesus the son of Mary Clear (Signs) and strengthened him with the holy spirit. Is it that whenever there comes to you a messenger with what ye yourselves desire not, ye are puffed up with pride?- Some ye called impostors, and *others ye slay*.[42]

It would be prudent of Islamic scholars to provide a list of prophets who were slain according to Islamic teachings before they can make categorical statements to dismiss the death and resurrection of Jesus Christ. I doubt they would do so, however, because the consequences could be costly for Islam and its propaganda campaign, as there is no such list of slain prophets. Prophet Muhammad recited these verses—before realizing what the death and resurrection of Jesus Christ entailed in Christianity—as an accusation against the Jews who had spurned him. He tried to make them feel guilty for what they did not do, in order that his message could be heard after he had been so widely rejected.

The Yusuf Ali translation of the Qur'an is one of the translations that tend to sway their readers with their disingenuous commentaries. For instance, in the aforementioned verse (Al-Maida, 5:70), which is close in meaning to the eighty-seventh verse of Suratul Al-Baqara (the second Qur'anic quoted above), he says:

> There is a double significance. First, reviewing the long course of Jewish history, we have come to the time of Jesus: they have often given the lie to Allah's Prophets, and even now they are trying to slay Jesus. Secondly, extending the review of that history of the time of Muhammad, they are even now trying

to take the life of that Holy Prophet. This would be literally true at the time words were promulgated to the people.[43]

It is appalling that Yusuf Ali selectively wrote a commentary on Al-Maida, 5:70, but did not include one with the verse in Al-Baqara. Clearly, he did that intentionally in order to conceal the meaning of the word "slay," which is in the past tense also in other translations of the Qur'an. He included "they go as far as" to the verse in Al-Maida to downplay the meaning of "to slay." Both Shakir and Pickthall translations have it as "some they slew."

Islamic scholars can play all the dirty games of hoodwinking the faithful, but the truth about the death and resurrection of Jesus Christ is evident. It is clear that Prophet Muhammad did not keep track of claims he made about Jesus Christ because he did not understand the depth of the Gospel message. He only realized too late that it was a daunting task to try to disprove the purpose of Jesus Christ's suffering and death. Islamic scholars divergent Qur'anic commentaries show that they picked the wrong topic to debunk and are left merely pontificating.

It is amazing that all the banal statements Prophet Muhammad made to downplay the significance of the crucified Jesus Christ, the Son of God, have backfired. That leaves Islamic scholars frantically trying to cover up the inconsistencies. I have met Muslims who would prevaricate, trying to defend Islam's claim to have a firsthand knowledge of a divine event that preexisted it.

15.8 His Second Coming

The Jesus of Islam is supposed to return at the end of the world for judgment. Muslims believe he is coming back to disown Christians, marry, and live on earth for forty years and then die. My brothers used to tell me, "We will see you on the Day of Judgment." They were confident that Jesus Christ would disown me, a Christian, when He comes back. According to one renowned scholar, "The place of his future grave is already marked out between the graves of Omar, the caliph, and Fatuma, Mohammed's daughter."[44] If this is indeed true, Muslims are in for a rude shock. It is pointless for them to mark a gravesite for Jesus Christ when there is ambiguity surrounding his fate in Islam.

My brothers are not alone. Apparently it is very difficult for Muslims to understand some divergent passages in the Qur'an that could elicit their quest for the truth. For example, prior to Prophet Muhammad becoming aware that Christians believe in the death of Jesus Christ on the cross for the redemption of sins, he received a revelation in Mecca before the migration to Medina in 622 A.D. This underscored that all the messengers who were sent before Muhammad were men who only survived on food, and none of them (including the Jesus of Islam) were exempt from death. The Qur'an states:

> Before thee, also, the messengers We sent were but men, to
> whom We granted inspiration: If ye realise this not, ask of
> those who possess the Message. Nor did We give them bodies
> that ate no food, nor were they exempt from death.[45]

Muslims should be lauded for their patience when referencing the Qur'an and the Hadith for guidance. Conversely, it must take gargantuan creativity to read these texts and not realize these accounts contradict on various topics, including the life and death of Jesus Christ. How Muslims would still contend that the Qur'an is excellent and infallible in light of the passages we have read is a mystery. Perhaps their adamant, aggressive, and blind defense of the Qur'an is the reason behind the confusion in Islam. A Little scrutiny of the Qur'an is necessary to realize that Prophet Muhammad concocted the Qur'an and no divine being was involved in it.

---

[1] Anwar G. Chejne, *Islam and the West, the Moriscos: A Cultural and Social History* (Albany: State University of New York Press, 1983), 80.

[2] Yahiya Emerick and Quasim Najar, *The Complete Idiot's Guide to Understanding Islam* (Indianapolis: Alpha Books, 2001), 101–102.

[3] Pickthall, Al-Maryam, 19:16–22.

[4] Al-Imran, 3:36.

[5] *Sahih Bukhari, Volume 4, Book 55, Number 641.*

6   Gro Nylander, *Becoming a Mother: From Birth to Six Months* (Berkeley, CA: Celestial Arts, 2002), 17.

7   Yusuf Ali, Suratul Al-Imran, 3:42.

8   Suratul Al-Nisa, 4:171.

9   Suratul Al-Maryam, 19:22–30.

10 Pickthall.

11 *Sahih Muslim, Book 1, Number 317.*

12 *Sahih Muslim, Book 25, Number 5326.*

13 Suratul An-Nisa, 5:46.

14 Pickthall.

15 *Sahih Bukhari, Volume 5, Book 58, Number 208.*

16 Pickthall.

17 *Sahih Bukhari, Volume 1, Book 5, Number 268.*

18 *Sahih Bukhari, Volume 4, Book 52, Number 74i.*

19 *Sahih Bukhari, Volume 4, Book 55, Number 635.*

20 *Sahih Bukhari, Volume 8, Book 78, Number 634.*

21 *Sahih Bukhari, Volume 8, Book 79, Number 711.*

22 *Sahih Bukhari, Volume 9, Book 93, Number 561*

23 Farid Esack, *The Qur'an: A User's Guide* (Oxford: OneWorld Publications, 2005), 102.

24 Gerald Massey, *Ancient Egypt: The Light Of The World, Part 2* (Whitefish, MT: Kessinger Publishing, 2002), 809.

25 Yusuf Ali, Al-Imran, 3:50.

26 Matthew 5:17–18, NKJV.

27 Belgic Confession of Faith, Article 25: Of the Abolishing of the Ceremonial Law. Retrieved from http://www.iclnet.org/pub/resources/text/ipb-e/epl-01/confa-02.txt on July 13, 2007.

28 R.C. Sproul and Abdul Saleeb, *The Dark Side of Islam* (Wheaton, IL: Crossway Books, 2003), 66, 67. Bracket mine.

29 Shakir, Al-Nisa, 4:157–158.

30 Psalm 90:10, NKJV.

31 *Sahih Bukhari, Volume 2, Book 23, Number 457.*

32 Luke 4:28–30, NKJV.

33 Meira Polliack, *Karaite Tradition of Arabic Bible Translation, A Linguistic and Exegetical Study of Karaite Translations of the Pentateuch from the Tenth and Eleventh Centuries C.E.* (Leiden, The Netherlands: Brill Academic Publishers, 1997), 3. Bracket mine.

34 *Sahih Bukhari, Volume 4, Book 55, Number 605.*

35 Matthew 20:19; Mark 10:33; and Luke 18:32.

36 NKJV.

37 Yusuf Ali, 3:55.

[38] Maulawi Sher Ali, *The Holy Qur'an* (Telford, UK: Islamic International Publications, 1997), 54, 55. Italics not part of the original Arabic. This translation has this verse as verse 56 because it has the beginning statement of every chapter of the Qur'an, "In the Name of Allah, the Compassionate, the Merciful," as verse 1.

[39] Pickthall, 3:55.

[40] Shakir, 3:55.

[41] Shakir, Al-Maida, 5:70. Emphasis mine.

[42] Yusuf Ali, Al-Baqara, 2:87. Emphasis mine.

[43] Yusuf Ali, Commentary Number 91. Bracket mine.

[44] Samuel Zwemer, *Moslem World 1907* (Whitefish, MT: Kessinger Publishing, 2003), 66.

[45] Yusuf Ali, Al-Anbiya, 21:7–8.

CHAPTER SIXTEEN

Is Prophet Muhammad the Promised Comforter?

slam is its own worst enemy. Contradictions are rampant in both the Qur'an and the Hadith. And with consensus lacking among its scholars—due to the apparent plethora of inconsistencies—ordinary Muslims are generally victims of the colossal confusion. There are various assertions Muslims have made about the mission of Jesus Christ, and this chapter deals with one of them: the outlandish claim that Prophet Muhammad was the Promised Comforter—the Holy Spirit—in the Gospel.

Islamic teachings purport that Jesus Christ prophesied the coming of Prophet Muhammad. Muslims categorically quote a verse in the Qur'an to ascertain their claim that Jesus indeed came to prepare the way for Muhammad. Even though the Bible clearly shows that the Promised Comforter is a spirit, Muslims still claim that this prophecy pointed to Muhammad. (There is a widely held belief among them that the early Christians and Jews must have removed from the Gospel the reference to Prophet Muhammad.) The Qur'an states:

> And When Jesus son of Mary said: O Children of Israel Lo! I am the messenger of Allah unto you, confirming that which was (revealed) before me in the Torah, and bringing good tidings of a messenger who cometh after me, whose name is the Praised One. Yet when he hath come unto them with clear proofs, they say: This is mere magic.[1]

A footnote on this verse states that "the Praised One" is the meaning of the Arabic word *Ahmad*, "a name of the Prophet of Arabia. The Promised 'Comforter' was believed by many Christian communities of the East to be a Prophet yet to come."[2]

This verse and the ensuing commentary clearly portray a Messiah who had supposedly come to prepare the way for Prophet Muhammad. Many Muslims go as far as quoting the Gospel of John, in which Jesus prophesied the coming of the Comforter, to bolster their claim.

16.1 Who Is the Holy Spirit in Islam?

Prior to digging into Jesus Christ's prophecy, let us first and foremost deal with the Muslims' understanding of the Holy Spirit. The Hadith clearly states that the Angel Gabriel is the Holy Spirit. The highly regarded Hadith collection of Sahih Bukhari mentions:

> Narrated Abu Salama bin 'Abdur-Rahman bin 'Auf: That he
> heard Hassan bin Thabit Al-Ansari asking the witness of Abu
> Huraira, saying, "O Abu- Huraira! I beseech you by Allah (to
> tell me). Did you hear Allah's Apostle saying "O Hassan ! Reply
> on behalf of Allah's Apostle. O Allah! Support him (Hassan)
> with the Holy Spirit (Gabriel)?'" Abu Huraira said, "Yes."[3]

Furthermore, according to an Islamic scholar, the Qur'an claims that the Holy Spirit is the Angel Gabriel. Suratul An-Nahl states:

> Say, the Holy Spirit has brought the revelation from thy Lord
> in Truth, in order to strengthen those who believe, and as a
> Guide and Glad Tidings to Muslims. We know indeed that
> they say, "It is a man that teaches him." The tongue of him
> they wickedly point to is notably foreign, while this is Arabic,
> pure and clear.[4]

The Yusuf Ali commentary on these verses states that the Holy Spirit is "the title of the Angel Gabriel, through whom the revelation came down."[5]

Whereas the Hadith lucidly shows that the Holy Spirit in Islam is the Angel Gabriel, contrary to Abdullah Yusuf Ali's surmise, the Qur'an is ambiguous on this subject; hence it exacerbates Muslims' confusion about the Promised Comforter.

Three crucial facts from the Qur'an and the Hadith disqualify Prophet Muhammad as the Promised Comforter whom Muslims claim Jesus prophesied would come. First of all, it is grotesquely odd that Jesus could have announced the coming of the Holy Spirit in Islam—the Angel Gabriel—because this angel had already appeared to prophets before Jesus. For instance, the Hadith states, "This is the same one who keeps the secrets (angel Gabriel) whom Allah had sent to Moses."[6] Second, the angel is also mentioned in the Qur'an and the Hadith as having delivered the pronouncement of Jesus' virgin birth to Mary.[7] Third, the same angel strengthened the Jesus of Islam, almost five centuries before the birth of Prophet Muhammad.[8]

16.2 Who Is the Authentic Holy Spirit?

The term "Holy Spirit," which Islamic scholars unequivocally apply to the Angel Gabriel, is a clue conspicuous enough that Muslims should eschew referencing the Bible to validate Prophet Muhammad's claim that he is the Promised Comforter. On the contrary, Muslims read the Bible with an intention not to learn objectively but to bolster Muhammad's claims. They misinterpret the two passages in the Gospel of John that portray the authentic Holy Spirit. John 14:15–17 states:

> If you love Me, keep My commandments. And I will pray the Father, and He will give you another Helper, that He may abide with you forever—the Spirit of truth, whom the world cannot receive, because it neither sees Him nor knows Him; but you know Him, for He dwells with you and will be in you.[9]

John 16:13–15 states:

> However, when He, the Spirit of truth, has come, He will guide you into all truth; for He will not speak on His own *authority*, but whatever He hears He will speak; and He will tell you things to come. He will glorify Me, for He will take of what is Mine and declare *it* to you. All things that the Father has are Mine. Therefore I said that He will take of Mine and declare *it* to you.[10]

These are the words of Jesus Christ to His disciples that Muslims claim to be a prophecy about Prophet Muhammad. For the sake of answering Muslims in a way that puts this matter to rest, let us analyze in portions what Jesus said and see if He gives any hint of Muhammad's birth. Here are statements mostly from the Qur'an and the Hadith that disprove Muslims' claim.

16.2.1 His Nature

Who is this Spirit that Muslims claim is Prophet Muhammad? To their dismay, the Gospel portrays the Holy Spirit—a spirit, not an angel or a human—as part of the Holy Trinity:

> And Jesus came and spoke to them [His disciples], saying,
> "All authority has been given to Me in heaven and on earth.
> Go therefore and make disciples of all the nations, baptizing
> them in the name of the Father and of the Son and of the
> Holy Spirit, teaching them to observe all things that I have
> commanded you; and lo, I am with you always, *even* to the
> end of the age." Amen.[11]

Jesus made it very clear that the Comforter is a spirit. That means if Muhammad were the Promised Comforter, he would have been invisible to the world. However, his family, relatives, friends and enemies saw him.

The Christians of the fourth century clearly understood the message of the Gospel and formulated their understanding of the Holy Spirit in a creed. A creed is:

> A confession of faith for public use, or a form of words setting
> forth with authority certain articles of belief... [It] may
> cover the whole ground of Christian doctrine and practice,
> or contain only such points as are deemed fundamental or
> sufficient, or have been disputed.[12]

One of the creeds, the Nicene Creed, clearly states that the Holy Spirit is "the giver of life, who proceeds from the Father and the Son. With the Father and Son he is worshipped and glorified. He has spoken through the prophets."[13] The early Christian church clearly articulated its position on the Holy Spirit. The writers of the Qur'an and the Hadith read the Bible in the seventh century but failed to grasp that the Promised Comforter is a spirit.

16.2.2 Sent by Jesus

This implication brings us to a turf Muslims would not like to tread despite the fact that they hold a claim to the Promised Comforter. The Bible clearly states that the Comforter came to glorify Christ who sent Him. John 15:26 states, "When the Counselor comes, whom I will send to you from the Father, the Spirit of truth who goes out from the Father, he will testify about me."[14] I know that not one Muslim would accept that Prophet Muhammad was sent by Christ to glorify Him. That would be blasphemous. The Gospel message, however, is quite explicit. The Holy Spirit came to continue the work of Christ. He did not come to bring change.

16.2.3 The Spirit of Truth

Jesus said that the Comforter is the Spirit of Truth. However, Jews, Christians, and pagan Arabs called Prophet Muhammad a liar. The Qur'an states, "And if they call you a liar, truly messengers before you were called liars, and to Allah are all affairs returned."[15] He is accused in the Hadith of deceiving his enemies, especially the Jews.[16] When Islam was in its preliminary stage, Prophet Muhammad lived peacefully with his neighbors. However, once he gained political power and will, he ambushed his unsuspecting enemies, oftentimes disregarding the mutual peace treaties that were in place.

The Qur'an does not support well Muslims' claim that Prophet Muhammad is the Promised Comforter, the Spirit of Truth, because it proves that he invented the "satanic verses." Muhammad recited these verses believing that they were revelations from Allah, only being told later that they were from Satan. Islamic scholars disagree on what really happened. A renowned Muslim historian, Abu Ja'far Muhammad bin Jarīr al-Tabarī (838–923 A.D.), had this to say in his *Ta'rīkh al-rasul wa'l muluk* (History of Prophets and Kings):

> The prophet was eager for the welfare of his people, desiring to win them to him by any means he could. It has been reported that he longed for a way to win them, and part of

what he did to that end is what Ibn Humayd told me, from
Salama, from Muhammad ibn Ishaq, from Yazīd ibn Ziyād
al-Madanī, from Muhammad ibn Ka'b al-Qurazī: When
the prophet saw his people turning away from him, and
was tormented by their distancing themselves from what
he had brought to them from God, he longed in himself
for something to come to him from God which would
draw him close to them. With his love for his people and
his eagerness for them, it would gladden him if some of
the hard things he had found in dealing with them could
be alleviated. He pondered this in himself, longed for it,
and desired it. Then God sent down the revelation, 'By the
star when it sets! Your companion has not erred or gone
astray, and does not speak from mere fancy...' [Kuran (sic),
53:1 and following]. When he reached God's words, 'Have
you seen Allāt and al-'Uzzā and Manāt, the third, the
other?' [53:19–20], Satan cast upon his tongue, because
of what he had pondered in himself and longed to bring
to his people, *These are the high-flying cranes and their
intercession is to be hoped for.*[17]

(The part in italics was a verse in Suratul Al-Fitr, one of
the satanic verses, which was abrogated, thus, it is not found in
the current Qur'an. The compiling of the Qur'an is discussed in
chapter four. Uthman, the Third Caliphate, ordered the burning
of divergent copies of the Qur'an to stem confusion among
Muslims. Some of the satanic verses could have been expunged
at that time.)

The truth is that Prophet Muhammad recited verses he had
supposedly received from Allah that acknowledged the validity of
three goddesses in Arabia. It happened when he faced stiff opposition from his tribe, the Quraysh, who had rejected him as a prophet.
Al-Tabari added:

When the Quraysh heard this [Muhammad's acknowledgment
of their idols], they rejoiced and were happy and delighted at
the way in which he spoke of their gods, and they listened
to him, while the Muslims, having complete trust in their

Prophet in respect of the messages which he brought from
God, did not suspect him of error, illusion, or mistake.[18]

The Hadith adds, "He [Muhammad] finished reciting Surat-
an-Najm [the above-mentioned chapter of the Qur'an], and all the
Muslims and pagans and Jinns and human beings prostrated along
with him."[19] Muhammad's reciting pleased the pagans in Mecca
so much that they prostrated in prayer with Muhammad without
even converting to Islam. Then Muhammad received another
revelation:

> Never sent We a messenger or a Prophet before thee but
> when he recited (the message) Satan proposed (opposition) in
> respect of that which he recited thereof. But Allah abolisheth
> that which Satan proposeth. Then Allah establisheth His
> revelations. Allah is Knower, Wise.[20]

This verse encouraged him because it shows that he was not
the only prophet whom Satan had deceived, resulting in his reciting
of the satanic verses. In addition, this verse abrogated the satanic
verse in Suratul Al-Fitr. It remains obvious, however, that had
Prophet Muhammad been the Promised Comforter, he would not
have "recited (the message) Satan proposed" because the Comforter
is a part of the Holy Trinity, and would not have had anything to
do with the satanic verses.

Muslims I know would not accept that Prophet Muhammad
recited the satanic verses. Their denunciation, however, is just to
cover up for Islam because the Qur'an elsewhere states:

> And they indeed strove hard to beguile thee (Muhammad)
> away from that wherewith We have inspired thee, that thou
> shouldst invent other than it against Us; and then would they
> have accepted thee as a friend. And if We had not made thee
> wholly firm thou mightest almost have inclined unto them a
> little. Then had we made thee taste a double (punishment) of
> living and a double (punishment) of dying, then hadst thou
> found no helper against Us.[21]

This verse confirms that Prophet Muhammad invented the satanic verses. Abdullah Yusuf Ali wrote the most widely used commentary of the Qur'an. He commented on the preceding verse:

> It happens with men of Allah, and it happened with the Holy Prophet [Muhammad], that they are tempted by the world with many things which appeal to the world generally, if they would make some small concession in their favour.[22]

Ali trivializes Prophet Muhammad's reciting of the satanic verses as "small concession" but tacitly confirms that Muhammad was a mere human whom Satan tempted and misled. Muhammad's invention of the satanic verses is proof that he was not the Promised Comforter, the Spirit of Truth.

16.2.4 The Purpose of His Coming

Islamic teachings claim that Prophet Muhammad had to come because Jesus' teaching to His disciples and the Jews were disobeyed, corrupted, or forgotten. The Gospel clearly shows that it was never on the condition of disobedience or corruption that the Promised Comforter had to come. Jesus told His disciples, "If you love Me, keep My commandments. And I will pray the Father, and He will give you another Helper, that He may abide with you forever—the Spirit of truth."

16.2.5 Who Would Accept Him?

Jesus clearly said that the world would not accept the Comforter because the world neither sees nor knows the Comforter. The world, in this case, means those who are not Christians. Nevertheless, non-Christians have accepted Muhammad, speak well of him, and endorse Islam. If he were the Holy Spirit, they would have spurned him.

16.2.6 He Was Present with Jesus at Pentecost

The Spirit was with the disciples at the time Jesus Christ was speaking to them. Prophet Muhammad was not born until 570 A.D., more than five centuries after Jesus addressed His disciples at Pentecost.

It is recorded in the Bible that the Comforter fully came on the disciples with power approximately ten days after Jesus Christ's Ascension. It is written in Acts 2:1–4:

> When the Day of Pentecost had fully come, they were all with one accord in one place. And suddenly there came a sound from heaven, as of a rushing mighty wind, and it filled the whole house where they were sitting. Then there appeared to them divided tongues, as of fire, and *one* sat upon each of them. And they were all filled with the Holy Spirit and began to speak with other tongues, as the Spirit gave them utterance.[23]

The coming of the Holy Spirit on the day of Pentecost was necessary to empower the disciples to be effective in witnessing and evangelism. The Comforter was to be in the disciples.

16.2.7 Continuity of Jesus' Teachings

Muhammad did not guide Jesus' followers into all truth as the Comforter does. His lifestyle as recorded in the Qur'an and the Hadith clearly contradicts all accolades and attributes Muslims accord him. Incriminating evidences in the Qur'an and the Hadith disqualify him, but Muslims ignore them and still contend that he was the Promised Comforter.

The Comforter was not supposed to speak on His own accord. According to the aforementioned Bible passages, He was to speak what He heard from Christ. On the other hand, Muhammad claimed to have his own revelation. The Hadith states:

> A'isha reported that Harith b. Hisham asked Allah's Apostle (may peace be upon him): How does the wahi (inspiration) come to you? He said: At times it comes to me like the ringing of a bell and that is most severe for me and when it is over I retain that (what I had received in the form of wahi), and at times an Angel in the form of a human being comes to me (and speaks) and I retain whatever he speaks.[24]

Two things are evident in this Hadith. First, Muhammad did not continue the mission of Christ as the Promised Comforter was supposed to because Muhammad had his own agenda, as was evidenced by new "revelations" coming to him. Second, he struggled to remember *wahi* (revelation from Allah). If he were the Holy Spirit, he would not have struggled to remember what was revealed. The disciples struggled to remember what Jesus Christ taught, but the true Comforter was there to ensure that they remembered it.

Prophet Muhammad received new revelations in the form of debilitating and deafening rings of a bell and also from an angel who came in the form of a man. The angel is supposedly Gabriel, who is also called the Holy Spirit in Islam. When Jesus Christ promised the Comforter, He implied that there would be no mediator between Him and the Comforter because the Comforter heard what Jesus taught the disciples.

16.2.7.1 Violence

When Prophet Muhammad came with his message, there was no continuity in the work of Christ in the Arab world. Instead, cities of people who rejected Islam were conquered, and people were either killed or enslaved and forced to pay extra tax. As one Islamic scholar puts it, "The posture of Islam, then, was clear from onset: It must prevail over all other religions."[25] This shows that, contrary to the prevailing notion in the Muslim world, Muhammad was not the Promised Comforter in the Gospel. If he were, he would have empowered the disciples to wage *jihad* against non-Christians, coercing them into accepting Christianity, which would have been in contravention with Jesus Christ's teachings in the Gospel.

16.2.7.2 The Doctrine of the Trinity

The Qur'an also shows that Prophet Muhammad went to the extent of opposing Jesus' teaching on the Holy Trinity without even understanding it properly. Jesus called Himself the Son of God frequently in the Gospel, but Muhammad contradicted His teachings and nicknamed Him the "Son of Mary." He emphatically told his followers that Allah could not have a son.

Muhammad went on record to falsely accuse Jesus of things He allegedly said about His mother that He did not teach His disciples in the Gospel. A few places in the Qur'an falsely accuse the Jesus of Islam of telling his disciples to take his mother, Mary, as a god, a part of the three gods.[26] This was never the case in the Gospel because Mary was a vessel whom God used to bring Jesus Christ into the world.

The Christian leaders of the fifth century deemed it necessary to write a creed in response to controversies over the divine and human natures of Jesus Christ. It is important to look back because the creed they wrote in 451 A.D. puts to rest Prophet Muhammad's assertion that the Virgin Mary is part of the Trinity. The Creed of Chalcedon states, "In these latter days, for us and for our salvation, born [Jesus] of the Virgin Mary, the mother of God, according to the manhood; one and the same Christ, Son, Lord, Only-Begotten, to be acknowledged in two natures."[27] God purposely used Mary to bring Jesus Christ into the world. As Christian theologian Erwin Lutzer puts it:

> We can say that she participated in the origination of human nature of a child who was divine. So it would be more accurate to speak of her as the mother of the God-man, recognizing that deity was miraculously joined with humanity in her womb. When the Council of Chalcedon used the phrase "the Mother of God," it did so not to honor Mary as much as to emphasize the deity of Christ.[28]

This creed clearly explains how Mary was viewed in the church. And it was in nowise as a part of the Holy Trinity. Were Muhammad the Promised Comforter, he would have proclaimed the right message because the Comforter was with Christ from the beginning. In contrast, Muhammad was carried away by his whims; hence, Muslims live in confusion or denial today.

16.2.7.3 Pilgrimage

Prophet Muhammad made it compulsory for his able-bodied followers to go to Mecca for pilgrimage at least once in their lifetime. He seemed totally oblivious to the teachings of Jesus Christ in this regard. Jesus did not endorse pilgrimage. On the contrary, we read in John 4:19–24:

> The woman said to Him, "Sir, I perceive that You are a prophet. Our fathers worshiped on this mountain, and you *Jews* say

that in Jerusalem is the place where one ought to worship." Jesus said to her, "Woman, believe Me, the hour is coming when you will neither on this mountain, nor in Jerusalem, worship the Father. You worship what you do not know; we know what we worship, for salvation is of the Jews. But the hour is coming, and now is, when the true worshipers will worship the Father in spirit and truth; for the Father is seeking such to worship Him. God *is* Spirit, and those who worship Him must worship in spirit and truth."[29]

Muhammad should have known better than to require Muslims to have, at the outset of Islam, Jerusalem, and then later on Mecca, as a holy city that they should pay homage to. He forgot that:

> With the coming of the Messiah, Jerusalem as a type would disappear. No longer would salvation be confined to a single people, and worship to a single city [because] the types of the old dispensations would find their fulfillment in Christ.[30]

16.2.7.4 Prayer and Fasting

He also instructed Muslims to observe different kinds of prayers than the Lord's Prayer that Jesus had taught the disciples to pray. He made it compulsory for Muslims to fast in a particular month with different rules to follow. Others could obviously see Muslims observing the fast contrary to Jesus' teaching against the kind of fast that cultivated hypocrisy.

16.2.7.5 Compassion

Had Muhammad been the Comforter, he would have continued with the message of Christ. He would have turned the other cheek for his enemy to smite, humbled himself, loved his neighbor as himself, showed empathy toward the handicapped, and respected other people's wives and widows. To the contrary, his actions were utterly contradictory to what Christ had taught.

The Qur'an states, "(The Prophet) frowned and turned away, because there came to him the blind man (interrupting)."[31] Muslim scholars spar over the meaning of these two verses; hence some Qur'an translations downplay their actual meaning. The Hadith clearly shows that Prophet Muhammad frowned because a poor blind man walked into the mosque and asked him where he could sit. Instead of showing him where to sit, Muhammad frowned and ignored him and talked with a more "important man" in the audience. He later addressed the poor man.[32] Some Muslims argue in defense that the blind man interrupted Muhammad. It is acceptable to ignore someone when another conversation is in progress. It is generally unacceptable, however, not only to ignore a blind man who was just asking where he could sit in a crowded mosque, but also to frown at him. Prophet Muhammad showed no compassion, which was uncharacteristic of the teachings of Jesus Christ of which the Comforter was supposed to remind the disciples.

In contrast, Jesus cared for the blind. It is written in several places in the Gospel that Jesus stopped to attend to the blind when He was surrounded by a horde of other people. To all appearances, His busy schedule was interrupted, but obviously He did not feel so, since He had compassion and healed them. On the contrary, Muhammad did not want the blind man to bother him. He even gestured, which the blind man could not see. Had he been the Comforter, he would have heeded the teachings of Jesus Christ to be compassionate.

16.2.7.6 Discernment

Prophet Muhammad lived a life that Muslims are embarrassed to discuss. All his biographies that Islamic scholars have written leave out significant parts of his life that would be nefarious by any moral or ethical standard. Non-Muslims who dare to expose his lifestyle are either threatened or labeled as bigots. For the sake of proving that Muhammad was not the Promised Comforter, let us look at how he flouted the teachings of Jesus Christ.

Prophet Muhammad married Umm Salama when her husband, Abu Salama, died. In fact, he went to her house when Abu Salama had just died. Muhammad even closed Abu Salama's eyes, which the Hadith states "were fixedly open."[33] Umm Salama was a very beautiful woman.[34] On the day her husband died, Muhammad went to her house under the guise of comforting her. The way he talked with her betrayed his motive to win her. Muhammad's behavior toward a widow who had not even buried her deceased husband was totally despicable.

Little is known as to whether the widow got any comfort that fateful day because Muhammad pitched his offer right away by telling her to pray, "O Allah! Forgive me and him (Abu Salama) and give me a better substitute than he."[35] Bizarre as it sounds, Muhammad married Umm Salama. He made his pitch while the grieving woman was newly bereaved of her own husband. That act is uncharacteristic of the Comforter whom Jesus Christ said would come. Jesus said, "Blessed *are* those who mourn, for they shall be comforted."[36] Muhammad could not be the Promised Comforter because he did not know how to mourn the Jesus way.

16.2.7.7 Discretion

The Promised Comforter was to remind Jesus' disciples of His teachings. He knew what those teachings were. Jesus said, "Let the little children come to me, and do not forbid them; for of such is the kingdom of God."[37] He received children and gave lessons to the audience when they were sitting on his lap. Muhammad, on the other hand, did not carry on the message of Christ like the Comforter would, and ended up marrying a six- or seven-year-old Aisha. The Hadith shows that Aisha was very young and was still playing with her dolls when they consummated their marriage at the age of nine. She said, "They took me, made me prepared and decorated me. I was then brought to the Apostle of Allah (peace be upon him), and he took up cohabitation with me when I was nine."[38] Had he been the Promised Comforter, he would have used some discernment and discretion and would not have married a child, not to mention more than one wife. (The Comforter is a spirit and cannot marry.) Marrying a minor is now illegal in all the countries that are signatories to the United Nations Convention on the Rights of the Child.[39]

Muslims I know argue that Aisha was about fifteen years old when Muhammad married her. That is not true according to the Hadith. Aisha herself said she got married to Prophet Muhammad when she was six or seven years old and consummated their marriage at the age of nine when she was still playing with dolls and her playmates.[40]

16.2.7.8 Divorce and Remarriage

The Comforter was supposed to carry out the teachings of Jesus Christ pertaining to divorce and remarriage. The Gospel of Matthew states:

> The Pharisees also came to Him, testing Him, and saying to Him, "Is it lawful for a man to divorce his wife for *just* any reason?" And He answered and said to them, "Have you not read that He who made *them* at the beginning *'made them male and female,'* and said, *'For this reason a man shall leave his father and mother and be joined to his wife, and the two shall become one flesh'?* So then, they are no longer two but one flesh. Therefore what God has joined together, let not man separate." They said to Him, "Why then did Moses command to give a certificate of divorce, and to put her away?" He said to them, "Moses, because of the hardness of your hearts, permitted you to divorce your wives, but from the beginning it was not so. And I say to you, whoever divorces his wife, except for sexual immorality, and marries another, commits adultery; and whoever marries her who is divorced commits adultery."[41]

Jesus quoted part of the Torah to show that God intended marriage to last until death. Prophet Muhammad disobeyed that teaching by convincing Zaid bin Haritha to divorce his wife, Zainab bint Jahsh, because Allah apparently told Muhammad that he should marry Zainab. (Divorce is justified only in case of infidelity; however, the couple still is technically married because only God can end marriage at the death of a spouse.) Zaid must have been distraught by the news, but he was compelled to obey what Allah's apostle had purposed. The Qur'an states:

> It is not fitting for a Believer, man or woman, when a matter has been decided by Allah and His Messenger to have any option about their decision: if any one disobeys Allah and His Messenger, he is indeed on a clearly wrong Path. Behold! Thou didst say to one who had received the grace of Allah and thy

favour: "Retain thou (in wedlock) thy wife, and fear Allah." But thou didst hide in thy heart that which Allah was about to make manifest: thou didst fear the people, but it is more fitting that thou shouldst fear Allah. Then when Zaid had dissolved (his marriage) with her, with the necessary (formality), We joined her in marriage to thee: in order that (in future) there may be no difficulty to the Believers in (the matter of) marriage with the wives of their adopted sons, when the latter have dissolved with the necessary (formality) (their marriage) with them. And Allah's command must be fulfilled.[42]

Allah revealed these verses in the Qur'an that justified Zaid divorcing his wife so that Muhammad could marry her. Even harder to believe, Zaid was Prophet Muhammad's adopted son. Forcing a son to divorce his wife so that his father may marry his daughter-in-law is unacceptable by any standard. In addition, Muhammad was already married to a handful of women when this egregious incident took place.

Islamic scholars argue that Allah was teaching Muslims against adoption which was widely practiced during pre-Islamic times in Arabia. Since there are a lot of decrees in the Qur'an without examples from Prophet Muhammad's lifestyle, shouldn't a mere verse outlawing adoption suffice without subjecting Zaid to pain? The Islamic scholars are apparently making excuses for Muhammad's offense. If he were the Comforter, he would have obeyed the teachings of Jesus Christ and would have also used some discretion. Like Jesus Christ, the true Comforter would not get married in the first place.

This is how it all started. Prophet Muhammad went to Zaid's house when he was not home and accidentally saw his wife who "was very lightly clad [and] succumbed to her charms."[43] (That was before veiling in Islam was invented.) Seeing her led Muhammad to want to marry her.

Once Muhammad married his daughter-in-law, he instituted a rule through a revelation he purportedly received from Allah in the Qur'an, 33:53, that no man should enter his house without being invited. Apparently Allah does not act fairly because Muhammad did not want men to seduce his wives in retaliation. The Hadith also adds:

> When Allah's Apostle married Zainab bint Jahsh, he made the people eat meat and bread to their fill (by giving a Walima banquet). Then he went out to the dwelling places of the mothers of the believers (his wives), as he used to do in the morning of his marriage. He would greet them and invoke good on them, and they (too) would return his greeting and invoke good on him. When he returned to his house, he found two men talking to each other; and when he saw them, he went out of his house again. When those two men saw Allah's Apostle: going out of his house, they quickly got up (and departed). I do not remember whether I informed him of their departure, or he was informed (by somebody else). So he returned, and when he entered the house, he lowered the curtain between me and him. Then the Verse of Al-Hijab was revealed.[44]

It is evident from this Hadith that Muslim women began wearing veils when Prophet Muhammad reached the uncomfortable realization that his new wife Zainab could be seduced.

16.2.8 Prophecy

The Promised Comforter is capable to predict what is to come. In fact, He has been foretelling future events even before the birth of Prophet Muhammad. This characteristic of the Comforter to prophesy perhaps is what confuses Muslims into thinking that Jesus foretold the coming of a prophet.

Since there is no record of Prophet Muhammad prophesying in the Qur'an or the Hadith, Islamic scholars argue that the Islamic understanding of a prophet does not require a prophet to prophesy. One of them wrote:

> The *nabi*, 'a giver of news,' does not mean in the Qur'an (as it mostly did in the Bible) 'one who gives news about the future,' but 'one who gives news from God'; he comes from God to warn against evil and to give good tidings to those who are good.[45]

Islamic scholars enlist the Bible's help, a book they allege had been corrupted, to bolster Muhammad's claim that he was a prophet. In deed in Exodus 7:1, God appointed Aaron to be a prophet without Aaron prophesying. In this case, Aaron spoke to Pharaoh the news which God had revealed to Moses. The Promised Comforter, however, is capable to prophesy and Prophet Muhammad did not. Therefore Prophet Muhammad could not have been the one whom Jesus prophesied would come.

16.2.9 Eternal

The Promised Comforter, the Holy Spirit, is eternal. He was to be with the disciples forever. He is still present today. Muhammad, however, died at the age of sixty-three years in approximately 632 A.D. The Hadith states:

> Narrated Abu Huraira: When Khaibar was conquered, a roasted poisoned sheep was presented to the Prophets as a gift (by the Jews). The Prophet ordered, "Let all the Jews who have been here, be assembled before me." The Jews were collected and the Prophet said (to them), "I am going to ask you a question. Will you tell the truth?'" They said, "Yes.' The Prophet asked, "Who is your father?" They replied, "So-and-so." He said, "You have told a lie; your father is so-and-so." They said, "You are right." He said, "Will you now tell me the truth, if I ask you about something?" They replied, "Yes, O AbuAl-Qasim; and if we should tell a lie, you can realize our lie as you have done regarding our father." On that he asked, "Who are the people of the (Hell) Fire?" They said, "We shall remain in the (Hell) Fire for a short period, and after that you will replace us." The Prophet said, "You may be cursed and humiliated in it! By Allah, we shall never replace you in it.'" Then he asked, "Will you now tell me the truth if I ask you a question?" They said, "Yes, O Ab Li-AI-Qasim." He asked, "Have you poisoned this sheep?" They said, "Yes." He asked, "What made you do so?" They said, "We wanted to know if you were a liar in which case we would get rid of you, and if you are a prophet then the poison would not harm you."[46]

The Jews in Arabia wanted to get rid of Prophet Muhammad because he had decimated their kindred. It is not clear if he ate the poisoned lamb on this very day. They eventually succeeded in their quest. Muhammad ate the poisoned lamb and, "The poison gradually took root in his system and the Prophet's health deteriorated."[47] He subsequently died from its complications.

Unfortunately for Muslims who contend that the Promised Comforter is Prophet Muhammad, the Spirit of Truth whom Jesus prophesied would come is eternal. The Qur'an and the Hadith's lack of unanimity on the Holy Spirit in Islam exacerbate the confusion among Muslims. It is about time that they put aside their pride and read the Scriptures others were already reading before the advent of Islam. Perhaps that would allay their confusion, and they would learn the Truth, which might comfort them.

16.3 Conclusion

One would wonder how Muslims wouldn't know salient inconsistencies in Islam. There are reasons. First, most of them reside in Islamic countries, which censor discussions about Prophet Muhammad's behavior or the authorship of the Qur'an. Islamic governments know discussing them would expose some of Islam's inconsistencies. These governments are known for censoring any criticism of prophets. This propensity, however, favors Prophet Muhammad because the rest of the prophets mentioned in Islam had nothing too embarrassing on record to require a permanent "gag order."

Second, those Muslims who live in non-Islamic countries do not have adequate Islamic resources to understand Islam objectively. For example, some Islamic *madrassa* teachers I knew in Kenya did not have the Hadith collections, which are valuable toward understanding Prophet Muhammad's behavior.

Third, Islamic leaders employ scare tactics to keep their faithful from either scrutinizing Islamic teachings or exploring Christianity as a viable option. In the first case they say it is a sin to probe Islam, Allah's perfect religion, and are quick to admonish one of the faithful who asks deep questions. Some of these leaders I have known tell the faithful who question Islam to say *asta ghfirullah,*

which means, "May Allah forgive me" in Arabic. An extreme case
of these scare tactics occurs in Kenya, especially in the Coast Province, where Islamic Arab missionaries once preached and it now is
believed that going into a Christian church and sitting in the pews
results into a "stamp" being sealed on the buttocks, thus earmarking
a churchgoer for hell.

Last but not least, Arab Muslims have something they can call
their own in Islam, and it is difficult, if not impossible, for them
to betray a religion that has given them something to brag about.
The Arab Republic of Egypt banned two European newspapers for
"insulting" Islam in September 2006. Reuters quotes Egypt's state
news agency MENA: "They published articles which disparaged
Islam and claimed that the Islamic religion was spread by the sword
and that the Prophet ... was the prophet of evil."[48] By all counts,
these accusations levied against Islam are compatible with what
any open-minded individual would extrapolate by reading the
Qur'an and the Hadith. Instead of addressing these allegations, the
Egyptian government outright banned these newspapers, perhaps
because the leaders knew there is not a vestige of truth in Islam to
dispel them.

---

[1]   Pickthall, Suratul As-Saff, 61:6.

[2]   Ibid.

[3]   *Sahih Bukhari, Volume 8, Book 73, number 173.*

[4]   Yusuf Ali, Surat An-Nahl, 16:102–103.

[5]   Yusuf Ali, Commentary Number 2141.

[6]   *Sahih Bukhari, Volume 1, Book 1, Number 3.*

[7]   Suratul Al-Maryam, 19:17.

[8]   Suratul Al-Baqara, 2:87–253 and Suratul Al-Maida, 5:110.

[9]   NKJV.

[10] NKJV.

[11] Matthew 28:18–20, NKJV.

[12] Philip Schaff, *The Creeds of Christendom: With a History and
      Critical Notes, 4th Ed. Volume I.* (Public Domain, 1877), 3, 4.

13 Retrieved from http://www.magnificat.org/inquiry/prayers.asp on July 13, 2007.

14 NKJV.

15 Shakir, Suratul Al-Fitr, 35:4.

16 *Sahih Bukhari, Volume 4, Book 53, Number 394.*

17 Gerald R. Hawting, trans., *The Ideas of Idolatry and the Emergence of Islam: From Polemic to History* (London: Cambridge University Press, 1999), 131. Emphasis mine.

18 W. Montgomery Watt and M.V. McDonald, trans., Ehsan Yar-Shater, ed., *The History of al-Tabarī: Muhammad at Mecca Volume VI* (Albany: State University of New York Press, 1988), 108. Bracket mine.

19 *Sahih Bukhari, Volume 6, Book 60, Number 385.* Brackets mine.

20 Pickthall, Suratul Al-Hajj, 22:52.

21 Pickthall, Suratul Al-Isra, 17:73–75.

23 Yusuf Ali, Number 2269. Bracket mine.

23 NKJV.

24 *Sahih Muslim, Book 30, Number 5765.*

25 Yahiya Emerick, *Critical Lives: Muhammad* (Indianapolis: Alpha Books, 2002), 298.

26 Suratul Al-Maida, 5:73, 116 and Suratul Al-Nisa, 4:171.

27 Retrieved from http://www.wcg.org/lit/church/pamphlet/3creeds.htm on July 13, 2007.

28 Erwin W. Lutzer, *The Doctrines That Divide: A Fresh Look at the Historic Doctrines That Separate Christians* (Grand Rapids: Kregel Publications, 1998), 53.

29 NKJV.

30 Don Doezema, *Upon This Rock Volume 1 Jesus Christ: His Earthly Ministry* (Protestant Reformed Sunday School Teachers Association, 2003), 84. Bracket mine.

31 Yusuf Ali, Surah Abasa, 80:1–2.

32 *Malik's Muwatta, Book 15, Number 15.4.8.*

33 *Sahih Muslim, Book 4, Number 2003.*

34 *Sahih Muslim, Book 9, Number 3508.*

35 *Sahih Muslim, Book 4, Number 2002.*

36 Matthew 5:4, NKJV.

37 Luke 18:16, NKJV.

38 *Sunan Abu-Dawud, Volume 3, Book 36, Number 4915.*

39 United Nations General Assembly, *Convention on the Rights of the Child* (September 2, 1990).

40 *Sahih Muslim, Book 31, Number 5981.*

41 Matthew 19:3–9, NKJV.

42 Yusuf Ali, Suratul Al-Ahzab, 33:36–37.

43 Karen Armstrong, *Muhammad: A Biography of the Prophet* (San Francisco: HarperCollins, 1992), 196. Bracket mine.

44 *Sahih Bukhari, Volume 6, Book 60, Number 317.*

45 Fazlur Rahman, *Major Themes of The Qur'an* (Minneapolis: Bibliotheca Islamica, Inc., 1980, 1989), 81, 82.

46 *Sahih Bukhari, Volume 4, Book 53, Number 394.*

47 Shaikh Safiur Rahman Mubarakpuri, *When the Moon Split: A Biography of Prophet Muhammad* (Houston: Darussalam, 1998), 303.

48 "Egypt Bans Europeans Newspapers for Comment on Islam," *Reuters*, September 24, 2006. Retrieved from http://today.reuters.com/news/articlenews.aspx?type=worldNews&storyID=2006-09-24T153740Z_01_L24839584_RTRUKOC_0_US-RELIGION-EGYPT-BAN.xml&archived=False on September 28, 2006.